Witchcraft and the Web

Weaving Pagan Traditions Online

WITH A FOREWORD BY PHYLLIS CUROTT

M. Macha NightMare

ECW PRESS

The publication of *Witchcraft and the Web* has been generously supported by the Canada Council, the Ontario Arts Council, and the Government of Canada through the Book Publishing Industry Development Program. Canadä

CANADIAN CATALOGUING IN PUBLICATION DATA

National Library of Canada Cataloguing in Publication Data.
M. Macha NightMare
Witchcraft and the Web: weaving pagan traditions online
ISBN 1-55022-466-2
1. Witchcraft. 2. Internet I. Title
BF1571.M2 2001 133.4'3'02854678 C2001-900538-5

Copyedited by Mary Williams.
Cover, interior design and typesetting by Guylaine Régimbald—SOLO DESIGN.
This book is set in ApolloMT, Percolator, and Brother.

Printed by AGMV L'Imprimeur, Cap-Saint-Ignace, Quebec.

Distributed in Canada by General Distribution Services,
325 Humber College Boulevard, Etobicoke, Ontario M9W 7C3.

Distributed in the United States by LPC Group,
1436 West Randolph Street, Chicago, IL, USA 60607.

Distributed in Europe by Turnaround Publisher Services, Unit 3,
Olympia Trading Estate, Coburg Road, Wood Green, London N2Z 6T2.

Distributed in Australia and New Zealand by Wakefield Press,
17 Rundle Street (Box 2266), Kent Town, Adelaide, South Australia 5071.

Published by ECW PRESS
Suite 200
2120 Queen Street East
Toronto, Ontario M4E 1E2.

ecwpress.com

Printed and bound in Canada.

PERMISSIONS

Diligent efforts have been made to contact copyright holders; please excuse any inadvertent errors or omissions, but if anyone has been unintentionally omitted, the publisher would be pleased to receive notification and to make correct acknowledgments in future printings.

Excerpts from personal correspondence by Shawn Arthur. All rights reserved. Reprinted by permission.

Excerpts from personal correspondence by Jen "Lhiannon" Bryan. All rights reserved. Reprinted by permission.

Excerpts from personal correspondence by Cat Chapin-Bishop. All rights reserved. Reprinted by permission.

Excerpts from personal correspondence by Grey Cat. All rights reserved. Reprinted by permission.

Excerpts from personal correspondence by Ceffyl. All rights reserved. Reprinted by permission.

Excerpts from personal correspondence by Cynthia. All rights reserved. Reprinted by permission.

Excerpts from "Technopagans" by Erik Davis. All rights reserved. Reprinted by permission.

Excerpts from "Pagans & Christians: The Personal Spiritual Experience" by Gus diZerega and published by Llewellyn Worldwide Ltd., PO Box 64383, St. Paul, MN 55164, 2001. All rights reserved. Reprinted by permission.

Excerpts from personal correspondence by Tom "Moose" Dixon. All rights reserved. Reprinted by permission.

"Grounding Ceremony" by Richard Ely and M. Macha Nightmare. All rights reserved. Reprinted by permission.

"The Charge of the Counsellor: A Statement of Ethics." by Margaret Hammit-Macdonald. All rights reserved. Reprinted by permission.

Excerpts from "Fantasy in the Study of Religions: Paganism as Observed and Enhanced by Terry Pratchett" by Graham Harvey and published online by DISKUS, Volume 6, 2000. All rights reserved. Reprinted by permission.

Excerpts from personal correspondence by Imajicka. All rights reserved. Reprinted by permission.

Excerpts from personal correspondence by Adam Jenkins. All rights reserved. Reprinted by permission.

Excerpts from personal correspondence by Sandy Johnson. All rights reserved. Reprinted by permission.

Excerpts from personal correspondence by Fritz Jung. All rights reserved. Reprinted by permission.

"Witchvox Code of Ethics" by Fritz Jung. All rights reserved. Reprinted by permission.

Excerpts from personal correspondence by Mark Kelly. All rights reserved. Reprinted by permission.

To my Sisters and Brothers in the Art

May our sacred rites generate waves and waves of compassion, understanding, pleasure, and love through all the worlds.

Spider Woman

At a remote time,
when there was no world
and nothing else alive,
I, Spider Woman, thought out into space.

I breathed, I sang, I thought,
and I spun a world into being
out of the purple glow at the beginning.

After finishing this world,
I populated it with creatures, and made the first woman and man,
Who in turn made your ancestors
Who in turn made all of you in this room,
And so it went.

Into the first woman and man
I spun a bit of my own being—
A web of wisdom and thought,
and connected this by a strand
to my own web.

However, over time, first woman and man and their descendants,
your ancestors, and you
have all seemingly forgotten you possess this web of wisdom,
and so you have lost sight of the meaning of life,
and have become proud and bitter,
gambling and fighting,
and even fancying you made yourselves!

You have *so* disappointed me!

And yet I have persevered,
Making three new worlds for you,
Each more real and perfect and complete than the last,
In each you have acquired new wisdom:
How to plant seeds,
How to stoke fire,
How to weave blankets, make pots,
Pray.

Now here we are in the fourth world,
Where you human beings have been mighty clever
with the crafts I have taught you.
You have fashioned a complex civilization, full of buildings and money
and technologies and habits,
Whose computer connections you have even dared to call
The World Wide Web.

But the purpose of your grand culture project
that so busies everybody is—what?
To grow more and more humans at the expense of all other life?
The *real* web that sustains you
The web which I wove,
The web which contains all matter, all beings, all thought, all action,
visible and invisible,
Space as well as Time
seems now lost to you.
Life itself has disappeared as you scurry about your business.

Today I challenge you and command you,
To wake from your reverie of abstraction and addiction,
To open your eyes and your heart,
To Me,
To My web,
To reality.

To see
You are not "in here"
Over and against the world "out there."
Rather, You are of the world, part and parcel;
Fashioned from the same starry web as the Earth, the stones, and the
trees,
your dog, your mate,
your enemy, your lover,
your computer, your mother.

You are My web, and that is all,
points of the same light,
connected.
Your neighbor is yourself,
And all of you are Mine.

If you don't believe me,
try calling Me in your mind,
Don't speak,
Yet I will answer
With an image or a word in the outer world.
Incredible coincidence, you say?

No,
synchronicities are the web illumined,
And that is all.

—Mary Kay Landon

CONTENTS

FOREWORD

A Witch is a wise woman, a cunning man, a shaman, an explorer of sacred realities, a weaver of unseen forces, a seer. A Witch is someone who is paying attention, someone with vision—who sees the unseen and who knows that vision is not just seeing, but foreseeing.

Witches have foreseen the infinite potential of the Internet, technology's bridge to the future. From its inception, Witches, and Pagans, have been a formative part of the creation of the World Wide Web, and more than any other religion, they have crossed this bridge into the frontier of cyberspace to explore, cultivate, and create. As much as Witches have created and contributed to these rich resources, the Net has contributed to the creation of contemporary Witchcraft. The astonishing speed with which the Internet connects people has helped spur the speed and size of our growth to such an extent that diverse sources now acknowledge Witchcraft as the fastest growing religion in America.

Witchcraft has mostly been a hidden religion—an inevitable consequence of the Witch hunts, and the distorted, negative stereotypes that emerged from its ferocious persecutions. Since the 1950s, however, modern Witchcraft has been characterized by a slow and careful process of emergence, organization, and liberation—though for most of the last fifty years only a few have been willing or able to publicly declare themselves practitioners of this ancient, modern religion. The consequences of such visibility, as I can attest from both personal experience as a Witch and as an attorney defending the rights of Witches, can be severe. But Witches cannot live, nor practice their spirituality, in fear. Confrontation with the terrors of oppression is profoundly liberating, for on the other side of fear is the empowerment of freedom.

But there are many who have been unable to risk "coming out of the broom closet." They live in areas where violence is easily used to intimidate, or they risk losing custody of their children or a much-needed job, or young Witches face the cruel harassment of fellow students and school officials. Assaults on our religious liberties stretch from the depths of the

Bible Belt to the heights of the ivy-covered walls of academia, from the media to the current Congress and administration. Times, however, are rapidly changing—and the Internet is one of the reasons why.

The Web has provided a source of profound strength and solidarity to countless individuals who once struggled, explored, studied, or practiced alone. With the anonymity provided by a computer screen, Witches have been able to reach out into a formerly hidden world to find support, education, information, networks of legal advice and counsel, organizations, and, most importantly, community. People have discovered that, no matter where they live, or what their circumstances, they are not alone. The Internet has provided a safety net—a web of magic and connection that has been a lifeline out of fear and isolation into a dynamic realm of activism and spirituality. The Internet empowers us as individuals and as a community. It has not only helped to engender this community, but it has also hosted and transformed it.

Web sites, listserves, e-correspondence—the Internet allows Witches to communicate, react, and respond with extraordinary speed and effectiveness. An act of bias is met with swift mobilization—with kindred aid and comfort, legal assistance, and media efforts. The Web hosts not one, but dozens of networks of activist assistance, information, and inspiration. Our connections in cyberspace become connections in terraspace—friendships are made, covens are found or formed, organizations take shape, and goals with plans of action emerge. We are no longer invisible—to one another, or the world. The weaving Witches do on the Web has made us luminously visible.

The Internet has become the world's town square, where we are free to speak with our own voices—to present the truth of who we are, what we believe, how we practice, and what our values are, uncensored by the prejudice or fears of others. And what we say is now accessible to anyone who wishes to listen, anywhere in the world, at any time. And as both our truths and our community become increasingly present in the world, we have a growing impact on the future. In a world at risk of annihilation, the Net carries our message that the Divine dwells within and all around us, that the Goddess is returning, the Earth is sacred, and Witchcraft is a spirituality of elegance, beauty, and rebirth.

The Internet enables us to grow not only as a spiritual community and as members of a global community, but also as individuals. Within it we have greater access to one another and to the most extensive and nourishing source of information that has ever existed. Witchcraft is a living, evolving spirituality—it is organic, and, like any living thing, it requires nourishment. The Internet provides an endless source of sustenance—for our minds, our souls, and our spirituality. We can learn about sacred sites, the religions of other people, deities, mythology, languages, philosophy, metaphysics, physics, mathematics, geology, history, architecture, art, dance, music, poetry, psychology, counseling, politics, and much more.

We can investigate the history and folk practices, cosmology and religious rites of our forebears. We can learn about sacred technologies and shamanic techniques, including altered states, divination, and energy and healing practices. We can investigate herbs, rivers, animals, weather, astronomy, or the biographies of inspiring figures. Beginners can learn how to cast a circle, and experienced practitioners can learn Sanskrit. The list is as infinite as our interests. And all of it enriches how we live and practice our spirituality. We can also teach one another. There are online classes, radio broadcasts, and self-publishing. We have created chat rooms and bulletin boards and sites where we can discuss techniques and experiences, issues and ideas, and share rituals and revelations.

The Web is where Witches are reconstructing the lost library of Alexandria, with rich resources exceeding the contents of this ancient temple of learning in ways that, until now, could only be dreamed of. The mysterious, energetic realms of cyberspace now host the knowledge of humanity throughout the ages and from all over the globe. All is literally available at your fingertips. And each keeper of knowledge and explorer of sacred mysteries on this Web of energy, light, and information is blessed by the guiding spirit of Hypatia, philosopher, mathematician, and acclaimed teacher at the university at Alexandria. Brutally murdered by a Christian mob, she dwells within each of us, just as the spirit of the great library of

Alexandria resides within the Web.

The Internet is also a temple of magic, a portal into realms of possibility and divinity. Circles, rituals, rites, and convenings are all held online. There are sites dedicated to deities and to sacred altars. There are spell workings and energy workings on the Web. Witches have transformed their holy outposts in cyberspace into safe and sacred space. Witches know that everything is energy, and our journeys along the pulsing paths of light coursing across the globe unite us as we weave a web of wonderment, wisdom, and divine revelation. We reweave connections, we enliven information with intuition, and we craft ourselves and our religion as we navigate the realms of cyberspace and cybermagic. We remember where we are and why we are here: all of life is divine and interconnected, and so, too, is the world revealed, woven, and made manifest upon the web of energy we call the Internet.

The path we walk within this web is as singular and unique as we are. But our magical journeys have shown us that we walk those paths in a shared and sacred landscape. Because we bring to it our sacred purpose—to nourish our spirituality both individually and as a community—the realm into which we all venture becomes charged with divinity. The same divinity that empowers the web of life empowers the web of light, and enlightenment, which we call the Internet.

It is a portal into realms of magic, a tool for making magic, and another form of divine energy with which to make sacred magic. There are patterns and connections, synchronicities and magical manifestations. Witches practice a spirituality of immanent divinity, a spirituality based upon our ability to experience the sacred within ourselves, and in the world. Our bodies are holy, and the Earth is holy, and Nature, as the embodiment of divinity, is our spiritual teacher. Has the Internet, and the prospect of cybermagic, returned us to transcendent and disembodied realms confined to the head? Will it endanger our spirituality by luring us into the culturally comfortable realms of abstraction?

I do not believe that is our destiny. We can choose to remain in our heads, or we can use this remarkable gift to open our hearts. For just as the Internet has nourished the growth of Witchcraft, Witchcraft is now nourishing the Internet. We carry the wisdom of Earth and body into the energetic dimensions of cyberspace. As Witches, we physicalize this realm of energy. We will not have the unique and necessary experience of casting a circle hand to hand, of feeling the heat and energy move from one Witch to another, of feeling the wind on our faces and the sun on our skin as we call to the elements, or of seeing and feeling the energy of the Goddess or God descend into and transform us. And so, we must always return to the Earth for our magic and our spirituality, to have the fullness of its divinity. But we can bring the power, the feeling, and the wisdom of those experiences into cyberspace and cybermagic. Just as we understand that the maxim "As above, so below" means that spirit and matter are one, increasingly our explorations on the Web will show us that "As within, so without." Our inner landscapes —which contain our spiritual, emotional, and physical feelings—will find ways of shaping the outer landscape of cyberspace.

What is our vision of the future? The Nobel physicist Richard Feynman wisely said that the only way to predict the future is to invent it. The magical frontier of cyberspace, with its chaotically infinite amounts of information, reminds us that at the furthest edges of chaos a pattern emerges—it is the pattern of spirals, the fundamental shape of life, from the molecules that constitute our DNA to the galaxies whirling around us. Let us nourish ourselves and our spirituality with the boundless wisdom the Web provides to us, and let us build temples in the realms of cyberspace, and in our hearts, that honor the spirit of Hypatia.

—Phyllis Curott, New York City, May 2001

ACKNOWLEDGMENTS

More than most books, this one is the result of the contributions, encouragement, and influence of many people. Much of my inspiration has come from them, their feedback has helped refine this book, and the mistakes are my own.

For sound and matter-of-fact advice, and confidence that I could do it, thanks go to my agent, Jennie Dunham of Dunham Literary. For seeing the potential, Emma McKay of ECW. For advice on the original proposal, John Hedtke ("Tiller"). For organizational help with this book and support since my very earliest days in the Craft, Diane Baker and the former Coven Raving.

For opening the world of feminist Witchcraft to me and then getting me in to the world of publishing, thanks go to Starhawk. For seeing potential and for offering encouragement, both in my personal and social growth within the Craft, for years and years, thanks go to Mevlannen Beshderen, Judy Harrow, and Brandy Williams. For divinatory guidance, my "Oracle in the Cave," Kat Suthon. For cheerful, competent, and generous support in creating and maintaining my Web presence, which is what got me this job in the first place, Elsa DieLöwin.

For help with computer catastrophe bail-out, Russell Williams, Chas S. Clifton, Pam Williams, Elvis Omar ben Tof, David Farrow, and Tom Caudle. For the discipline of the "Book in a Week" group, Jennifer Stevenson. For her lyrical foreword, Phyllis Curott. For consultation on matters of international interfaith, Donald H. Frew, and on interfaith higher education, Anne Hill.

For participating in my informal information gathering and my cyberweaving listserve, thanks go to Ginger Wages, Laura Spellweaver Wildman, Chris Classen, Melissa Oringer, Marilyn R. Pukkila, Panthera Orbweaver, BaAset, and Nanx. Help in specific areas was provided by the following folks:

- Sharing their experiences on early online webweaving—
  Carol Maltby and Magenta Griffin.

- Sharing insights about online ritual and online teaching—Jehanna Silverwing, Tom "Moose" Dixon, Abby Willowroot, Adam Jenkins, and Ceffyl.
- Allowing me the opportunity to experience online teaching directly—Cat Chapin-Bishop and Kirk White of Cherry Hill Seminary, and my wonderful classmates in Boundaries and Ethics.
- Providing information on online broadcasting—Sandy Johnson and Mark Kelly.
- Speaking on behalf of college students—Murph/Barda.
- Sharing her beautiful voice of Spider Woman—Mary Kay Landon.

For consultation on weaving metaphors, thanks go to former Holy Terror coven sister Beth Bone Blossom Stanford. For reality checks over the years, my sister in Reclaiming, Vibra Willow, who contributed much of the glossary, as well. For intellectually stimulating looks at a Nature religion practice in cyberspace, Shawn Arthur and Grant H. Potts.

For sympathy, encouragement, and a discerning eye, Grey Cat. For his Faggot Witch perspective on our movement, for keeping me from stepping in something malodorous, and for complimentary appraisals of my work, Sparky T. Rabbit. For morning chats "over the back fence" of e-mail, and for cheering me each step of the way, Patricia Monaghan.

For generously helping me keep my balance and perspective, for sharing their unique perspectives on the presence and growth of Paganism and Witchcraft on the World Wide Web, even though they'd never even met me, Fritz Jung of The Witches' Voice and Lhiannon/Jen Bryan of DrakNet.

And last, but most, to Corby Lawton, for keeping me fed, rested, and massaged, for taking me on walks in the fresh air in our beautiful coastal hills, for laughter and love.

INTRODUCTION

As with every other area of human endeavor, the ancient/future religion of Witchcraft has been profoundly affected by the advent of the Internet. Witchcraft has experienced tremendous growth and change over the past twenty years, and this growth has expanded beyond measure with the popularity of the Internet. Cyberculture seems to have a special appeal to Witches and Pagans. We Witches have readily embraced the Net, e-mail, the World Wide Web, chats, and the many other attendant features of cyberculture.

With the Diaspora, the Jews remained bound as a people by their sacred text, the Talmud, in spite of having no homeland. The endless discussion of passages and meanings the text generated held the Jewish people together. They became known as the People of the Book. I see Pagans, especially Witches, as evolving into what I will call the People of the Web.

The overarching metaphor of this book is the web, which encompasses the motifs of weaving, looms, spiders, shuttles, warp and woof. Certain threads will appear and disappear in these pages, only to be picked up elsewhere. I have indicated where a thread is dropped and where you can find it again. This, I hope, will make following them more fun; I also hope that it makes the book more demonstrative of the concepts I'm putting forth. Some threads are left dangling or unraveled. These threads invite you—and me, and us—to follow them to see where they lead and how they may be woven back into the tapestry.

Prior to the advent of the Internet and the World Wide Web, Witches and Pagans were isolated from one another. We did have working groups, commonly called covens, and we had "traditions," or families of covens whose members had learned from each other and passed on teaching via lineages. If and when a coven grew large, it "hived": a covener who had been adequately trained took some others with her and formed a new coven, or simply left and created a coven from scratch. However, several covens and traditions could exist in the same city, or even in the same neighborhood, and never even know about one another. While some of this fragmentation was countered by rural Pagan festivals, where friendships were born, most Witches lived their lives in the figurative broom closet. Discretion was the safe and prudent approach when it came to our religion. We kept ourselves, and our groups, to ourselves.

The Net changed all that. On the Web, isolated individuals and groups found one another. On the Web, networks were woven around common concerns and goals. The Web allowed community to be created where none had been. The anonymity of online communications liberated witchen folks to express their thoughts and feelings and experiences in relative safety. So, in a sense, the Web became our church. By following the filaments from node to node, by overlapping and interconnecting our weavings, Witches have woven a culture in cyberspace that is manifesting in terraspace.

The Net has given us, and everyone with Internet access, unprecedented networking capabilities. It has facilitated the building of community, both online and off. It has allowed previously fragmented groups to find each other and previously isolated people to find community. It has fostered the growth of Pagan rights organizations, Pagan publishing, organizing in general, and mobilization for Pagan safety and civil rights. The Net has provided us with unlimited resources to learn about our ethnic and cultural heritage, to reconstruct ancient rites, and to bond around these sharings.

All these changes have engendered the unique phenomenon of online teaching. We can now perform rituals and magical workings in cyberspace, when once we could only practice them in terraspace. As well, the Internet facilitates national and international spells. It has inspired the formation of online covens and has even led to the creation of new Craft traditions that exist exclusively in cyberspace. While the Internet has fostered online teaching and online magic, it has also increased our need for guidelines to evaluate any ventures we may be contemplating.

The Pagan movement and Pagan culture have been radically altered by these factors. In this book, I explore some of what I consider to be the more remarkable aspects of computer culture as it affects the national and global populations who follow Pagan paths. I invite you to pick up a thread and follow it with me through the complex and exquisitely rich tapestry that is contemporary Witchcraft and Paganism.

This book is an Internet baby. It was conceived on the Net, gestated on the Net, and birthed on the Net. The idea for it was manifested through the Net: the publisher found me there. My qualifications to write it were determined, in part, by my presence on the Net. Many of the notions expressed herein come from my own experiences as a Witch who uses her computer and her online connections. More important, however, is the fact that I'm writing from the perspective of a "terraspace" Witch—by which I mean that I'm a person who was trained in Witchcraft, magic, and ritual, and who continues to practice, in person, in a physical space with others, in real time.

My thoughts about the cultural effects that the Internet has had on Witchcraft have been greatly enhanced and refined by online communication with others via the wonderful medium of the e-list and other electronic communication. To help me write this book, I solicited a small group of cybersavvy Pagans to subscribe to an e-list and discuss some of the ideas I was working on. Throughout the book, I refer to them as my coconspirators. Some of my colleagues in this venture are longtime close friends; some are rather newer close friends whom I encountered online; some are interested and knowledgeable people whom I know casually, in person or not. Some live in other parts of the globe. All of us, in some way or another, gave birth to this printed work, filtered through my perceptions and understandings; the book is what I could relate to you of this synthesis.

Before we start, let me clarify some words I'll be using throughout the book. *Paganism* is a broad term that encompasses many Earth-based or Nature-oriented faith traditions, most of which do not revere a single father-sky-god as a monolithic entity. I say *Pagan* rather than *Neopagan* because the prefix *neo* implies that there was once a "paleo" Paganism that had a group identity and some shared values, beliefs, and practices. There was no such phenomenon. *Pagan* simply means "country dweller" or "peasant," and the term was used by the Romans as they expanded their empire across much of Europe, Africa, and the Middle East. Subsequently, it was adopted by other empire builders, such as England. To them, a Pagan was what we today might call a "hick."

Another term used to designate the indigenous peoples of conquered lands was *heathen*, or "dweller on the heath." Ironically, the early Roman Empire was created by people whom today we might call Pagans, in the sense that they were not Jews, Christians, or Muslims. The Roman armies were comprised of many men who worshiped a Persian god called Mithras. It was not until some centuries later, after Julius Caesar expanded the empire to the hinterlands, that the Emperor Constantine decreed Christianity to be the state religion.

The most numerous, and very likely the most visible, of the walkers on Pagan paths are Witches. *Wicca* is a subset of Witchcraft (yet in no sense less worthy). It is considered by many to be "purer" than Witchcraft because it is firmly based in British cultural heritage. Wicca has a goddess-and-god dyad; mixed-gender covens; a high priestess, and usually a high priest (often referred to by the acronyms HPS and HP); a degree system that indicates levels of competency and personal growth; a prescribed series of seasonal and working rituals; a common Book of Shadows (a book containing rituals, spells, pathworkings or guided meditations, songs, chants, and other materials found to be effective for that tradition); and, usually, a specific set of deities. Wicca is one of many lineage-based witchen traditions.

Aside from the Wiccans, there are several other kinds of Witches: those who work in same-sex covens, circles, groves, or other groups; those who work with a female deity or deities only; those who work within an egalitarian, nonhierarchical group; and those who work alone, called solitaries. These Witches may or may not have a Book of Shadows.

The practice of Witches and Wiccans is "Witchcraft," or "Craft," but many Pagans prefer the term *Wiccan* to *Witchcraft*. It serves to distinguish Craft from sorcery, "black magic," conjuring, and other practices that often earn their practitioners the sobriquet "Witch." However, in the context of this book, I'll be using the term *Witch* to mean "a practitioner of the Craft."

Another term for this is *Crafters*.

Just as all Witches are Pagans but not all Pagans are Witches, so, too, all Wiccans are Witches but not all Witches are Wiccans. That said, many use the two words—*Witchcraft* and *Wicca*—interchangeably. This book is about the cultural effects of the Internet on Witchcraft. The adjective I'll be using is *witchen*. I will use the word *Pagan* when I mean Witches, Druids, Asatru, and Pagan paths including Witchcraft.

I've provided further aids to understanding terminology used in this book in the form of sidebars and a glossary that defines the witchen terms that appear in boldface throughout the book.

Now, step with me into Spider Woman's sticky, lacy web.

Chapter 1

People of the Web

Nature and Webs — The Nature of the Web

As my late witchen friend Judy Foster often said, "If we Witches do anything, we look for patterns. It's what we *do*." The patterns of Nature are, in many ways, mimicked by the patterns of the Internet. I speak as a Witch, a priestess, and a layperson, not as a natural scientist, a technologist, or an engineer.

In popular culture, Witches are often depicted with spider webs nearby—in a doorway or window frame, hanging from a fireplace mantel; the places spiders weave their webs when they live in human habitations. I look at spiders and their choosing to live in a particular home as a good sign, a sign that the spider has blessed the home. There is a goddess among some Indians of the American Southwest called Spider Woman, or Grandmother Spider. Spider Woman's words begin this book.

**As the crickets' soft autumn hum is to us so are we to the trees as they are to the rocks and the hills.[1]
—Gary Snyder**

Witches generally see all life as interconnected. What is done in one place travels along the fibers and affects other places. When a thread is cut, the fabric is weakened. When a new thread is spun, the fabric is strengthened and renewed.

Spiders weave their webs in spirals. The galaxies whirl in spirals. DNA molecules form spirals. Vast galaxies, the compact universe of the spider's web, microscopic DNA molecules—all share this form. The macrocosm and the microcosm.

Solar systems form patterns as planets, on their discrete paths, circle their suns, creating interconnected webs. Even though they are not connected by tangible filaments, they are energetically linked. Spiders spin webs of filaments issuing from their own bodies, stretching them out to connecting vortices where they join with other filaments. When one of these threads is cut, the entire web is torn. An animal comes crashing through the underbrush and inadvertently tears the spider's web. The spider repairs it. She may not be able to restore it to its original pattern, but she is able to rebuild her home and her means of obtaining food.

In a fit of housecleaning, I take my broom and lift the spider webs from the corner of the room, destroying a spider's home. I apologize and tell the spider that she can rebuild it in the same place if she wants to, and I will not disturb it until I repaint the room or take down the curtains to wash them. If I find her loose in my house, I will carefully take her outdoors. I will never, ever kill her. I feel that she blesses my home, the people in it, and the activities we engage in by choosing to take up residence here. Still, her webs can be sticky and creepy. They fill with the empty carcasses of devoured insects, and I don't like to have them sticking to my skin, hair, and clothing. Usually, however, spider constructs her home in inaccessible places where we inhabitants of the house won't disturb her very often.

Only three weeks before this manuscript was due to

the publisher, I lost everything in my computer. Diagnoses offered by various computer professionals differed, but that didn't alter the result of the calamity. I had become dependent on this machine—and its wider electronic connections with e-mail, listserves, chats, and Web sites—for most of my professional pursuits. All my financial records existed in electronic form within my accounting software. All my databases and mailing lists existed in my computer. All the research for this book and other writings lived there, too. All drafts, all reviews and workshop descriptions, all correspondence and contacts lived within the mysterious inner world of this iMac I'm typing on. Most of my recent backup copies were on my main hard drive.

VIRUS: **A piece of programming code, usually disguised as something else, that causes some unexpected and usually, for the victim, undesirable event. It is often designed to spread automatically to other computer users.**

In the computer lexicon, a Trojan horse is a program that contains malicious or harmful code. This code is concealed inside apparently harmless programming or data; from there it takes control and does its special form of damage—such as ruining the file-allocation table on your hard disk. The term comes from Homer's *Iliad*. In the Trojan War, the Greeks presented the citizens of Troy with a large wooden horse in which warriors were hidden. During the night, these warriors emerged from the wooden horse and overran the city.[2]

They tell you always to back up your work, that it's not a matter of *whether* your computer will crash, but *when* it will happen. I cannot say that I felt invulnerable to such things, but I did think that I was less susceptible because of the kind of computer I use. Ironically, I was in the process of downloading software that I believed would lessen the likelihood of my computer being infected by a virus or a Trojan horse when the loss occurred.

I'm not excusing my laxity in neglecting to make external backups of my work. What I am doing is trying to ascertain the cosmic message behind this event, the reason it happened. I also want to try looking at it as an opportunity similar to the one that spider experiences whenever her home is wrecked. So, I hope that the contents of this book reflect Spider Woman's way of reweaving that which has been rent.

Christians, Jews, and Muslims are known as the People of the Book. Pagans, however, have always realized that one book is never enough. Pagans are not the people of the book; Pagans are the people of the library.[3]
—Steven Posch

People of the Library

We Witches are amazingly literate people. Step into any

Witch's home, and you'll find yourself surrounded by shelves and shelves of books. It's not unusual to enter the small apartment of an urban Witch and be confronted by a hallway lined with books. Those fortunate enough to have more indoor space often devote an entire room to their libraries. There are even community collections housed in private-membership libraries, such as the New Alexandria Library in Minneapolis.[4]

The type of reading material you'll find in a Witch's personal library is quite diverse. She may keep obscure and popular texts on Greek mythology alongside books on Renaissance clothing, Kaballah, orchid gardening, bats, **geomancy**, Norse languages, and Hindu cults.

GEOMANCY: Divination by means of lines and figures or by geographic features.[5]

My library, for instance, contains little science fiction, although this is a popular literary genre among Pagans. Instead, I collect books on feminist theory and women's history dating back to Second Wave Feminism of the late 1960s and early 1970s. I also have what one witchen friend terms "an inordinate appetite for contemporary fiction": American, Irish, biblical, Native American, African American, East Indian, South American, noir, pop. In my library, you won't find much in the way of romance or mystery writing, but there's lots of mythology, folklore, history, and psychology. One of my favorite genres is biography—from former Israeli Prime Minister Golda Meir to Eleanor of Aquitaine, from crime novelist James Ellroy to tree activist Julia Butterfly, from Lord Byron to labor activist Joe Hill.

My reading informs my perceptions of the world around me. I take inspiration from such contemporary fiction writers as Barbara Kingsolver and Dorothy Allison; African Americans Toni Morrison and Alice Walker; Spokane/Cœur d'Alene Indian Sherman Alexie; South

American magic realists Isabel Allende and Gabriel García Márquez, and North American magic realists Barbara Gowdy and Jane Urquhart; East Indian, Anglo-Indian, and American East Indian writers Gita Mehta, Chitra Banerjee Divakaruni, and Salman Rushdie.

Common to my library and those of many other Pagans are the works of anthropologists like Claude Lévi-Strauss, Mircea Eliade, and Joseph Campbell. Possessing the books of these authors does not necessarily mean that we agree with all of their ideas, or, if we do generally agree with them, that we swallow them whole. Nor do we share a common book of law, advice, lore, gospel, or liturgy.

British scholar Graham Harvey claims that "the formation and development of Pagan identities almost always features significant literary sources."[6] Most of us read voraciously, exploring a wide variety of topics and genres. We also write a lot: short and epic poems; chants and songs; articles and opinion pieces; ritual liturgy and litanies; letters to the editor; books of all kinds. The Reverend J. Gordon Melton of the Institute for the Study of American Religion in Santa Barbara, California, claims that "The first holy books of the Neopagans were anthropological texts."[7] And many Pagans and Witches declare their interest in still other literary genres—such as fantasy, utopian fiction, feminist theory, ecology—claiming that these writings have profoundly informed their theology and practice. Let's follow some of these threads of influence.

NATURAL SCIENCES

Many Pagan folk work in the fields of conservation and ecology—as microbiologists, botanists, ichthyologists, or cartographers. "I worship the ground I walk on" is a popular Pagan saying. We are life affirming, we rejoice in being alive and in being a part of this mysterious, glorious web of life. We love to witness the changing of the seasons and the cycles of life revolving around us. From seed to shoot, from blossom to seed; from egg to quail to food for a fox.

We don't share a vision of life, even when we're looking at the same things—each of us has a different way of experiencing the world. Some of us garden, or canoe, or work with injured sea creatures. Others work in laboratories surrounded by glass, steel, and plastic, with test tubes and cultures in petri dishes. Still others count bird species or watch the migrations of elk.

I know I am not alone in my fascination with satellite photos of our blue-green planet, photos made possible by the technology that sent satellites out of the gravity field to orbit the Earth. I watch the weather reports on television and visit a Web site to check the forecast at my destination if I'm going on a trip. In addition to revealing the distribution of land masses, continents, oceans, and polar ice caps, these photographs show the endlessly whirling and swirling patterns of storms, murky clouds of matter from within the Earth, released by volcanic eruption.

Geology: Richard Ely has been a geologist all of his adult life. He has also been a Pagan priest for most of that time. In his earlier years on a Pagan path, Richard used to think that geology had nothing special to offer to the development of Pagan sensibilities. He was mistaken, as he has come to discover. In the course of exploring the connections between Paganism and Earth sciences, Richard wrote a wonderful article called "The Nine Layers of Gaia," which was published as part of a *PanGaia* magazine column called "Scientific Mysticism: Mysteries and Magick of the Physical World."

I was so moved by simply reading Richard's meditation that I was inspired to learn it. And by learning it, by learning to feel and sense it, I learned more about my land, the land that supports me. I wanted to spread this knowledge to others by creating meditations of my own, so I rhapsodized to Richard about this refreshing and very real way to **ground**. Because he has a geologist's expertise, Richard knew exactly where I could find the precise geological information that I need to create a meditation.

GROUND: To connect yourself, your body, and your feelings in a circuit with the Earth. To consciously become connected to the energy of the Earth, usually through a meditation. This is considered essential to being able to focus and do magical work, and to prevent psychic distress.

Since we first talked about this, several years ago, Richard has generously helped me, a nongeologist, to create "geologically correct" meditations that I've used in many parts of the country. Each area has its own distinctive geology, so each meditation is different to a depth of about twenty-five miles. The Pagans I've done these meditations with have liked them; in a sense, they are more grounded than the basic tree-of-life meditation. Richard and I continue to plan them via e-mail.[8] Paganism, magic, minds, Earth science, and e-mail have joined together to form a vortex/node in the web of life where many strands intersect and connect.

Geologically Correct Grounding Meditation for Burlington, Vermont

[To be spoken slowly.]

Take a deep breath, then another, then a third, so that we are all breathing in unison. Stand with your feet shoulder-width apart. Press them into the ground. Feel the solid Earth that supports you. Honor the Earth.

Now center yourself in your body in your heart chakra. Bring your awareness to your heart, and allow it to open in a way that displays and invites love. Then will your energy and your awareness to descend through your lower chakras, down your legs, and into the soil.

Will your energy to descend further, imagining it as twin red cords that spiral around each other as they emerge from your feet.

We are standing on the remnants of a highly deformed continental shelf that accumulated between 550 and 440 million years ago along the shore of the Iapetus Ocean (the precursor of the Atlantic Ocean). Trilobites and armored fish populated the waters of this sea. Take a moment to imagine yourself standing on the shore of that ancient sea. Feel the latent consciousness of those extinct organisms lingering in the rocks.

Four hundred and forty million years ago, the Iapetus Ocean basin closed, and ancestral North America collided with ancestral Europe, one of several collisions that formed Pangaea, a supercontinent that included almost all of Earth's present-day continents. Great mountains rose up along the suture line where the continents collided.

Today, we are standing on the roots of those mountains, deformed shallow marine carbonate and shale, which were part of that ancient continental shelf that was thrust westward into the interior of ancient North America. Again, take a moment to feel the latent consciousness of those extinct organisms lingering in the rocks.

Two hundred and twenty-five million years ago, the Atlantic Ocean began to open, and present-day Europe separated from North America.

Now, send your awareness down further. Twenty-five miles or so down, we pass through the base of the crust and into the mantle. The temperature is around nine hundred degrees Fahrenheit. See the red Hadean glow of these rocks, feel their density. Garnet and olivine are typical minerals here. The rocks grow hotter and softer as your energy and awareness descend.

Sink your roots deeper and deeper. Eventually, at a depth of about eighty miles, we come to the base of the North American plate and enter the softer rocks of the asthenosphere, the mantle upon which North America slides as it drifts westward.

Sink downward through the Earth's mantle into hotter, denser rocks that glow yellow, then white, coming at last to Tartarus, at the base of the mantle, the shadow realm to which the old gods were banished. This is the place where anticontinents float on liquid metal, beneath a silicate sky, bordered by seas of magma from which rise eighteen-hundred-mile columns of molten rock, connecting that shadow realm with ours. These rocks do not melt because of the immense weight of the rocks above. Slowly, a few inches a year, the mantle flows, stirred by the heat of radioactive decay.

Pause here, and connect your energy with whatever powers you find compatible.

Molten rocks of the nickel-iron core are at eighteen hundred miles. Descend another thirteen hundred miles through liquid metal to the core. Here, at the center, is a great body of crystallized iron, the crystalline heart of Mother Earth. Bind your energy to this great crystalline body, and honor it as Mother's heart.

Now, ascend the path you earlier descended, bringing with you the cord of energy that is connected to the heart of Mother Earth. Pass through the liquid metal skin of her crystalline heart, through the glowing rock, meeting again the roots of those mountains of deformed shallow marine carbonate and shale, the ancient continental shelf, coming to the living soil of Vermont, and, at last, arriving in your own body, centered in your heart.

When your heart energy is joined with the heart energy of Earth, will the combined energies to rise through your upper chakras, emerging from your crown to rise to the cosmic heights, to the celestial in a fountain of love. Let the lower and upper energies mingle for a time, and then call them down, back to your heart center, where you pause and cherish them. Then will the energies to descend to the core of the Earth, while you stand as the world tree stands, a bridge connecting the great above with the great below.

Blessèd be.

— Richard Ely and M. Macha NightMare (© 1999)

WEB CAM: A cam, homecam, or Web cam is a video camera, usually attached directly to a computer, whose current or latest image is requestable from a Web site. A live cam is one that is continually providing new images that are transmitted in rapid succession, or, in some cases, in streaming video. There are now estimated to be several thousand sites with cams. The first cams were positioned mainly on fish tanks and coffee machines. Many of today's live cams are on sex-oriented sites. For travel promotion, traffic information, and the remote visualization of any ongoing event that's interesting, Web cams seem like an exciting possibility, and they will probably become more common as users get access to more bandwidth.[10]

Geomancers like Paul Devereux further explore old and new ways of understanding and connecting with the Earth's energy flows. In *Earthmind: A Modern Adventure in Ancient Wisdom*, Devereux, with John Steele and Reclaiming Witch David Kubrin, describes the many ways that our ancestors communicated with Gaia herself and suggests methods (including fasting and entrancement) whereby we may do the same. Devereux, Steele, and Kubrin also map several of the sacred places where communication is most likely to be effective.

Looking from Earth to the sky above, we find that there are Web sites—scientific, not Pagan—where a live camera has been set up inside a passage grave so that people all over the globe can watch the light enter the underground chamber at the precise moment on the morning of the Winter Solstice.

Astronomy and Archeology: Maes Howe is a megalithic chambered cairn in Orkney, Scotland. In 1996, an American druid named Lowell McFarland posted a message on the Internet asking if anyone was thinking of putting a camera in another cairn, New Grange, located in Ireland, in connection with the Winter Solstice sunset and sunrise. This inspired archeo-astronomist Victor Reijs to install a **Web cam** in Maes Howe; his aim was to better understand the alignments of this ancient structure, as well as to promote research, education, and tourism.

In 1997, photographer Charles Tait, who had been viewing the Winter Solstice sunset with his grandfather since his early boyhood, came upon Reijs's Maes Howe Web site. The ensuing collaboration between Reijs and Tait led to the live broadcast of the sunset on the Internet.[9] Over eight thousand hits were recorded in a three-week period in December of 1997, around the time of the Solstice; I was among the 950 people who visited the site on December 21, 1997.

The successful experiment of viewing the midwinter sun at Maes Howe via a Web cam involves a unique union of ancient and future technology. It opens endless Internet technology possibilities; it also offers us new ways to view our world and new ways to explore our religion. Many of the people who watch these extraordinary celestial events do so in the context of their celebration of the **sabbat**.

SABBAT: One of the eight days of the solar year, including the Winter and Summer Solstices, and the Autumn and Spring Equinoxes, which mark the turning of the Wheel of the Year.

Ornithology: Even those of us who don't travel can learn more about the Nature part of our Nature religion—through books, television, and video, and now through Web sites. If I want to know about a particular animal or tree or geological formation, I can surf the World Wide Web. I can, for instance, learn about the nesting habits, growth, and development of the peregrine falcon, because the Eastman Kodak Company, in cooperation with the Rochester Peregrine Falcon Project, has placed a human-made nest box on top of the Kodak Tower in Rochester, New York. Like the Maes Howe chambered cairn, the box is monitored by a Web cam. Websurfers can see four views of the nest box and its occupants, which change each minute.[11]

While ornithology is not a branch of Witchcraft or Paganism, the conservationists who mounted the Rochester

Peregrine Falcon Project are endeavoring to find new ways of living on our Earth and understanding it better. These are also the expressed values of many Witches. One could question the decision to intrude on the lives of these wild birds, but if we consider that their habitats have been damaged by encroaching humans, then we can see that the project's modification of their nests has helped ensure their survival as a species. It may not be the ultimate answer; nevertheless, it is a valuable contribution.

If you love birds and want to learn more about them, including how to attract them to your own backyard, visit the Backyard Wildlife site and view, via a Web cam, a backyard feeder near Fort Worth, Texas.[12]

Trees, Our Mother's Lungs: After I take a walk in the woods, when visual memories of the leaves, the bark, and the configurations of the trees are still fresh in my mind, I can take out a tree-identification book and browse through it until I find the particular tree that I want to identify. Or I can visit The National Arbor Day Foundation Web site.[13] There, I'll be asked whether the tree has needles and cones or leaves, flowers, fruit or nuts; these questions will guide me through all the other characteristics that make one species different from another, until an identification is possible. I can also look up a tree by name and find out what zones it lives in. I can view diagrams and a glossary. The foundation supports tree planting in urban areas and the effort to protect rain forests.

The Web allows me a range of involvement in tree-related activities, from reforestation to activism.

Some witchen working groups are called groves, or nemetons—sacred circles of trees. A Crafter may have a totem tree, may call herself Oak or Willow or Leaf, may devote his life to direct action against logging old-growth redwoods. Our Pagan beliefs, sensibilities, and values may impel us to take such action.

Fire: I'm creating a ritual using thirteen exquisite leather goddess masks made by artist Lauren Raine.[14] One is Pele, who haunts Moana Loa volcano. I need to learn more about her, and I cannot go to Hawaii. I want to give her voice to the mask wearer in the ritual, so I search the mythology and deity sites on the Web. I look for online shrines, poetry, and images, but I find little of substance. Where I do, eventually, find what I need is at the National Park Service site on Hawaiian volcanoes, at Aia La o Pele[15] and other travel sites, and at cultural-heritage sites like that of the Halau o Kekuhi dance troupe.[16] By doing this, I've skipped the library and entered the World Wide Web. The information that I gather on my quest brings a new dimension to the ritual art I create. (The thread of deities and online shrines reappears in chapter 4.)

Oceanography: One of my favorite scientific sites is the Monterey Bay Aquarium Research Institute (MBARI).[17] Just beyond California's Monterey Bay lies an underwater canyon the size of the Grand Canyon. In the dark depths of the sea, strange life abounds; unimagined species create their own peculiar ecosystems in which to thrive. Oceanographers at MBARI use an ROV (remotely operated vehicle) to explore regions of the ocean floor where the pressure is too great for humans to withstand. Sailing out to the canyon every weekday, they manipulate the ROV from aboard their vessel. They collect specimens and observe the underwater world. The ROV—wouldn't you know it?—is equipped with a Web cam, which records their work and broadcasts it live on the institute's

Web site.

These technological wonders may not seem all that remarkable to scientists, students of science, or people who spend a lot of time exploring the seemingly limitless World Wide Web. But for me, a layperson, a Witch, a woman who loves the sea and who grows uncomfortable when I'm away from it for long, this is an incredible resource. It opens my eyes to much more than I could ever experience on my own. I can see the Goddess in the mighty waves that crash upon the rugged coastal cliffs. I can hear her voice roaring in storms. I can feel her lull me when I float in calmer waters. And now, through the technological advance of the Web cam, I can visit the mysterious ocean depths where ninety-five percent of our precious planet's creatures live.

Grounding myself using the imagery of the very Earth I stand upon; viewing the midwinter sun rise and set from inside Maes Howe; finding out about reforestation from The Arbor Day Society; learning about Pele's behavior, gifts, appearance, and family online; marveling at the life hidden from us miles below the surface of the sea—all of these things inform my spirituality. They motivate magic. If we so choose, we can incorporate what we're learning in exercises, chants, songs, invocations, and other liturgy.

SOCIAL SCIENCES

A number of Witches are so intrigued by the social sciences that they make them their life's work. Wendy Griffin is one. A sociologist who has examined our society from a Goddess-revering perspective in her anthology *Daughters of the Goddess: Studies of Healing, Identity, and Empowerment*, Wendy is among the many scholars researching our Pagan past and present.[18]

Psychology and Psychotherapy: Jungian psychologist Clarissa Pinkola Estés is the author of *Women Who Run with the Wolves*, a book that has inspired many to seek insights and revelations in traditional tales. Coincidentally (if you believe in coincidence), Reclaiming's WitchCamps base magical work on tales. (To reconnect with the Reclaiming thread of this book, see chapter 5. The thread also reappears in chapters 6 and 7.)

Some WitchCamp sessions have been built around group and individual exploration of a folktale, fairy tale, myth, or bit of lore. WitchCampers and teachers spend an entire week exploring sections and themes of a given story, such as "The Ballad of Tamlin," "The Twelve Wild Swans," or the Mesopotamian stories of Inanna, translated from the Sumerian. Each night, they share a ritual linked to one part of the story. During the day, they may act out, dance, or make masks or costumes of individual characters from the story. They also go into the story in guided meditations.

The practice of magic can have therapeutic value for us when we perform rituals that have been constructed in such a way as to stimulate or reveal hidden parts of ourselves. Elements of what we learn from various psychological schools can be applied in magical situations. Witchcraft isn't therapy, nor was it ever meant to be. But its practice can indeed be therapeutic for those who want to bring about changes in their lives, or who seek greater self-awareness and healing.

Estés's book is just one example of writing on psychology that has enriched and enlivened the magical practices of groups and contributed to the personal growth and self-awareness of individual Witches.

History and Biography: The reading of history also informs and inspires our religion. We strive to relearn the ways of our ancestors. We reconstruct the ways of peoples and cultures of earlier times, and often of distant places. We research in conventional books, but we also have the benefit of the vast resources residing in cyberspace.

Some of us look to history for healthier, more balanced ways of living on the Earth. We seek knowledge of our forebears: how they lived, where they lived, what they ate, what sheltered them from the elements, what their architecture and cooking implements were like, what forms of food cultivation, animal husbandry, hunting, fishing, and planting they practiced. We can visit the places on Earth where our ancestors walked, the land that sustained them. And if, for whatever reason, walking that land is not an option for us, then we can explore it in books, art, music, dance, cooking, and at Web sites.

We may have intimations of previous lives lived in another historical place and time. This notion assumes a belief in reincarnation, a common belief among Witches and Pagans. Reincarnation is a topic that is too complex and too remote from this book to devote much time to here, but it does warrant mention. Through the ages, many fine minds have grappled with this concept and discussed it at length. There are books aplenty on **reincarnation**. In some societies, it is called the transubstantiation of souls. Not all of us believe in reincarnation in a literal sense, but it's safe to say that most Pagans see the patterns of life, the turning of the Earth, the changing of the seasons, the phases of existence, from birth through initiation to consummation to repose to death.

REINCARNATION: Most, but not all, Witches believe in some kind of reincarnation or rebirth —either in the sense that we all get recycled because everything comes from the Earth and our bodies go back into the Earth when we die, or in the sense that our individual identity, our spirit, becomes connected to a new person or life form.

We may be taken with a particular historical personage, or a constellation of people. Author and Tarot authority Mary K. Greer, for instance, was deeply interested in four women who lived in Western Europe at the turn of the nineteenth century.[19] With some male colleagues, these women formed the Order of the Golden Dawn, a magical lodge and working group involved primarily in Western ceremonial magic. At a time when most people bowed to convention and didn't stray from prevailing theological doctrines, the magicians of the Golden Dawn pushed boundaries to explore unknown psychic territory. These four women—Florence Farr, Moina Mathers, Annie Horniman, and Maud Gonne—are our magical foremothers.

Greer's fascination with these women led her to write their collective biography, calling it, appropriately, *Women of the Golden Dawn*. Her work inspired me to call the Golden Dawn women to join a group of us at table at a women's **Samhain** ritual. In my tradition, Reclaiming, we respect those we call the **Mighty Dead**. These are people on a magical path who have gone before us and are no longer living. I consider the women of the Golden Dawn to be among our Mighty Dead, and that's why I invited them to our sacred circle. In this way, both Mary Greer and I—and, I hope, the women who were in the circle to which Florence, Moina, Annie, and Maud were invited—applied biography to our practices.

If we want to take things further, we can explore the many Web sites that are related to these women, their collaborators in the Order of the Golden Dawn, and the methods they employed—such as Kaballah, astrology, Tarot, and **pathworking**. We can re-create their rituals as we have received them, or we can take elements and exercises from their workings and weave them into our own rituals in ways that are meaningful or appealing to us.

SAMHAIN: Also known as Halloween, Hallows, or Hallomas. Falling on October 31 in most traditions, midway between the Fall Equinox and the Winter Solstice, Samhain is the Witches' New Year, a major holiday. On it, we honor our Mighty Dead, celebrate our ancestors, mourn those who have died in the past year, and seek to contact the spirits of the dead.

MIGHTY DEAD: Those who have died and who are widely acknowledged as great priestesses, priests, and/or teachers of the Craft. The term is used in Reclaiming and Faery traditions of Craft.

PATHWORKING: A guided meditation.

RECONSTRUCTIVE AND HISTORICAL SCIENCES

Archeology: We have already seen that by combining archeology, technology, astronomy, tourism, and Paganism we can explore that which is ancient using tools that are new and relatively untried. And we can add recent archeological research to that list of tools.

One of the most prominent scholars to have influenced Witches is the late Marija Gimbutas. Dr. Gimbutas, born in Vilnius, was the daughter of two doctors who were political activists and members of the Lithuanian intelligentsia. Lithuania was the last European country to be Christianized, so its ancient Pagan traditions survived into the twentieth century. Her parents instilled in Marija a passion for education, political and aesthetic freedom, and intellectual achievement at a time when Lithuania, recently released from czarist tyranny, was being occupied by Polish forces. Speaking or writing in their native languages was forbidden, yet Marija's parents smuggled books.

With the encouragement of her family, Marija began collecting folklore at the age of fifteen. She absorbed the mythology of the indigenous Indo-European pantheon. She watched the changing of the seasons and observed the traditional ways of the people who worked the earth. She investigated aspects of Lithuanian culture, especially death practices and prehistoric burial sites. She collected folklore and ancient songs. She studied archeology, ethnology, and linguistics, gradually becoming a remarkable interdisciplinary scholar.

Marija fled the Soviet advancement on Lithuania in 1944. In 1949, she came to the United States. She published; lectured, researched; received awards, grants, and honors; and directed several major archeological excavations in southeast Europe. By the time she died, in 1994, Dr. Gimbutas had published countless papers and books. Her most important works, as far as modern Pagans are concerned, are *Goddesses and Gods of Old Europe* (1974, 1982), *The Language of the Goddess* (1989), and *The Civilization of the Goddess* (1991).

Although there are scholars who dispute the hypotheses that Dr. Gimbutas puts forth in her books, especially the later ones, she has garnered great admiration and appreciation among Goddess worshipers, Witches, and other Pagans. Her writings sit on bookshelves in many Pagan homes, some dedicated feminists are making a film about her life,[20] and she has inspired Web sites.

Catal Hoyuk: In the late 1950s, an archeologist named James Mellaart discovered the site of a city known as Catal Hoyuk on the Anatolian plains of southwestern Turkey. This city existed for about two thousand years during the time period of 7000 to 8000 B.C.E. (Before the Common Era), and it is the world's first urban center. Some of its spectacular sculptures and paintings are nine thousand years old, and they provide a direct window into Neolithic life. In the 1960s, Mellaart began excavating Catal Hoyuk.[21] Soon afterwards, the site became famous internationally, due to its large size and the density of its settlement, as well as to the spectacular murals and other art that was discovered inside certain dwellings. Excavations were resumed in 1993 by an international team of archeologists led by Dr. Ian Hodder. There were many things about this site that puzzled those who were seeking to uncover its mysteries.

So why is such an obscure endeavor as the excavations at Catal Hoyuk mentioned in a book about Witchcraft and the Internet? Because Witchcraft is a living, evolving faith tradition. And because some of the scholars who have begun interpreting the findings at Catal Hoyuk, including archeologist Marija Gimbutas, have posited that the existence of artifacts at the site gives credence to the belief that there were ancient matriarchies.

Most groups, reconstructionist movements, and political movements refer to a "golden age" in an attempt to justify their authenticity. This is as true of feminist Witches (Dianics—not quite the same as Witches who are feminists) as it is of any other group. Many believe that the architecture and artifacts of the people who lived in Catal Hoyuk confirm the fact that it was a female-centered society. So passionate have discussions on this point become that a section of one of the Catal Hoyuk Web sites is devoted to the dialogue.[22] (The thread of Dianic Craft and matriarchy reappears in chapters 6 and 7.)

Mythology and Folklore: Witchen author Margot Adler tells of having been immersed in Greek mythology when she was a child. She dressed up and acted out the tales. When I was a little girl, my mother read stories of the Greek and Roman goddesses and gods to me. I spent many hours listening, entranced and dreaming of the possibilities. My mother also read the stories of the Brothers Grimm to me, and those of Hans Christian Andersen, as well as other fairy tales. One of the series that most intrigued me was the Oz books, beginning with *The Wonderful Wizard of Oz*, by L. Frank Baum. Another of my favorite writers was eccentric Victorian mathematics teacher Lewis Carroll. I followed the White Rabbit down the hole. I stepped into the looking glass. I played with cards and kittens and chess pieces and teapots. I know that many of my coreligionists have had similar experiences. The books read to us in childhood—our early exposure to classical mythology, fairy tales, and biblical lore—fueled our imaginations.

Adding darker shadows to my growing store of supernatural imagery were the works of Edgar Allan Poe. In my first year of college, I jumped at the chance to take a literature class in mythology and folklore. My interest in these genres continues. They stir my imagination and remind me that there are other ways of seeing the world, other ways of knowing.

The primary piece of liturgy shared by all Witches is known as the Charge of the Goddess (see chapter 5). The Charge has its foundation in a book of folklore and an ancient Greek tale. The book is *Aradia; Or, The Gospel of the Witches*, written by American Charles Godfrey Leland in the last years of the eighteenth century and based on interviews with a Tuscan Witch named Maddalena. The tale is "The Golden Ass" by Lucius Apuleius, and it was written in the fourth century C.E. (Common Era).

Folklore is oral, and it derives from the people of the land, mainly peasants—hunters and fishers, farmers and falconers, herders, artisans, brewers and cooks. We Witches have our own oral culture, which has, in some ways, begun to move into cyberspace. There are now Web sites, not specifically Pagan, where urban legends, modern myths, and other such oral pop ephemera are collected.

Dr. Sabina Magliocco conducted field research in a small Sardinian village. She has explained some of the folkways of her beloved villagers and how these folkways manifest themselves today; she has also described what has survived, and in what forms, and discussed how these things may be seen as magical practices. In

1999, Sabina edited a special Wicca issue of *Éthnologies*, the journal of the Folklore Studies Association of Canada. Currently, she's completing a study of Neopagan altars. Sabina, herself a Witch, now studies contemporary Pagan folkways. With another folklorist, Holly Tannen,[23] Sabina also collaborates on studies of Pagan songs and Pagan humor. Their presentations at Pagan gatherings draw big crowds of fascinated folks.

Science Fiction, Fantasy, and Utopian Fiction: For many of us, the door to Craft was our interest in science fiction. This broad genre includes fantasy fiction and utopian fiction. Graham Harvey says that fiction, not works of theology, textbooks, or manuals, is "the primary literature of Paganism." Fiction writers may be informed by science, and they may address theology, but they are free to venture wherever their imaginations will take them. Harvey claims that "Pagans have rarely written tracts, creeds, manifestos, discourses, and other polemical literature. They have tended, rather, to express their vision and experience in poetry and novels."[24]

"The primary literature of Paganism," Graham goes on to explain, "is neither theology, textbooks nor 'how to do it' manuals, but fiction . . . Fantasy literature is perhaps the nearest contemporary literary form to the story-telling (around fires and sometimes in pubs or front rooms) that is typical of many Pagan events and celebrations. It also contains enchantment and magic that are at the heart of Paganism today. Experimental enchanting ritual and engaged story-telling represent and reveal Paganism far more than explanatory sermons."[25]

A series of medieval Welsh tales of the Cymri tribes forms an epic known as *The Mabinogion*. Translations of the tales, with scholarly interpretation and commentary, are available in bookstores; but when a fiction writer filters them through her own imagination and experience and rewrites them for contemporary readers, they are revived. This is what Evangeline Walton has done in a four-volume series called *The Island of the Mighty*. The tales of *The Mabinogion* are probably better known—at least in the Pagan movement—through Walton's books and the novels of other fantasy writers than they are through scholarly direct translations.

As Graham Harvey points out, "the narrative form allows and encourages an exploration and encounter that linear, hierarchical, systematic distillations prevent."[26] There is a Pagan church whose creation was inspired by a science-fiction novel. The novel is *Stranger in a Strange Land*, by Robert Heinlein, and the church is the Church of All Worlds (CAW).[27] Heinlein's novel does not view women in a way that most feminist Witches are comfortable with—and that includes me. Nonetheless, it has struck a chord in many people, prompting them to refine their thinking, beliefs, and practices to a level far beyond anything presented in the novel.

I think it's safe to say that Marion Zimmer Bradley's novel *The Mists of Avalon* has opened the door to Craft for more people, especially women, than any other. Bradley retells the timeless and compelling Arthurian legend from the perspective of its female characters. She depicts Arthur's sister, Morgaine, as a priestess of the Goddess and Avalon as the island home of all the Goddess's priestesses. In *Firebrand*, Marion Bradley retells the story of the Trojan War, a tale from a completely different time, place, and culture, recounting the events from the perspective of Cassandra, the seeress who was not heeded.

Diana L. Paxson is another novelist who writes what I

consider to be historical fiction, although her books are marketed as sci-fi/fantasy. With Adrienne Martine-Barnes, Paxson authored a trilogy called *The Chronicle of Fionn MacCumhal*, about the Fenians of Ireland. Irish deities live in the pages of Fionn's chronicle. In addition to other titles dealing with Irish and Welsh lore, Diana Paxson has written another trilogy, called *Wodan's Children*. These three books retell the stories of Siegfried (the wolf child) and Brunhild (the raven-haired Walkyrja), which have come down to us through the thirteenth-century epic poem called *The Nibelungenlied*. Wagner drew partly on these tales for his Ring Cycle operas, but Paxson takes quite a different look at the Norse magical and spiritual heritage.

The novels of Bradley and Paxson display several elements that are common in Craft and Paganism: feminist sensibility and empowered women; a foundation in earlier societies; and an attitude towards the nonrational or inexplicable experiences and phenomena that are attributable to divine influences. For instance, the character of Angus in Paxson's *The Sword of Fire and Shadow* (book 3 of the Fenian trilogy) is shown as he is in lore, as the Irish god who was Diarmid's father. Another novel by a different writer, but based on the same tales, portrays Angus as Diarmid's foster father—fosterage being a common practice in ancient Celtic cultures—rather than as Diarmid's divine parent.

Graham Harvey sees fantasy writing "as a mechanism for exploring possibilities and potentials: as a form of ritual or prelude to a transformative rite of passage. Fantasy does not necessarily misdirect people away from consciousness-raising, it need not be an opiate, but can be the much-needed catalyst for change."[28]

Other popular books with Pagan themes are *Lammas Night*, by the British author Katherine Kurtz, which deals with the magical defense of Britain by Wicca covens during World War II; *The Book of Kells*, by R.A. McAvoy, a time-travel story set in ancient Ireland with two archeologists as the main characters; *The Moon under Her Feet*, by Clysta Kinstler, about Mary Magdalene; and *Ariadne*, by June Rachuy Brindel, about a matrifocal Minoan Crete and its encounter with patristic Greek society.

Science fiction with a strong feminist attitude, by such writers as Ursula Le Guin, Joanna Russ, and Marge Piercy, informs some witchen folk. Other authors write of ancient matriarchies and remote times, when women characters were free of cultural constraints that inhibit their behavior and limit their choices. Pagans also read utopian fiction, such as Starhawk's *The Fifth Sacred Thing*; Dorothy Bryant's *The Kin of Ata Are Waiting for You*; and Sally Miller Gearhart's *The Wanderground: Stories of the Hill Women*.

A list of the works of science fiction, speculative fiction, historical fiction, and utopian fiction that inform and inspire Pagans would fill a volume of its own. Writing and reading these works allow us to explore new ways of being in the world, new technologies, new social systems.

From science fiction, in which imaginative speculation knows no limits, the mind proceeds to scientific theory, to experimentation, to proven fact, to invention. These are the steps that have led us to computers. In science-fiction fantasy, we find ancient ways of wisdom, but the genre is also a vehicle for projecting future possibilities.

Witchcraft and Computer Culture

What is it about the Internet that it adapts so well to our ways and our ways adapt so well to it? For one thing, Witchcraft has always respected scientific pursuit, scientific thought, and the technologies that have been realized by science. Witches are rational. We appreciate the Internet as a scientific construct. At the same time, we are intuitive and sentimental. By that I mean that we heed and value our experiences. And we care about our heritage, the ways and work of those from whom we descend.

Various formal and informal surveys conducted in recent years at, among other settings, Pagan festivals, have disclosed that a seemingly disproportionate number of Witches and Pagans work in the computer industry. This was true when Margot Adler's *Drawing down the Moon* was republished in 1986, and the trend is even more pronounced now. Erik Davis likens us to "Dionysian Nature worshipers who embrace the Apollonian artifice of logical machines."[29]

Another of my coconspirators, Ceffyl, of Knoxville, Tennessee, is a cofounder of KAPOW (Knoxville Area Pagans and Wiccans). Ceffyl, who was reared in the computer culture by parents who were a programmer and a technical writer, and who has been exposed to computers her entire life, says of the Internet, "It's another tool, like circle or **athames**, that can be useful in our work." She continues:

ATHAME: A ritual knife, usually two-sided.

> My primary uses of the Internet include teaching online, holding circles online occasionally, and creating learning-based environments on Web sites. (See, for example, <http:northwind.faithweb. com/

firstdegree>.)

I've been using computers since 1978, and currently work as a technical writer for an Internet imaging company. My parents were also in computer-related fields (programmer and technical writer), so I've been around them most of my life.

Computers do not seem odd or unnatural to me. Connecting to another person via an instant messenging program (like **ICQ**) is very easy and natural for me. Being in a chat room is the next best thing to having the person with you live—you can still read their auras, moods, and energy state through the network, just like you would if they were sitting next to you.[30]

ICQ: "I seek you." A downloadable program that will let you know when friends and contacts are also online, page them, and allow you to chat with them. ICQ enables you to send messages, files (single, multiple, or whole directories), and URLs directly to your friends' desktops. In addition, you can initiate an IRC-style chat session or voice and video-voice connection, and play games with the other ICQ members you are in touch with. Your contact is signaled of an incoming event as soon as it arrives and has immediate access to it.[8]

Witchcraft respects both rational, scientific pursuit of knowledge and emotional, intuitive, experiential perceptions. This makes it especially welcoming to modern technology and computer culture.

Pagans who work on the Net, who work in the computer industry, or who make it their business to become adepts in computer technology and culture are fondly referred to as "technopagans." Erik Davis describes these people as having "one foot in the emerging technosphere and one foot in the wild and wooly world of Paganism."[31] Technopagans see the patterns of magical technologies and schema within the workings of computers and electronic media. Jody, for instance, works on computers all over the United States from her own computer in her San Francisco office. She has studied the medieval Jewish metaphysics of the Kaballah, which she sees patterned in her work with computers. I am neither a computer technician nor a Kaballist, so it is beyond my abilities to

CHAOS MAGIC: To many, the term "chaos" denotes disorder, or complexity beyond understanding. But this is not what chaos magic is about. In essence, chaos magic is concerned with throwing out what its practitioners see as the unnecessary paraphernalia and rigid structures of magic and getting down to the core. Those who practice it move away from the complex beliefs and symbolism of other magical systems and instead employ a basic magical framework that produces results through methods unique to each practitioner. This framework provides a set of tools and techniques that often involve sigils, gnosis (or altered states of consciousness, achieved through a variety of methods), ritual, humor, and rigorous self-assessment.

The web of beliefs and symbols used by other magical systems is often seen by chaos practitioners simply as a set of tools rather than an end in itself. Thus, chaos magicians select the beliefs and symbols that best meet their needs in any given situation. A practitioner might, for example, use the Kaballah in the morning, H.P. Lovecraft's Cthulhu mythos in the afternoon, Egyptian mythology in the evening, and a system based on *The Rocky Horror Picture*

explain exactly how Jody sees this. However, I think this is a stimulating theory for magicians, Kaballists, and technopagans to explore.

Erik Davis attributes this to what he considers a basic desire on the part of technopagans "to honor technology as part of the circle of human life, a life that for Pagans is already divine. Pagans refuse to draw sharp boundaries between the sacred and the profane, and their religion is a frank celebration of the total flux of experience: sex, death, comic books, compilers."[32]

I am not a technopagan like Ceffyl and Jody, so I sought information, advice, and opinions from several technopagans in weaving this book. You will see the colored threads they have added to the tapestry.

On the way to becoming People of the Web, we Witches researched the many things that interested us in books, periodicals, newspapers, manuscripts, and other printed materials. We now do much of our research online. I asked my coconspirators to describe the ways that their personal and/or coven practices have been impacted by the Net, apart from the fact that it has allowed them to meet others of like mind, and even potential coveners. I know of people who've done a lot of online research on a specific ritual, sacred technology, deity or dyad or pantheon or ethnicity. Earlier, I explained how I found tales of Pele on the Web and drew from them in writing liturgy for Pele to speak.

One of my coconspirators, Adam, lives in Australia.[33] He is a self-described technopagan who has some traditional Alexandrian Craft training and a current passion for **chaos magic.** Adam says:

I find the Internet to be an essential resource as a Pagan. I look up deities constantly, especially when I'm interested in a particular one. But I also have used it extensively, both through e-mail lists and the Web, to learn about specific areas—such as chaos magic—when I find that I have an interest in the area.

In practice, I would say that the main influences for my spirituality now are about five percent books (although for general knowledge about Paganism and Pagan history that would climb dramatically), perhaps ten percent inspiration, about the same (ten percent) for real-life discussions (as much as I wish that was higher), and about seventy-five percent Internet. But then I'm weird, just like the rest of us.

The remarkable effect that the Internet has had on Witchcraft and Paganism is that it has become our community. Cynthia, a Virginia Witch, explains:

I believe the Internet has given Witches a "church," for lack of a better word; a meeting place and even better an anonymous meeting place. A woman who wanted desperately to be around other Witches but was so afraid of all the hype surrounding Paganism wrote to me, "I want to come to your meeting, but I am afraid you will take my measure and never let me escape." She could safely ascertain what was fiction and what was the truth over the Net. Whereas before she may never have ventured out of her broom closet because of all the stereotyped witchlore.

***Show* late at night (although I would rather not speculate on the type of spells for which *The Rocky Horror Picture Show* would be deemed suitable).**

Such magicians may even employ Wiccan symbolism and call on the Wiccan God and Goddess, or use Christian saints and symbols. The important thing is not which symbols they use, nor which belief system they employ, but which system will be most effective for the particular tasks they have in mind. Indeed, the system doesn't even have to be "real"—practitioners are welcome to create entirely new and unique belief systems if they so choose.

Chaos magic is an exciting method of approach. Its extreme degree of flexibility, when compared to other systems, has allowed its practitioners to tackle almost any goal they may choose, while exploring new territory, techniques, and tools (such as the Internet). But the most interesting thing about chaos magic is neither its forms nor its flexibility: it is the attitude of the chaos magician. Practitioners use techniques, not because they were taught to use them, but because they work. In the end, a chaos magician uses what feels right, being far more interested in the performance of magic than in the theory.

As to what makes the Internet appealing to us; simply, it gives us a voice we never had before by presenting the number of Pagans no one would have believed existed in a medium that doesn't have morals like other forms of media. It is our words, uncensored and stripped of the Hollywood image. For the first time, our work, words, thoughts stand side by side with everyone else's with equal weight and without editorial comment.[34]

COWAN: A person who is not a Witch, just as a Gentile is a person who is not a Jew.

PENTACLE: A five-pointed star figure, with one point at the top, which is enclosed in a circle. Tool of the North. The pentacle is used to achieve psychic balance and to enable people to experience various connected energies in a concentrated way; each of its points is associated with different powers and qualities.

Reclaiming and Faery traditions of the Craft use two, and sometimes more, tradition-specific pentacle schema: the Pentacle of Iron, the points of which are sex, self, passion, pride, and power; and the Pentacle of Pearl, the points of which are love, law, wisdom, knowledge, and power. In addition, each pentacle point corresponds to a "point" of the body when it assumes a pentacle position (arms straight out to the side, legs wide apart): head, hands, and feet.

The Vastness of the Web — E-Connected Witches and Pagans

The World Wide Web is so vast that no one can know every part of it. But how vast is vast? In researching this book, I found that not only is it impossible to obtain an accurate count of how many Witches and Pagans there are in the world (or in the Americas, or in the United States), but it is also impossible to determine the percentage of people with Internet access. This is something that the Net and Craft have in common. Still, with increased public understanding and more widespread acceptance of Paganism, we are coming closer to knowing approximately how many people follow Pagan paths.

The choice to follow such a path is not without risk. I have known Witches who have had their homes firebombed. And witchen parents who have lost custody of their children in divorcing their **cowan** partners. Witches and other Pagans have lost their jobs and been evicted from their rented homes and business premises. Witchen teens have been harassed and even suspended from school for wearing jewelry, such as **pentacles**, that indicates they might be Pagans.

So, while Witches are no longer subjected to the kind

of persecution they endured in the past, many still feel the need to hide their identities from intolerant communities. (Fortunately, there is a constitutional separation of church and state in the United States, which guarantees freedom of religion.) All of this has made assessing our exact numbers an impossible task, but I have been able to gather several figures that shed some light on the dimensions of the Pagan population.

The Pagan Educational Network (PEN) estimates of the number of Pagans living in the United States range from 150,000 to 600,000.[35] Again, because of a tradition of secrecy among Witches, and because the movement has no central authority, accurate estimates are hard to make. Yet all leaders within the Pagan movement report that growth is meteoric, with the demand for teachers, resources, and festivals outstripping the supply.

The Wiccan/Pagan Press Alliance (WPPA) is the movement's only association of Pagan presses. Silver RavenWolf, director of the WPPA, estimates that there are 600,000 Pagans in the United States, based on WPPA memberships. There are over 150 member publications of the WPPA, which does not include the thousands of smaller, locally circulated newsletters.

The Church of All Worlds (CAW), founded in 1962, is one of the oldest Pagan organizations in the United States.[36] Until recently, CAW published the *Green Egg*, and it was the oldest magazine in the Pagan movement. *Green Egg* publisher emeritus Oberon Zell-Ravenheart estimates a Pagan population of half a million in the United States, based on the magazine's database. Not long ago, this database listed over thirteen hundred groups and approximately seven hundred periodicals. Many, but not all, members of CAW consider themselves to be Witches.

John Machate, coordinator/CEO of the Military Pagan Network (MPN), estimates that there are ten thousand practicing Pagans in the U.S. military (active duty, guard, reserve, and dependents).[37] This figure is based on surveys conducted for MPN and is accepted by the Armed Services Chaplains Board. The *Military Chaplains Manual*, published in 1978, contains information about Witchcraft for the military chaplains of any faith. A major contributor to the manual is a Witch.

A survey conducted in 1998 found that nineteen percent of Unitarian Universalists identified their practices as "Earth-centered," a term broadly connoting a Pagan worldview. This would indicate that in the Unitarian Universalist Church alone there are over 95,000 Pagans (or people with practices and beliefs similar to those of self-identified Pagans). Many Unitarian Universalist churches support congregations called Covenant of Unitarian Universalist Pagans (CUUPS).[38] Among the CUUPS Pagans, many specifically identify themselves as being Witches.

Llewellyn Publishing, based in Minnesota, is the largest publisher of Pagan books in the United States. The company's current catalog lists over four hundred titles, with an average print run of 47,000 copies each. A significant number of Llewellyn's titles deal with Witchcraft and topics related to Craft, and Llewellyn's market consists of many Witches.

Witchen author and activist Phyllis Curott says that there are millions of Witches in the United States, citing a 1991 estimate provided by Reverend J. Gordon Melton of the Institute for the Study of American Religion in Santa Barbara, California. Ten years ago, Melton claimed that the Pagan population in the United States was

130,000, and that it doubled in size every eighteen months. Basing her figures on Melton's 1991 estimate, Curott claims that the present Pagan population is from one to three million—or between 0.5 and 1.0 % of the nation's population.

Since its founding in 1997, The Witches' Voice (Witchvox, or TWV) has grown to become the most popular Pagan site on the World Wide Web.[39] As of summer 2001, The Witches' Voice averages over 1,500,000 actual pages viewed (nearly eight million hits) per moon cycle. Its contact/networking section lists over forty thousand Pagans, events, groups, and shops worldwide.

When breezes pass through webs or weavings or attached strings, they evoke sound. When threads are plucked, they sing. When a web has become sufficiently large and encompassing—and the witchen web has done so—it acquires a voice. In many respects, this voice issues from a phenomenal two-thousand-page Web site called, appropriately enough, The Witches' Voice. Throughout this book, just as you will see threads appear and then disappear only to resurface somewhere else, so, too, will you hear the sounds of The Witches' Voice.

Chapter 2

FOLLOWING THREADS: WAYS OF LEARNING

How Learning Takes Place on the Web

When Margot Adler's classic study *Drawing down the Moon* was reissued in 1986, the author included in the appendix the results of an informal survey she'd conducted during the process of updating her book. Adler had found a preponderance of computer professionals among her Pagan respondents. What could account for this? Is there something about computer thinking that makes it especially compatible with Craft? I asked my coconspirators. Grey Cat said:

> I believe that there are two reasons why so many of us feel comfortable on the Internet. One is because our religion is pretty much not hostile to science and invention. We don't have the need to keep things as they "were" in order for our faith to remain strong. The second reason is that we don't have the cultural prejudice about "other" sorts of communications. The "between the worlds" quality of the Internet isn't nearly as strange to us as it may be to the "average American."

And Adam said:

> I think that both Witchcraft . . . and the Internet are extremely compatible in the way in which you learn. Traditional teaching methods are basically linear, but the Internet encourages you (and, in fact, almost forces you) to take a nonlinear path. You pick and choose the answers that are right for you, rather than learning from a set of established dogma in a linear fashion. Thus, the Internet encourages people to follow Pagan-style religions, where they can choose the aspects of their religion that are right for them. I guess the terms most often used to highlight this are to say that Witchcraft, the Neo-Pagan movement, and the Internet are postmodern and tend to use postmodern learning methods, while most other churches are modernist, teaching an absolute set of truths, and thus do not fit in well with the new paradigms of the Internet.

COVEN: An autonomous group of Witches who meet regularly to do magic. Traditionally, a coven had thirteen members and met under a full moon. Today, a coven may be any size, and its members may be women or men. In some traditions, there is an accepted set of coven leadership and membership requirements. In the Reclaiming tradition, covens set their own rules. Most covens meet privately and are not open to visitors; occasionally, however, a coven may declare an open ritual and invite outsiders to join for that ritual only. Coven membership is gained through personal contact. Often, coveners become very close and consider each other as family. Covens are also known as "circles" or "groves."

Contemporary Witchcraft draws on many, many sources, and individuals, **covens**, and traditions combine these sources in ways that work best for them.

The Net is ideally suited to this type of learning. Erik Davis puts it succinctly when he says that "Magic is the science of the imagination, the art of engineering consciousness and discovering the virtual forces that connect the body-mind with the physical world."[1] Adam offers a more practical explanation:

> [T]he Internet leads you to learn by choosing your own path, in any topic, be it religious or secular, and this is a very postmodern concept of learning.

> Thus [for whatever topic] . . . I want to learn about . . . I have at my disposal hundreds of arguments from every possible point of view, and it is my job to choose which ones I want to listen to. It is the same with spirituality. If I want to learn about spirituality and have access to the Internet, I will be drawn to choose bits from a large number of sources, rather than taking all my information from one source. The resulting mix will be uniquely my own, rather than something dictated by an individual tradition.

I asked my coconspirators whether they found Craft and the Net compatible with their practices. In response to that, Adam wrote:

> First, I see computer networks as being energy networks, and as being very real, in much the same way that this world is real. This e-mail exists, and is real, even though I can't touch it. So, given that, I think computers and cyberspace are something we can work with, in much the same way we work with energy in other forms when doing a pathworking. It is at most a different kind of energy . . . The second area where I think they are compatible is that of how we work with the respective energies . . . [Computer] programming is all about creating with words and concepts, rather than with hands. Magic is, I think, similar—we create with words and ritual, rather than with physical objects. Tools, much like keyboards and monitors, are there to direct the words and intent, rather than being essential in and of themselves. Computers provide us

with a new set of tools with which to direct our intent, and possibly with a new space to direct it into, but they still use many of the same paradigms, and hence are very compatible.

Mark Kelly, a Seattle Witch and creator of the online radio broadcast *Earth Radio International*, replied:

> The Web is a living example of what we Witches are always yapping about: everything is connected, you can't do anything without affecting something else, and so on, and so on. The Web is the making of that ideal. I can connect my little Web document to any other resources in the entire world without cost, without worry, and without restriction. What's mine isn't, in fact, really mine . . . it's all part of the whole **egregore** of the Web . . . Often, we're moving in opposite and opposing directions, but the fact is that it takes energy to add to the Web, and most additions are intentional . . . It's not that the Web is a magical tool so much as it's a magical act . . . [The ceremonial magician in me says] that the magical concept at work is hypertext. The tool employed is **HTML**. The result of the magical act is the Web.

EGREGORE: A kind of group mind, which is created when people consciously come together for a common purpose . . . [It] has the characteristic of having an effectiveness greater than the mere sum of its individual members.[2] —Gaetan Delaforgem

HTML: This stands for "hypertext markup language"; it is coding for mounting text on the World Wide Web.

Ceffyl, of Tennessee, wrote that "Networks are giant energy systems, and Pagans . . . seem to specialize in dealing with forces like that. It's part of our belief system (animism). So, connecting to a network of computers is rather like connecting to the divine in everything. That universal life force also moves the electrons over the networks." And Rune, of Sylvan Grove, claimed that the

Internet, "being composed of energy, has more in common with etheric or astral-type things than physical." She then added, "The wires and servers and such simply being the physical manifestation of 'it.' With 'it' having an existence beyond those mere components."

Taking a similar perspective, SilverPeace, a student at a Midwestern college and an active member of one of the many Pagan student groups proliferating throughout the United States and Canada, wrote, "This medium is suited to Witches because it is truly magical, since all it is is energy. Data on a server is only little bits of digital code that when sent to another computer via phone lines or satellite in an energy form is translated to something that is pleasing to the eye or ear. What is magic but the transmission of energy from one person or thing to another?"

Another way the Net fosters learning is as a powerful medium for dispelling rumors. The Net gives us the opportunity to present ourselves to the e-connected world in ways that we feel are truer to who we are than the representations put forward by those who aren't Pagan. Not only do we learn from each other, and perhaps see each other more clearly, but we also teach others about who we are, about the things that matter to us, our causes, our tastes, our personalities.

Obviously, there's much more to be said about how we learn. Studies of learning fill volumes. Schools, colleges, universities, and hospitals employ many people and use many computers to study ways of learning. Through the voices of my coconspirators, I have explored some of the ways that Witches learn on the Net. Now I'll describe some magical ways of learning.

SACRED TECHNOLOGIES

It is beyond the scope of this book to provide a detailed presentation of all the sacred technologies that have been developed over the ages and throughout the world, technologies that we contemporary Pagans, living in a multicultural, multiracial, borderless global village, are exposed to. Instead, I'll give brief descriptions of a few of the more popular ones.

MAGIC: The art and practice of changing consciousness at will.

As we learn various sacred technologies, we discover which work best for each of us. And each time we perform them, we respond to their transformative influences more readily. We employ these technologies to attain a conscious connection with the divine, to look within ourselves, and to explore realms beyond this time and place.

Let's assume that we want to understand something from an alternative perspective, or from a combination of alternative perspectives. We've looked at a situation from every angle; we've considered every possibility; we've examined every factor; and we've expounded every theory. Now we want to understand it from a metaphysical perspective, from a cosmic perspective, from a holistic perspective.

CIRCLE: A sacred space in which a ritual, or any kind of magical work, is done, either by an individual or a group. Often, people stand in a circle to begin a ritual, but during the ritual they may move about in any configuration and are still said to be "in circle." A circle is also a concept fundamental to the thealogy of modern Witchcraft, generally referring to the cycle of life, death, and rebirth, and to the interconnectedness of everything in the universe. The word "circle" is also a synomym for "coven"; used as a verb, it means to join others in a sacred space.

The first thing we must do is consecrate a space. I would choose a space that is in some ways removed from ordinary reality. Sacred spaces, holy places, or power spots are found throughout the world. The Wailing Wall is sacred to the Jews. Muslims worldwide are enjoined to make pilgrimages to Mecca. The pyramids of Egypt were erected to enshrine the remains of sacred personages, and those of Central America were designed as sites for the performance of sacred rites. The list goes on and on: the River Ganges; the mounds of Illinois; the Rock of Cashel; the baths of Sulis, in Britain; the statues of Easter

Island, in the Pacific Ocean; the temples of Machu Picchu, in Peru; Niagara Falls; the Dakshineswar Temple to Kali Ma, in Calcutta; Uhuru, in Australia.

Some sacred spaces have been made by humans, and others were discovered by humans. The cave of the oracle at Delphi, Greece, where prophecy was spoken, may have had certain properties—perhaps fumes from something molten, deep in the Earth, or fragrances of herbs known to facilitate divination—that allowed the sybil more intimate access to the divine.

Not only do Witches recognize and appreciate these numinous world locales, but we also find special natural places close to where we live. Of course, we don't all have access to remote natural places. It is a fact of contemporary life that people are nearly everywhere. Since most of us would like to keep the little wilderness that remains pristine and untouched by human presence, we create sacred spaces for ourselves, through ritual, wherever we might be when we prepare to focus ourselves to do **magic**.

As often as not in our modern world, the most secluded spaces for performing our rites are at our homes—a backyard garden if we're lucky, but usually an indoor space.

The nearly universal initial step in preparing a sacred space is the creation of a sacred **circle**. This may be done in many ways: we may sweep an area clean; mark it in sand; cut it from the air with a blade; trace the shape in grain, flour, or colored powder; tread it, sing it, **asperge** it, **cense** it. A circle is said to be **cast**, **cut**, erected, and ultimately sealed. Casting a circle reinforces our sense of safety, of being protected from unwanted intrusions. This sense of trust in the sanctity of the circle enables us

ASPERGE: To purify ritually by sprinkling with salt water; often, this is done by dipping a fragrant branch, such as rosemary, into the water and sprinkling it over the participant in a ritual.

CENSE: To purify, using incense or the smoke of a smudge stick.

CAST: To "cast the circle" is to define the boundaries of the sacred space, usually a circle in which a ritual is about to take place.

CUT: To cast a circle, or to ritually leave or enter a circle after it has been cast by carefully opening a space to pass through and closing it after crossing the boundary.

ENERGIES; ENERGY RAISING: The use of various techniques, such as rhythm, movement, and voice, to increase and intensify the focused energy of a group. Such traditional techniques as chanting, drumming, and dancing can be employed to direct and release the energies that will effect the group's intent. The most easily observable indication that energy is elevated is heat: the room becomes warm, and the people who are raising the energy begin to sweat. Energy raising can magically empower a spell, healing, or other working; and when energy is raised to a peak, we shape it into what we call a "cone of power" and "release" it, either by directing it towards something, or by grounding it (that is, by allowing excess energy to drain into the Earth and become absorbed).

ELEMENTS OF MAGIC: The four substances (Air, Fire, Water, and Earth) necessary to the creation and sustenance of life. Each is associated with one of the four directions; a particular tool; certain qualities and powers that exist in the outer, physical world and within each person; certain colors, life forms, and natural phenomena that correspond to each direction. We begin at the East by

to travel more easily out of ordinary consciousness. It also serves to focus and contain the energies we summon forth or raise, so that we can better manipulate and direct them towards our desired goal.

The circle delineates a semipermeable but distinct boundary that acknowledges the mundane as separate from the place we call "between the worlds." It is a space outside of space, and a time outside of time, with no beginning and no end. Once we take steps to purify the space and the participants and to cast the circle, a shift in consciousness begins to take place. Words, gestures, the aroma of incense are the basic sacred technologies and technologies that assist us in making the shift.

Once a space has been demarcated as a sacred circle, we honor the cardinal directions with words and gestures; that is, we address East, South, West, and North. We summon these **energies** to bless and balance the activities that will take place within the circle.

Most Pagans ascribe certain **elements** to each of the four **directions**, though the specific ascription may differ from one group to another. We call this process creating sacred space. How, then, do we create sacred space online? We'll look at ways this might be done when we talk about cyberrituals and cybermagic in chapter 6.

Even prior to casting a circle, many of us will create altars to hold meaningful objects—for example, feathers, rocks, seashells, bones, a blade, a **wand**, a candle, a **cup**, a pentacle—that are symbolic of the element. Creating an altar prepares us to enter sacred space and to shift consciousness. It may be approached as a devotional task to strengthen the preparatory experience; a preceremony ritual bath is another act of preparation. Donning ritual garb, jewelry, or implements, or taking off all of our clothing, can help move us towards another reality.

The purpose of the circle may be celebratory, such as honoring the turning of the **Wheel of the Year**. It might also be to perform a rite of passage for an individual, couple, or group to consecrate a change in status. Examples of rites of passage are a birthing; a baby-naming ceremony; a young woman's first blood; a marriage; an initiation into a coven, sisterhood, or brotherhood; a graduation or the completion of a degree, either secular or magical; a birthday or anniversary; a career advancement or job promotion; the signing of a contract; the buying of a home, car, or business; a dying; a memorial or funeral—virtually anything we feel is worthy of ritualizing. Birthdays are festive rites of passage, whereas other such rites are somber occasions; but most call for some sort of concluding celebration.

Depending on the reason for the circle, we employ different magical techniques. If we are celebrating, we want to sing and dance and feast. Singing raises our spirits, dancing raises our energy, feasting brings pleasure to the senses—all celebratory.

Singing, or other kinds of music, can also be used to evoke sorrow and tears. For a healing ceremony, we choose music—something soothing or hypnotic—that is very different from the music we select for a celebration. A lullaby, a song or a chant that comforts and brings sleep, is appropriate for a healing circle when the subject of the healing is in pain or carries so much tension that she needs help to let go of it.

We seek to learn from our gods. We do this by talking with them, by performing devotional acts, by inviting them into our circles, and even by inviting them into our bodies. Many Craft traditions are ecstatic in nature.

calling in the element of Air, progress to the South and the Fire element, to the West and Water, to the North and Earth, and, in some traditions, to the Center, representing Spirit, Ether, and Now.

DIRECTIONS: East, South, West, North (also known as the quarters), and Center. Each direction has an element and particular powers and qualities associated with it. The Center is the center point of the circle.

WAND: Tool of the South. Usually handcrafted by its owner, a wand is a rod or stick, from a few inches long to an arm's length, which may be embellished with carving, crystals, feathers, or other objects of significance to its owner. Used to direct energy.

CUP: Tool of the West; used to hold salt water, water, or any drink used in a ritual. In some traditions, the cup is symbolic of the female. It may be a goblet, chalice, bowl, or other vessel capable of holding liquid.

WHEEL OF THE YEAR: The eight major holidays, called "sabbats," of the solar year, which mark the turning of the Wheel.

By that I mean that we seek "ex-stasis," to be out of the stasis, beyond the ordinary. When we do this, we rely more on intuitive knowledge, we act spontaneously and without inhibition.

The shifting of consciousness that I frequently mention here is a type of ecstasy. In addition to the combinations of ritual methods discussed earlier—preritual bathing, altar building, space sanctifying—the easiest and most accessible means of shifting consciousness is fasting. Fasts can last for several days, just for the day of the ritual, or for several hours before the ritual. I advise people not to do magic on a full stomach: the digestive process tends to slow us down. The time to eat is after a working has been completed, and then it's very important to do so; we must reground ourselves in our bodies and restore the energy we've used doing magic.

In addition to fasting, another easy method of moving from the mundane to the magical is to change how we are breathing. There are a number of breathing techniques that can aid our magic. Most of the ones that I know are yogic in origin. I was fortunate to have as one of my early teachers a woman who taught voice, deep-breathing techniques, Hindu toning into the **chakras**, and Mongolian overtone chanting.

CHAKRAS: Literally, "wheels." The term derives from Hindu beliefs. A chakra is one of seven energy vortices located throughout the human body, beginning at the base of the spine and ending just above the crown of the head. These are "opened" or stimulated through certain physical movements and psychic/mental/spiritual techniques, so that the energy can be released and utilized.

Sustained chanting, done over a period of minutes or hours, creates within the chanters a state of enchantment. They become enchanted. Breath work, chanting, and enchantment are my favorite ways of shifting consciousness and of empowering my magical acts.

Prolonged ecstatic dancing—the kind that Sufi whirling dervishes do, or rave dancing, or the dancing young adults did when I was one (wild dancing in parks and light-show illuminated dance halls)—is another way to achieve an altered state of consciousness. Many Witches perform worship and devotionals by offering their bodies in praise; it is their primary method of worship. There are other sensory methods of awakening alternate consciousness besides dance and vocalization. Stimulating the skin by slapping, pinching, pricking, abrading, tickling, and other means of tactile sensory stimulation also has a consciousness-changing effect.

With dancing, song, and chant go rhythm. Drums of all kinds—gourds, bones, maracas, castanets, rattles, systrums, spoons—are sacred tools of transformation. We use them in our magic. We enhance and reinforce our dance using the rhythms tapped with our feet and reverberating within our bodies. We synchronize our voices and music to the rhythms of the percussion instruments. Drumming is a sacred art performed by the priest/esses who control the structural foundation of a ritual. Through their drumming, they are able to accelerate, decelerate, deliberate, syncopate, and otherwise help to raise, shape, and direct the energy of the circle.

Another means of changing consciousness and entering into communion with the divine is by using **entheogens**. These are organic substances—usually plants, such as mushrooms—the ingestion of which engenders experience of other worlds and other entities. A common substance that can be entheogenic is wine, which brings us the ecstatic experience of the god Dionysus. Wine is not usually employed in this way, but it and other alcoholic beverages can induce an out-of-the-ordinary state of consciousness. Vegetarians may eat meat for sacramental purposes.

ENTHEOGEN: God within; god- or spirit-facilitating. An entheogen is a psychoactive sacramental, a plant or chemical substance taken to occasion primary religious experience—for example, peyote cactus, as used in the Native American Church.[3]

All of these techniques—fasting, breath work, chanting, ecstatic dancing, sensory stimulation, rhythm—

change our energy levels and affect what we are doing with energy. Most of them raise energy—that is, they stimulate and invigorate, inclining us to faster, louder, higher, more intense activity. We empower our magical workings with the energy we raise in circle. It is the way we use the energy we raise that sanctifies our acts. The expression we often use to describe this is "raising a cone of power." The raised energies cannot be measured by any objective method, but the temperature of the participants and of the chamber in which they're working will rise discernibly.

Once the circle has been cast and the directions, or quarters, have been honored, we begin the invocations and workings. An explanation of how this happens will emerge as we look at more ways of learning.

INTUITION

We experience intuitive knowledge in several ways. One way is by seeing things—we have vision, we are clairvoyant. Another is by experiencing emotions—we feel sorrow or joy or apprehension, and we know in this manner. Also, we experience physical sensations within our bodies—chill or tightness or tingling; this is a kinesthetic type of intuition. Clairaudience, or hearing, is another intuitive gift. It is with our senses and feelings that we intuit. Vision, sound, emotion, and physical sensation are all part of being a living, breathing organism. Intuition is *of this world*: it is a mundane phenomenon.

We may confuse intuition with desire—see or feel what we *wish*, rather than what is. Our vision may be colored by our desires, and thus inaccurate. It is important that we discern the difference between desire or fantasy on the one hand, and true intuitive knowledge on the other.

Pagans and Witches value and respect intuitive knowledge. Many practice intuitive skills, such as **divination**. Reading **Tarot** cards, runes, bones, and other items is common among Pagans. We also read palms, see auras, and palpate skulls, using intuition more often than formulas. Rune says, "When I 'look' at my computer and its connections, what I see is very similar to what I see when 'looking' at people, magical workings, and astral beings."

DIVINATION: The practice of seeking guidance or gaining insight or foretelling the future through magical techniques, such as reading Tarot cards, scrying, or reading tea leaves.

TAROT: A set of cards with five suits and symbolic pictures, used for divination. There are many different versions, and most have a guidebook. Tarot cards are the precursors of modern playing cards, and they are known to have existed in Europe as early as the fifteenth century. The cards are believed to have been used primarily by gypsies and Witches until recent years, when their use became widespread.

How does one intuit over the Internet? Some say it's easy. Some say they cannot do it. I, for one, am not very intuitive over the Internet—it's quite easy to fool me. And when I asked my coconspirators about this, Cat Chapin-Bishop, a therapist by profession who's been a Witch a long time and possesses a certain online sophistication, responded:

> I'm not at all convinced I can [intuit online] . . . I've been right a lot—made some solid friends. And certainly I've nourished spiritual ties via the Web . . . But I've been wrong a lot, too, and I never entirely know how good my reading of a person is until I know them from personal contact, too.
>
> Unless a person is more psychic than I am, at least, I don't think the Web is a friendly medium for intuition . . . I feel head-blind when I'm out of contact with body language/aura/facial expressions.

Yet Abby Willowroot thinks that intuitive readings of personality, character, authenticity, and integrity are easier to accomplish online. Abby has been an active online presence in the Goddess movement since layfolks began to use PCs. She sees magical will as an electrical energy that's easily measured and evaluated online. She insists that "subtle energies . . . are delivered along with the pixels." Abby explains:

> Several years ago, I became aware that excitement, loneliness, bravado, and other emotions not contained in words were readily discernible. The same paragraph written by six different people seems to have the ability to communicate to the reader differently. The "energy" of the writer, especially when it is a strong emotion, is carried along with the **pixels** and becomes an unseen, but easily detected, part of the whole . . .
>
> The processes of thought and emotion are both chemical and electrical based, as are the computer and the Internet. In computers, the necessary chemicals come through the intrinsic properties of minerals (silicon, silver, gold) used in their manufacture. The electrical is the transmission of information via electrical impulses, like in the human brain. In both human brains and computers, chemical and electrical elements are necessary for the information to be transmitted.
>
> Energy is electric, and that same force that transmits energy from person to person, even across long distances, seems to also be a factor on the Internet. This energy can be as tangible as the unspoken emotion in a voice transmitted over telephone lines. Highly charged emotions are, of course, the easiest to detect at a distance. One could argue that phone lines only transmit words, but clearly they transmit much more—they transmit voice. I believe that the Internet also transmits a unique kind of "voice" as well. One that can be perceived, recog-

PIXEL: A tiny, individual dot of light, the basic unit from which the images on a computer or television screen are made.[4]

> nized, and understood on a deeper level than words or images. It is this intangible quality of communication over the Internet that has made friendships, romances, and other connections on the Web as "real" for those who share them as any other "real life" relationship.
>
> On a metaphysical level, we are all aware that energy can be sent and received without the hardware. Why, then, is it hard to believe that it is also possible to transmit this energy when hardware is involved? One thing the computer provides, that I believe enhances the transmission of energy, is the tendency to create an almost hypnotic focus in the user. When you are deeply focused and interfacing with electrical energy and a means of mass transmission, your energy gets transmitted.

Moose of Ozark Avalon, in Missouri, is another Witch whose magical training was done in terraspace but who now participates in online rituals. These rituals bring Moose, and those who celebrate with him, satisfaction.[5] About intuiting online, he writes:

> I posit that the intangible nature of the Net makes it ideal for "knowers" to intuit. *How* I intuit over the Net is exactly how I intuit in other venues. It boils down to recognizing the Net as another realm of consciousness, one that can be affected magically.
>
> It also helps to have an affinity with the element of air. In online ritual settings, the data coming through the modem must get through the cast circle. Electricity looks a lot like air to my subconscious mind.

Some of my coconspirators claim that they can read others well when their only communications have been via computer. This ability, or inability, to read applies to online ritual, too. I was trained to do **ritual** that allows for spontaneity; I work out a general plan and purpose and arrange a few things to work with, but I have no script. For this to succeed, it's essential that I develop a high degree of familiarity and trust. I'm puzzled about how this can be done strictly online.

RITUAL: An occasion when an individual or a group uses traditional practices to focus energy for an identified purpose, such as healing, transformation, empowerment, protection, or celebration. The basic elements of a ritual in the Reclaiming tradition are grounding and purifying; casting the circle; invoking the elements; invoking deity (or deities); magical working; sharing food and drink; and opening the circle.

So, once again, I turned to my coconspirators, asking them how they experienced people online whom they'd never met in person. Could they communicate intuitively with people in cyberspace who were strangers to them in terraspace? Sandy, a witchen Web mistress in the San Joaquin Valley of California, reflected:

> I think we are talking about the essence of communication. We read people's actions, physical demeanor, when meeting them in person. Speaking to a person over the phone, you sense things in their voice—their speech patterns, if they are being sarcastic, and so on. In text, which is where most of the Internet-related communication we have been talking about lies, there are subtle insights into a persona. For instance, the style they type in. Do they stick with the default fonts, or do they add flourishes like backgrounds and color? Does one have a particular way of phrasing something, like using a lot of ellipses or not finishing sentences? There is a lot to be said of one's spelling and grammar as well—although that could be deceiving. My husband's written skills are really embarrassing, spelling and grammar are just awful, but he is a

brilliant man. He can come across seeming like a real idiot or jerk because of his poor writing skills, when he really is very good at verbal communication and the verbal expression of ideas.

I have a lot of first-time contact with people in e-mail, and I just get intuitive impulses from reading their messages. I can tell if it's a child writing (I have a penguin page that gets lots of hits from children), but there are times where I have gotten very well-written letters from people whom I thought were much older than what I had read into their messages.

In real life we can make these types of misjudgments, too. I know there have been times when I might have gotten a strange or weird vibe from someone and stayed wary until getting to know them more and just finding out they were on . . . [antidepressants] or something and are genuinely cool people.

I think the essence is how one communicates, whether it's body language, verbal, or written. I think we all leave subtle clues to our personality in our messages. I personally don't ever feel much of a need to portray myself any other way than who I am. I sometimes feel the Internet allows people the freedom to be themselves as much as it offers them the freedom to be someone else.

SPELL: Focused energy, directed towards a particular result, using a carefully chosen set of objects and ingredients, words and incantations, gestures and timing (such as a particular lunar phase). The purpose of a spell is to create a change in physical or nonphysical realms. In most traditions, spells are governed by ethical principles. A spell may be created in the form of a physical charm, or something may be charmed. The act of creating a spell is called "spellcraft" or "spellworking."

SPELLWORK AND PRAYER

Witches cast spells. We can create a **spell** for anything. If it doesn't work, we can redesign it. It is important, however, that we ask ourselves *why* we want to cast a particular spell. Whether or not we truly believe that spells can work, it is essential that we reflect on our motivation for doing a particular spell. Performing spells that seek to interfere with the free will of another person is unwise—in fact, such work is strictly forbidden in some traditions. Furthermore, most Witches (but by no means all) believe in a principle known as the Law of Threefold Return, whereby that which a person puts out into the world returns to her three times over. For those who might be tempted to do spellwork for selfish ends, to manipulate another, to harm someone, the Law of Threefold Return is a cautionary check.

The casting of spells often involves herbs, stones, natural objects, coins, talismans, oils, candles, bags (or other wrappings), or a **poppet**. Candles may be "dressed," or anointed with oils that have special properties, and inscribed with words or symbols. We **charge** a spell, or set it in motion, using breath, song, chant, liturgy, dance, or other form of energy raising.

When we do a spell that we want to "seal" by dancing, we might use a simple step and a repetitive chant together to raise energy. Beginning softly and slowly, we gradually allow the energy to build, the volume of our voices to increase, the pace of our steps to quicken. When we have done this long enough and intensely enough, we achieve a state of enchantment. We change our consciousness.

Witches may seek the potency to make their spells effective through supplication to a **deity**. We might involve several different deities in our workings and spells, depending upon the kind of work being done or the kind of spell being cast. We choose the one (or ones) most likely to influence our work in a positive way. Just as others ask God, Jesus, Allah, a saint, an ascended master, or a bodhisattva for a special favor—like an intervention

POPPET: A small, handcrafted doll, representing a particular person, used in spellcasting. A poppet may contain cloth, hair, or an object belonging to the person it represents.

CHARGE: To infuse with energy that is directed towards a particular purpose. A charged object holds magical energy and releases it to work the magic.

DEITY: Most modern Witches believe in a pantheon of Gods and Goddesses who are associated with many religious traditions around the world, both modern and ancient. Most commonly, Witches call on the deities of Celtic, Greek, and Roman cultures, but many also call on Egyptian, African, Scandinavian, Native American, Chinese, and Indian gods and goddesses. Most Witches are careful not to appropriate other people's spiritual practices or beliefs; but, since we also recognize that different cultures affect each other when they come in contact, we are open to the influence of religions that are harmonious with Craft.

that will avert a life-threatening situation—so, too, do Pagans. The act of speaking to a deity is an act of prayer.

Prayer can be amplified on the Net. Other religions recognize this. According to the *Rocky Mountain News*, of Denver, Colorado, nearly a million people have been praying and connecting each month at a site called Beliefnet.[6] Beliefnet encompasses many religions, and it even has two regular Pagan columnists: Starhawk and Margot Adler.

The following story, reported in the *Milwaukee Journal Sentinel*, demonstrates how prayer not only promotes change in the world around us but also unites people of vastly different worldviews in common causes.

> The phone rang. It was crushing news. [Mrs. Norman's] 10-year-old nephew had run into the road and been smacked by an oncoming car.
>
> Then, she prayed.
>
> Then she asked the world to pray.
>
> With moist palms, her fingers slipped over the keyboard at her computer in the kitchen, key by key, typing: "Please pray . . . Nathan was hit by a car . . . several attempts to arouse him have been unsuccessful."
>
> In moments, dozens of people from around the world responded to the plea posted at the Beliefnet.com Web site.
>
> And then one day, there, in the stream of comforting postings came yet another shock: the prayers of a woman identifying herself as a Pagan and a Druid.
>
> "She said she believed in Witchcraft," said Norman, 46, a Christian. "I thought, 'Oh, my God, I don't understand this. How do I deal with this?'"

In the weeks that followed, young Nathan recovered, beating the odds.

And Norman shed her fears about the Pagan woman.

She treasured everyone who "screamed to God for help" with her, regardless of their creeds.

"It has caused me to be a lot more open," she says. "These were all beautiful thoughts. Now I can see that."[7]

INVOKE: To call a spirit or deity into the circle.

Clearly, the Net is transforming how we experience religion.

ASPECT, ASPECTING: A magical technique whereby deity is summoned, or drawn down, into an individual. That individual, working with a partner in whom she has complete trust, allows her ego to be released, or diminishes her mundane, mortal personality, to a point sufficient to allow the divine to enter, speak, and act. If the aspecting is truly deep, the subject will be unlikely to remember anything that she has said or done while in that state, which can last for several hours. She will be exhausted and hungry afterwards, and it is critical that her working partner attend to her needs so that she can return fully to ordinary consciousness. Also known as "drawing down the moon," particularly among the British traditions of the Craft.

INVOCATIONS, EVOCATIONS

We Witches invite goddesses and gods into our sacred circles. We welcome their presence and their power to influence what we're celebrating. We ask goddesses or gods to bless our ventures and projects and to fortify our spells. We invoke them by calling their names, by speaking to them, through supplication, devotional acts, and prayer. The altar we erect for a particular occasion may contain an image, painting, or statue of the deity or deities we are choosing to invoke. To please and entice them, we might place their sacred flowers on our altars, burn a variety of incense that is sacred to them, sing to them, or set out their favorite foods. This is a form of prayer.

The words **invoke**, *evoke*, and **aspect** are often used synonymously. Strictly speaking, they are not synonyms, but for the purposes of our discussion we needn't differentiate. A more thorough explanation of aspecting follows. (This thread resurfaces in chapter 4.)

SHAPE SHIFTING, ASPECTING, MASKS, AND ONLINE PERSONAE

There are several mystical phenomena found in witchen traditions that have a special appearance and application in cyberspace and in online rituals and magical workings. These sacred technologies are aspecting, shape shifting, and mask wearing. All are related, and there are several areas of overlap. It is my contention that these technologies can be compared, in both positive and negative ways, to role-playing games and to the exploration and development of online personae.

HIGH PRIESTESS, HIGH PRIEST: A trained and skilled woman who conducts rituals or who embodies Goddess, and her male working partner, who conducts rituals with her and may aspect God. These are standard roles in most older, and many newer, structured traditions. These terms are not used in the Reclaiming tradition.

Traditional covens are small and intimate. They are guided by a **high priestess** (HPS) and possibly a **high priest** (HP), who are often a married or committed couple. They may or may not be people of the same gender. The HPS and HP conduct their rituals with the assistance of coveners of different levels of training and experience. In some covens, these ritual roles are rotated from **esbat** to esbat, sabbat to sabbat, or season to season.

ESBAT: A monthly full-moon ritual celebrated regularly by most witchen covens.

In less traditional covens, these roles may not exist at all, or they may exist in a modified form. For example, my first coven, Holy Terrors, was a group priestesshood. Each member was assumed to be capable of performing every aspect of conducting ritual, and specific duties would rotate from coven meeting to coven meeting. (The patterns of traditions and coven structures reemerge in chapter 5.) Furthermore, we didn't feel that the usual designation of "high priestess" accurately denoted how we thought and felt about our roles, so we coined the term "deep priestess." Each of us was deepening our magic, delving deeper into the world of spirit, as well as into our deeper selves. And, since Holy Terrors was a coven of women, we had no priest—high, low, deep, or shallow.

TRIPLE GODDESS: The Maiden, Mother, and Crone, associated with the new, full, and waning phases of the moon, are the most familiar triad in the Reclaiming tradition. Other Triple Goddesses recognized in various cultures and historical periods are the Fates, Clothos, Lachesis, and Atropos; the Moirae or Graeae Sisters; the Norns or Wyrd Sisters; and the Morrígan. The Goddess Brigit, or Bhride, is associated with the forge, the flame, and the well.

GODDESS: The Earth, also called "the Mother" and "the Great Goddess", because the Earth is the source of life. When we die, our bodies are returned to the Earth. Through the Earth, we are connected to the mystery and beauty of the cosmos, and Witches consider her sacred, worth dedicating their lives to protecting. Qualities of the Goddess are those associated with the Earth, such as endurance, fertility, abundance, sustenance, compassion, creativity (birth), destruction (decay), and rebirth. (See Deity.)

There are covens that are even less traditional than Holy Terrors was, and in these the various ritual roles, including that of aspecter, might be assumed by anyone in the coven, regardless of gender: a man might perform the duties of the HPS; a woman might perform the duties of the HP. Or two men might perform the roles of HPS and HP as working partners.

The most common of the mystical phenomena that are traditional within Craft, and that can be seen online, is aspecting. Perhaps because of the importance to many Witches of the Moon Goddess archetype—the **Triple Goddess** of Maiden, Mother, and Crone, easily seen in the changing phases of the moon—the phenomenon of aspecting is also known as "drawing down the moon," especially among British traditional Witches. This is usually done with a priestess as the subject into whom the "moon," or the **Goddess**, is drawn. When the **God** is summoned, he is drawn into the body of a priest, and the process is called "drawing down the sun."

The Triple Goddess, Plus One

Many American Witches, perhaps even most, honor the Goddess in her triple aspect as Maiden, Mother, and Crone. This is especially true of Dianic and other gynocentric traditions. Sacralizing the stages of a woman's life serves to empower us, to enable us to see the divinity of all we are. In addition, these three aspects of the Goddess can appear in any color, shape, or form.

Most maiden goddesses, such as Diana or Persephone, are portrayed as slim and fit. Many mother goddesses, however, are depicted with abundant figures, denoting comfort, protection, nurturance, prosperity—enough to eat for all; she has plump breasts and a soft belly and thighs. This body type is not valued in popular American iconography. Examples of mother goddesses are Demeter in Greek myth, and White Tara, Mother of Compassion, in Tibet. Perhaps the best-known mother goddess in the West is Mary, Mother of God.

The least appreciated aspect of the Triple Goddess is the Crone, or Hag. In our youth-fixated culture, the beauty that comes from a long life filled with rich experiences, a life that produces lines on the face and flesh that responds to the pull of gravity, is not valued. Older women are dismissed, even mocked. To treat older women in such a way is to ignore the wealth of knowledge and wisdom that women—and men—have gained from having witnessed the passing of many seasons.

There have been triple goddesses, such as the Matronae, throughout much of history. There is a triple Bridget in Ireland: Bridget of the Forge, Bridget of the Flame of Inspiration, and Bridget of the Healing Waters. (These are just the main attributes of Bridget. She also invented keening, the intense wailing used to grieve the dead; whistling up the wind; bee keeping; and mead making, among other things.) From Norse mythology, we know the three Wyrd Sisters, who sit at the base of Ygdrassil, the World Tree. And then there are those other-than-human entities, the Fates, or Moirae—Clothos, the spinner of the thread of life; Lachesis, the weaver or measurer; and Atropos, charged with the task of cutting the thread at life's end—who are often considered deities, as are the three Graeae Sisters, who share one eye.

One goddess who can be either a single persona or three is Ireland's Morrigan, or Great Queen, or Phantom Queen. She is the Washer at the Ford who washes the garments of those about to die in battle; she can appear in the shape of a raven or crow, shrieking over the battlefield and feeding on the bodies of the slain; or she can reveal herself as a beautiful young maiden. As Macha, one of the Morrigan's aspects, she is consort, mother of twins, swift of foot, and she can take the form of a gray mare. It was Macha who cursed the warriors of Ulster, declaring that in the hour of Ulster's greatest

GOD: All that is born, grows, and dies; animal and plant life. Sometimes, the sun is considered to be the God because every year it grows bright in summer, fades, dies, and is reborn. The qualities of the God are those of plants, such as growth, vitality, reaching maturity, rising, and falling; they are also the qualities of animals, such as wildness, freedom, vulnerability, innocence, and ecstasy in Nature. (See Deity.)

need, its defenders would be struck down by pain, like women in childbirth.

Seeing Goddess in all women enriches our lives. I'm of the belief that imaging Goddess as Maiden, Mother, and Crone first occurred after the publication, in 1948, of Robert Graves's *The White Goddess*. But no matter how ancient or recent this construct is, it has tremendous power to affect our lives. I don't believe that because this Triple Goddess concept is newer than other Goddess concepts it is any less powerful.

In addition to the three stages described here, some Witches are now exploring the notion of the Saga (pronounced "say-ga," the term is related to "sage"). The Saga is the woman who is past her childbearing and rearing years, yet she is still actively engaged in the community. The Saga is a vital woman, not a woman in repose, like the Crone.

A less common variation of this mystical phenomenon involves an aspecter and her tender, instead of a priestess and a priest. (You may also hear a tender described as a "wrangler," but I dislike that term.)

I will now describe what happens in the most commonly used forms of aspecting. (Please do not use this text as a manual for learning to aspect; what I offer is for explanatory purposes only.) A woman acting as HPS works with a companion HP. The HPS will be the aspecter, and the HP will help her to prepare for and assume the role of Goddess. The HPS must have complete trust in her HP and in her coven if this technique is to accomplish its full benefits.

Using various sacred techniques and technologies—such as fasting, ritual purification, scents, clothing, jewelry, ritual implements, chant, or song and other forms of invocation—the HPS prepares herself, and allows herself to be prepared by others, for the working at hand. Technologies can vary from group to group, or individual to individual. As a priestess becomes more adept at achieving the state of consciousness necessary for her to aspect Goddess, she learns which techniques work best for her, and so does her HP working partner(s). It is essential, however, in order for the aspecting to be effective, that she release her ego, or diminish her mundane, mortal personality, to a point sufficient to allow the divine to enter, speak, and act.

When that point is reached, deity is summoned, or drawn down, into her person. If the aspecting is truly deep, she will be unlikely to remember anything that happened. She won't recall what she said or did. This state can last for several hours, and she will be exhausted and hungry when it's over. It is critical that the working partner tend to these needs when the aspecter returns to ordinary consciousness. The aspecter may think she's fine, but she needs the close attention and ministrations of someone she trusts and knows well to help her fully return. She should not be allowed to drive or go out alone until her working partner is completely certain that she is in her normal, everyday state.

Of course, aspecting can be faked. It can be used to advance a personal agenda in a way that brooks no opposition: "The Goddess said it." It can be exploited for personal aggrandizement, for claiming attention. But when an aspecting is authentic, it is unmistakable—mysterious and wondrous and beauteous. There are several things that tell me an aspecting is authentic. The subject's gestures, carriage, and body language, her voice, speech patterns, and dialect or accent, are not those she displays in mundane life. And when I look into her eyes, someone else looks back at me.

I haven't experienced aspecting online, but my co-conspirator Ceffyl has: "One time Deity decided to come through and speak to another person. I could feel her knocking and wanting to talk to someone. I had no idea who, until I got online, opened ICQ, and couldn't take my eyes off their name. I've had the same kind of thing happen for other people, but that was the first time it happened online."

A technique related to aspecting is shape shifting. This is just what it sounds like: a person changes his shape from his normal, human, form to another form. The most common shift is probably from human to animal. The change can also be from human to mythical beast, such as a dragon, griffin, or unicorn. Or a person may take on the appearance of the deity who is speaking; when aspecting is full, the aspecter may appear to others in the form of the deity invoked.

I experienced shape shifting as a child while running through a field with my head thrust forward, hair flying behind me like a mane, haunches churning, narrow feet and delicate ankles carrying me over the grasses. I don't know whether anyone else saw me as I saw myself and felt myself to be.

When I was serving as death priestess to my friend Raven, during the intense final hours of his life, he and I were big glossy black birds, flying together. Others who vigiled around Raven's deathbed saw visible changes in both of us, but I don't know whether what they saw was precisely two black birds. The literalness of shape shifting and its visibility to others are not relevant to this discussion.

Another effective method of changing consciousness

and identity is mask wearing. Mask wearing has been used for sacred purposes by many peoples, in various times and places, throughout the world. Among those peoples are Witches; one of those times is now; and one of those places is here. A seeker can find an abundance of resources about the use of masks—in libraries, on Web sites, from mummers and false-face societies, from studies of international folklore, from schools of theater and puppetry.

Mask wearing is, simply, obscuring—or replacing, or substituting—one's visage with another visage. The face you put out to the world is one you have chosen, perhaps even created. It may be a fantasy mask, a portrait, a deity, or a creature. It is not your ordinary face. It is not your everyday identity. It is a persona that you deliberately construct, just as you do when you choose a costume, a hairstyle, makeup, or jewelry.

And where do these techniques interact with computer culture? One way is through names and naming. The first thing we do when we sign up for e-mail is select a screen name. It will be our initial persona for different types of online communication. Many people adopt several screen names, using them to separate their professional identities from their magical, or playful, or sexual, or shopping personas.

Naming is a powerful act. That which we name we can address and have some control over. By naming a thing, we give it definition. Naming is useful when confronting demons, either real or imaginary, because when we name them, or find out their names from them, we have gained some power over them. Naming also helps us to pattern our lives, to imbue our lives with whatever qualities we seek in taking the name. For instance, Julie Rabbit doesn't conduct herself in the same way Julie Wolf does.

Not long ago, Witches guarded their identities closely. Our ancient/future religion was misunderstood. Frequently, we even misunderstood one another, mainly because we didn't know each other. People used magical names in their magical work, so members of a particular coven might not even know the mundane names of their fellow coveners. It was a safety precaution; it kept Witches from revealing—inadvertently, or under torture—the identities of their coreligionists, thereby protecting them from persecution.

Witches may take, or receive, names at an early stage of their walk on a magical path, or after extended study and practice. We may do it more than once, changing our names as we attain new thresholds in our individual lives. Taking the name of a goddess whose attributes, qualities, and characteristics we wish to cultivate in our own lives is a common step towards empowerment among feminist Witches. Others may adopt the name of a deity for any number of unique personal reasons. If we are to undergo an initiation, elevation, or other rite of passage, we may add a name or replace an existing name in honor of the event. We may even swear oaths in those names.

Our names are where our identities begin. Online, we can name ourselves whatever we want, and we can do this any number of times—one for each e-mail account. We can give ourselves the name of a deity or deities, a power animal (Bear, Gazelle), a totem bird or fish (Hawk, Salmon), a plant or tree (Oak, Lily, Mugwort), a quality or emotional state (Serenity), a meteorological phenomenon (Rain, Thunder, Cloud, Sunshine, Zephyr, Sirocco). We can take the name of an ancestor, a historical figure, a time (Autumn, April, Tuesday). Or any combination we choose.

Another way that sacred techniques intersect with computer culture is through our bodies. Just as we are not restricted by our names, we are not bound by our bodies. We can move easily through the entire spectrum of gender and sexual identities when we are online. We can be female, male, androgynous, old, young, slender, round, strong, delicate, fair, ruddy, dark, short, tall. Skin, hair, eye color, and body configuration can all be assumed in an online persona. Through the Net, we are free to switch our gender or race and to make other "body changes" of the sort that can be done in terraspace rituals. In doing so, we have much to learn from the "edgewalkers" among us—those who are gay, bi, or transgendered, priest/esses in particular. We may even transcend species, becoming a goat, an owl, a butterfly, or a juniper.

This Net capability allows anyone with the equipment and the connection to participate fully, regardless of physical limitations. One of the great boons of Internet communication is its leveling effect on those who are differently abled. The Net permits these people to participate as equals with able-bodied folks.

So, it's easy to see how choosing a screen name and creating an online identity, or several, are forms of mask wearing—the mask being the new name and the altered behavior. Behind a monitor, we can inhabit whatever body we choose. We can interact online as anyone we want to emulate, impersonate, or, in the case of aspecting, speak as.

As I have said, I am not skilled at intuiting online. I find it hard to tell when certain people are joking or being insulting. Due to the limitations of written language, online communication cannot convey tone of voice and other inflections that shade and shape meaning. My

VR: Virtual reality. This is the simulation of a real or imagined environment that can be experienced visually in the three dimensions of width, height, and depth, and that may additionally provide an interactive experience visually, in full real-time motion, with sound and possibly tactile and other forms of feedback. The simplest form of virtual reality is an image that can be explored interactively with a personal computer, usually by manipulating keys or the mouse so that the content of the image moves in some direction or zooms in or out. Most of these images require installing a plug-in for your browser. As the images become larger and interactive controls more complex, the perception of "reality" increases. More sophisticated efforts involve such approaches as wraparound display screens, actual rooms augmented with wearable computers, and haptics joystick devices that let you feel the display images. Virtual reality can be divided into

- The simulation of real environments, such as the interior of a building or a spaceship, often with the purpose of training or education.

- The development of an imagined environment, typically for a game or educational adventure.[9]

friend Abby, however, can identify people from their e-mail messages:

> In my own experience, there are a number of individuals that I instantly "recognize" by their energy. Even if they are writing to me under another screen name, I usually identify them before they identify themselves. It is not language use, or typing, or anything easily identified. I recognize them by their "presence." The same way you can recognize someone you know well if they walk up behind you. Frequently, before you turn around, you have already recognized their presence. With the continued use of the Internet for both business and personal communications, our ability to be sensitive to the unwritten "voice" will become an increasingly important part of online communication.

I asked my coconspirators for their thoughts on the connections between the sacred technologies of aspecting, shape shifting, and mask wearing and the phenomenon of online persons. Adam said that he had opinions on the subject:

> Yes, heaps of them . . . It is one of my major areas of interest, especially in **VR** [virtual reality]. The first place I really saw some sort of connection between spirituality and the Internet was on MOOs . . . [O]ne of the interesting things was the notion of adopting online personas by "shifting" your form, or wearing a new mask, if you like. It is intriguing to watch people change as they adopt new personas within a MOO and to then translate that

> process into a spiritual setting. I haven't really looked at the notion outside of VR, though, as that is where most of my interest has been.

I became involved with MOOs in the first place because of online shape shifting—in a manner of speaking. When I was working on my philosophy thesis, a fellow postgrad gave a paper in which she argued that MOOs herald a new world for feminism since they liberate women from gender-based stereotyping online. Unfortunately, her argument devolved into "Women will be treated equally online because they can change their gender to male," which I always thought misses the whole point about equality. Still, the paper succeeded in arousing my interest in MOOs.

MOO: The acronym stands for "MUD, object oriented." "MUD" itself stands for "multiuser dungeon" (or, for people who want to move away from the "dungeon" idea, "multiuser dimension").

Legba is a longtime Pagan and dedicated MOOer. She is used to wearing borrowed bodies. Legba claims that "the false dichotomy is to think that cyberspace and our RL [real life] bodies are really separate. That the 'astral' is somewhere else, refined and better." She goes on to describe her experience of shape shifting in cyberspace: "Gender fucking and morphing can be intensely magical. It's a very, very easy way of shapechanging. One of the characteristics of shamans in many cultures is that they're between genders, or doubly gendered. But, more than that, morphing and Net.sex can have an intense and unsettling effect on the psyche, one that enables the ecstatic state from which Pagan magic is done."[10]

The anonymity afforded by Internet communication allows people to feel safe about revealing themselves. Not seeing another person, perhaps a stranger, across the room, but instead viewing that person on a monitor in the coziness of one's home, can foster a sense of intimacy that may not be well founded. Is this approach advisable? It's much harder to tell whether an aspecting is genuine when a person at a keyboard somewhere else on the planet is deliberately deceiving others. Appearance, odor, temperature, color, breathing, voice, touch—all of which are absent from online connections—are vital triggers for intuition. We'll pick up this thread in later chapters.

Chapter 3

SPINNING THE THREADS: NETWORKING

PRE-NET DAYS AND NIGHTS

There were days when we were few and fragmented. For generations, we Witches have kept our beliefs to ourselves. Due to the anti-Witchcraft laws in effect in England, which weren't repealed until 1951, and to a pervasive hostility throughout Western culture towards any minority religion, especially one that does not revere a male god above all, we were in constant peril. Anyone known to be a practitioner of Witchcraft, a practitioner of magic, an explorer of the arts of divination, a worshiper of any deity but Yahweh, Jesus, or Allah (particularly in Occidental countries) took great care not to reveal themselves to neighbors or coworkers. Discretion was the order of the day—and the night. Witches came together in small working groups, called covens. Coveners often referred to one another and addressed one another by "magical" names only. This emphasis on secrecy has kept us fragmented, mistrustful, and disempowered.

But most longtime Witches will agree that despite our troubled history our Craft has a rich and varied heritage.

We have drawn on many sources; in today's multicultural world, we blend sacred technologies, schema, deities, and liturgy from many different times and places. Some of us have chosen to develop our practices from within a particular ethnicity or cultural pantheon. The more popular of these are Celtic, Norse, Hellenic, and Egyptian. Many also look to the Goddess of the Americas, Nuestra Señora de Guadalupe Hidalgo, formerly called Tonatzin, particularly Witches of Mexican ancestry.

I am dedicated to the Hindu Kali Ma, to whom, in my Macha persona, I bear a striking resemblance. In Irish lore, champions customarily took the heads of their slain enemies. For them, these heads, called "Macha's acorn crop," were symbols of certain qualities they admired in their enemies, qualities that the champions now "owned." Kali is frequently depicted wearing a necklace of skulls or rotting heads, or a skirt made of severed arms, usually considered to represent the surrender of ego; her adornments are also graphic reminders of the impermanence of individual human life.

My former coven sister, Cerridwen Fallingstar, used to say that she practiced the "magpie tradition" of Witchcraft: she picks and chooses what works for her. Some might call this cultural appropriation, but I prefer to think of it as cosmic recycling. Cerridwen also used to say, "I'm practicing my religion just the way my ancestors did. I'm making it up as I go along." Craft embraces magpies like Cerridwen and those who find greater satisfaction in concentrating on a particular culture or pantheon. Some of these people are reconstructionists, and others claim unbroken lineage. What matters is that they have found unique ways of making the Craft work for them.

Beyond individual approaches, there are certain fundamental aspects of the Craft that don't vary. Witchcraft is a Nature-based religion whose practitioners worship Goddess, the immanent life force within us all and connecting everything, manifest in both female and male images of the divine, most especially female. To Witches, the Earth is alive, and all life is sacred and interconnected.

Certain traditions (similar to denominations) of Witchcraft have existed in Europe, North America, and Australia since the early twentieth century; some claim lineages going back hundreds of years or more. (See chapter 5, where the traditions thread reemerges.) A revival of interest in the Craft occurred in the late 1960s and early 1970s, with the weaving together of an array of threads: a new focus on Western ceremonial magic; an exploration of intuitive, nonlinear modes of perception; the search for meaning and spirit in materialistic contemporary culture; renewed respect for folk traditions; honor for our direct experience of Nature and of our bodies; concern for the survival of the Earth and our quality of life on our planet; women's sense of oppression, anger; and the profound need to honor life experiences with ritual.

As this revival was occurring, so was a revival of interest in the magical arts within the context of Second Wave Feminism, a movement characterized by grassroots consciousness-raising groups and a yearning for female empowerment. A desire for a feminine image of the divine also surfaced within the more conventional churches, synagogues, and temples, but feminist Witches pushed the boundaries and took Goddess worship several steps beyond anything that could have been manifested in the established, majority faith traditions.

Concurrently, a greater awareness of ecology and conservation issues was developing. We began to look more closely at the ways in which humanity had interfered with the free flow of natural forces. We had dammed mighty rivers and flooded canyons and valleys for power and irrigation purposes; we had destroyed huge sections of land through strip mining and quarrying, in the process destroying the health of miners; we had allowed the proliferation of internal-combustion engines, thereby increasing petroleum mining and refining and toxic emissions; we had permitted the clear-cutting of majestic old trees, causing flooding, landslides, and the obliteration of wildlife habitats; we had ushered in agribusiness, monocrops, and a proliferation of processed foodstuffs; we had brought on overpopulation and urban sprawl; we had subjected ourselves to a host of environmental ailments and stressors. Many people who were profoundly disturbed by these developments found their way to a Pagan path.

Principles of Wiccan Belief

In 1974, one group of American Witches meeting in Minneapolis adopted the following set of principles. Adherence to these principles is not required of anyone, but they do reflect the thinking of many modern Pagan Witches in the United States and elsewhere.

The Council of American Witches finds it necessary to define modern Witchcraft in terms of the American experience and needs.

We are not bound by traditions from other times and other cultures, and we owe no allegiance to any person or power greater than the divinity manifest through our own being.

As American Witches, we welcome and respect all teachings and traditions and seek to learn from all and to contribute our learning to all who may seek it.

It is in this spirit of welcome and cooperation that we adopt these few principles of Wiccan belief. In seeking to be inclusive, we do not wish to open ourselves to the destruction of our group by those on self-serving power trips, or to philosophies and practices contradictory to those principles. In seeking to exclude those whose ways are contradictory to ours, we do not want to deny participation with us to any who are sincerely interested in our knowledge and beliefs.

We therefore ask only that those who seek to identify with us accept these few basic principles:

1. We practice rites to attune ourselves to the natural rhythm of life forces marked by the full of the Moon and seasonal quarters and cross-quarters.
2. We recognize that our intelligence gives us a unique responsibility towards our environment. We seek to live in harmony with Nature, in an ecological balance that offers fulfillment of life and consciousness within an evolutionary concept.
3. We believe in a power far greater than that which is apparent to the average person. Because this power is far greater than ordinary, it is sometimes called "supernatural," but we see it as lying within that which is naturally potential to all.
4. We conceive of the Creative Power of the Universe as manifesting itself through polarity—as masculine and feminine—and we believe that this same Creative Power lives in all people, and functions through the masculine and the feminine. We value neither above the other.
5. We value sex as pleasure, as the symbol and embodiment of life, and as the interaction source of energy used in magical practice and religious worship.
6. We recognize both an outer world and an inner, or psychological, world—sometimes known as the Spiritual World, the Collective Unconscious, or the Inner Planes—and we see in the interaction of these two dimensions the

basis for paranormal phenomena and magical exercises. We neglect neither dimension for the other, seeing both as necessary to our fulfillment.

7. We do not recognize any authoritarian hierarchy, but we do honor those who teach, respect those who share their greater knowledge and wisdom, and acknowledge those who courageously give of themselves through leadership.
8. We see religion, magic, and wisdom in living as being united in the way one views the world and lives within it—a world view and philosophy of life which we identify as Witchcraft, the Wiccan way.
9. Calling oneself "Witch" does not make one a Witch, but neither does heredity itself, nor the collecting of titles, degrees, and initiations. A Witch seeks to control the forces within her/himself that make life possible in order to live wisely and well, without harm to others and in harmony with Nature.
10. We believe in the affirmation and fulfillment of life in a continuation of the evolution and development of consciousness, giving meaning to the Universe we know and our personal roles within it.
11. Our only animosity towards Christianity, or towards any religion or philosophy of life, is to the extent that its institutions have claimed to be "the only way" and have sought to deny freedom to others and to suppress other ways of religious practice and belief.
12. As American Witches, we are not threatened by debates on the history of the Craft, the origins of various terms, the legitimacy of various aspects of different traditions. We are concerned with our present and our future.
13. We do not accept the concept of absolute evil, nor do we worship any entity known as "Satan" or "the Devil," as defined by the Christian tradition. We do not seek power

through the suffering of others, nor do we accept that personal benefit can be derived only by denial of another.

14. We believe that we should seek within Nature that which contributes to our health and well-being.

Witchcraft, whether it is of the more formal, ceremonial kind or the hedgewitch or conjure-man variety, has always passed on from person to person. An individual might seek a one-on-one apprenticeship with a solitary practitioner, and that practitioner might agree to teach her. More often, though, we learned the Craft within the context of a coven. Prospective new members were carefully scrutinized and then perhaps invited to a meeting; this is how the covens expanded. The prospective member and one or more coven members might have met in a coffeeshop or a park for casual conversation before the decision to extend an invitation to circle was made. Eventually, a prospective member might have been invited to a ritual, maybe a festive sabbat ritual.

Gradually, we learned the practices of the group—the procedures, tools, colors, liturgy, and so forth. As we progressed in our learning, we, as candidates, relied on the entire group to check our experiences, but usually we had a mentor, or sponsor, who took special responsibility for our training. We were in a safe environment where we were free to deepen our magic and our knowledge and understanding of the Craft. This process allowed us a steady, self-paced integration of witchen spirituality into our lives.

This is the way I learned the Craft—gradually, in an intimate group setting. My coconspirator Grey Cat, a grandmother Witch who lives in rural Tennessee, describes this phenomenon as "cellular growth."

> The classical pattern of the growth of a new religious movement [which does not apply to initiative Wicca] begins as a cellular growth pattern, moving out geographically from the original group/leader. It moves outwards from town to town with a variable limitation of distance, depending on available forms of transportation and local definitions of "too far." All groups in each of these will be similar, due to physical and emotional closeness to the source group/individual. The effect of the Internet on groups of this sort is felt primarily in the increased ability of students to locate the group.

Cat is high priestess of a hierarchical New England coven,[1] trained back when we still kept to the shadows. She talks about her own coven situation as it relates to the Internet:

> Of Stepchild Coven's seven current members, four only came into contact with the coven originally via the Internet (or the earlier Echonet bulletin board system). Without electronic communication, our coven would be myself, my husband and a friend of a friend. Every other recent addition to the group has been sparked by a Web contact . . . We are far from an open group—closed, oath-bound to secrecy, and damn choosy about who we circle with. It's not possible to join us without being already a close, trusted friend—but, as it happens, most of those friendships began online.

FROM BROOM CLOSET TO RURAL FESTIVAL

Prior to the 1980s, the Pagan population in the United

States generally hid in their broom closets. We kept our spiritual beliefs and practices hidden, because it wasn't safe to reveal them. The mainstream culture was predominantly Judeo-Christian and intolerant of differentness. At best, Witches seemed exotic to the adherents of mainstream culture. At worst, and unfortunately most typically, they viewed Witches as devil-worshiping sinners. As I mentioned earlier, we were subjected to scorn, discrimination, and social ostracism. Some of us had our homes vandalized or even firebombed. People known to practice the Craft risked losing their jobs or their homes. Judges, the judicial system, and social services favored the nonwitchen parent in disputes and custody battles involving the offspring of mixed—Pagan/non-Pagan—unions.

But gradually, as the social revolution of the 1960s transformed America, Craft folks began to find one another. During the 1970s, the occasional conclave of Witches and Pagans was organized; at these gatherings, we participants became better acquainted with one another, made magic together, shared skills, built trust and solidarity, and resolved to support and defend one another. These early events, held in rural camp settings or in hotels, drew occultists of every stripe, not just Neopagan Witches.

In the Northeast, several people began organizing in various forms, beginning in the early 1970s. New England Covens of Traditionalist Witches (NECTW) was founded in 1972 by a hereditary Witch from New Haven, Connecticut. Her family tradition, which was made public in the late 1960s, was blended with popular occultism and handed down in its present form. It still exists.[2]

The People of Holy Earth tried to develop a Pagan

community in Massachusetts in the early 1970s. The Massachusetts Pagan Federation was established in 1976. One of the longest-lasting witchen federations began with a group of Witches from northern and southern California who organized themselves into a group called the Covenant of the Goddess (CoG) and incorporated with the California Secretary of State in 1975.[3] Today, the group encompasses approximately fifteen local councils; it has sixty-one member covens and ninety-five **solitary** members.

SOLITARY: A Witch who practices alone, not in a coven.

The Keepers of the Ancient Mysteries (KAM) was very active in the mid-Atlantic region during the mid-seventies. The Midwest Pagan Council was started at about this time, and the first pan-Pagan gathering was held in 1977. The first Gathering of the Tribes in Georgia took place in 1978. Two other well-known Pagan festivals that continue today are Heartland, in Kansas, and Spiral, in Georgia.

The EarthSpirit Community of Massachusetts produced its first Rites of Spring in 1979, and it went on to produce Twilight Covening in October, as well as Feast of Lights, an indoor gathering. EarthSpirit's festivals have not only survived, but also Rites of Spring, in particular, has grown to become one of the most well-regarded festivals in the United States.

The Church and School of Wicca, formed by Gavin and Yvonne Frost, also began holding hotel-based conferences, or "cons," in the mid-seventies. Today, Pagan cons are mounted in several cities and on both coasts.

Another established annual gathering is Pagan Spirit Gathering (PSG), held over a week's time at the Summer Solstice. Produced by Circle (founded in 1974), in the Midwest, and now in its twenty-first year, PSG has become an annual pilgrimage for many Witches and Pagans.

When I began to search actively for others of like mind, before I was truly convinced that I was a Witch, I found a small, relatively discreet training group advertised at a local free university. My teachers were a man and woman who belonged to a coven and to a larger tradition (or group of related covens). This particular Craft tradition was called NROOGD (for New Reformed Orthodox Order of the Golden Dawn—I have never known its members to use the full name).[4] NROOGD is a self-created, or reconstructed, syncretic tradition whose members gave themselves that highfalutin name in good humor. They are unrelated by training, nor do they trace a lineage from the Order of the Golden Dawn, a group that flourished in England in the early part of the twentieth century. These Witches, in spite of being creative autodidacts when it came to magic, were careful to maintain secrecy about who they were, what they did, and when and where they met.

As I learned the Craft, I learned that what was drawing Pagans and Witches together were the festivals, mostly those held in remote rural areas. It was the 1980s, and in certain parts of the country, where there were sizable numbers of Pagans, Pagan gatherings of one kind or another were taking place nearly every weekend from May to October. Some of us created a lifestyle of going from one festival to another, weekend after weekend, all summer long. We had good camping and cooking gear, campers and RVs, and elaborate tents adorned with colorful banners or flags bearing the emblems of our traditions or covens. We erected festive temporary villages, which inspired in us a feeling that we belonged to a tribe.

These festivals proliferated all over the Deep South and

the Midwest; there were fewer in the Northeast, the Southwest, and on the West Coast. California, the largest state, but one whose population was at that time comprised primarily of newcomers, had only about a half-dozen regular Pagan gatherings.

Perhaps this is because California, and the West Coast in general, are so diverse and multicultural that they have always been more tolerant of the eccentric and unusual. The East Coast is heavily populated with European immigrants, whereas the Pacific Rim has large Asian and Hispanic populations. Craft heritage is primarily Western European, although it has grown more and more eclectic, taking inspiration and techniques from the Native peoples of North America, from the Orient, from wherever inspiration comes. Still, I remember attending a weekend-long Pagan festival in 1981 on public parkland in Oakland, California. It was organized, on a shoestring budget, by the late bard and Faerie shaman Gwydion Penderwen and his friend Stephan Abbott, along with assorted friends and helpers. We all camped out in the hot, dry, golden coastal hills.

Of course, there are far too many Pagan festivals to list here. Fortunately, in recent years, various sociologists and other scholars have found us intriguing. They have started to collect data, analyze it, and, most importantly, immerse themselves in our festival culture. While an academic's view of us may not accurately reflect the way we see ourselves, scholars often fall in love with the subjects of their study. It's not uncommon for those who've endeavored to study us to join us—in the rarefied atmosphere of a rural Pagan festival, in our sacred circles, and on a Pagan path. Some contemporary scholars of Paganism were actually Pagans of one kind or another first, before they embarked on a formal study of the phenomenon. (I recommend that those who are interested in finding out more about Pagan festival culture read Sarah M. Pike's study *Earthly Bodies, Magical Selves: Contemporary Pagans and the Search for Community*.)

Although a number of Pagan groups and festivals no longer exist, many have continued to thrive. And those that didn't survive broke ground for the ones that followed. Today there are many, many such manifestations of Paganism, and they are far more visible than their predecessors.

How has this festival culture been affected by the Web? Fritz Jung of the Web site The Witches' Voice (TWV or Witchvox) observes:

> Festivals are but a tiny fraction of our community's events. Witchvox has featured over twelve thousand events in just the past four years. They happen constantly and include full moon/sabbat circles, Pagan night outs, workshops, public and private circles, political rallies, big and small fests, and many, many more types of events. We have seen the same growth curve in local events that we have seen with the Net community itself. Pagans are getting together in big ways these days.
>
> Events listings at TWV are at an all-time high, and the pages that feature/celebrate events have been viewed close to 1.1 million times in the past five years.
>
> Festivals are springing up everywhere, and pretty big ones, to boot. We just attended a "first festival" in our area that attracted close to three hundred [people], and this will no doubt double when

> they repeat it. Why? Because it was very well done, and because the need was there. We've seen that happen with other fests 'round the planet, as well.
>
> What I have also noticed is that festivals grow with friends telling friends, and attendance growth doesn't seem to be all that affected (with rare exception) by who . . . the guest speaker(s) [are]. We have a continually growing local fest that has been going on for over a decade (twice a year), and of late it has been top-heavy with "personalities." Thousands of dollars were spent to do this. This last time they cut way back on famous names; attendance once again increased. My observation is that it is the people/community that predominately build these fests. Yes, some will come to share the magic, wisdom, and talents of guest speakers, but the actual attendance draw of "big-name Pagans" (in my opinion) is grossly overestimated. BNPs who expect" special treatment" are tolerated briefly but not asked back. BNPs who hang with us regular folk are cherished and become regulars.
>
> There are so many nonfamous folks who do a wonderful job with workshops and rituals. In fact, there are folks who have only been doing this for a few years who are truly an asset to us all.
>
> It really comes down to not who you are . . . but what you actually do. As we all know, there is, and has always been, no shortage of titles, degrees without depth, hype, and big fat claims.

According to Fritz's observations, the general mix of people who attend the festivals has remained consistent. The ratio of givers and takers is the same.

It's been a boon to have more festivals to choose from. Now, it's easier for people to attend festivals near to where they live, and organizers are more confident that they can draw a sufficient crowd. Explains Fritz, who lives in Florida, "Mercifully, the days of having to travel hours/days to get to *any* festival are waning. Many Pagans we met at Starwood [a well-known New York festival] over the years came from Florida. They have little reason to make that trip anymore. They have some wonderful fests right here."

The older, established Pagan festivals may not have maintained their rapid growth rates with the advent of the local festival, but this isn't necessarily a bad thing. Overall, the effect of the Net on festivals and festival culture has been positive. As Fritz reminds us, "Fifty folks working magic, camping, or hanging out 'round the fire will always be more intimate than a thousand, but the option to just hang with a smaller group will always be there, and is actually preferred by many."

ZINES

Around the time that we Witches were starting to peek out of our broom closets, we began producing simple newsletters with small, select circulations. These were typewritten, sometimes even handwritten with calligraphy headlines, and run off on pre-photocopy-machine duplicators; some were photocopied, hand collated, and mailed to subscribers in plain, unmarked envelopes. Most of these publications lasted for a while, then faded away. Some folded after accomplishing what they'd set out to do; others vanished when their creators' interests or priorities shifted.

Among the more notable of the Pagan publications

that were, until quite recently, still in existence are *Harvest*, out of New England, and the *Green Egg*, published by the Church of All Worlds. The *Green Egg* Forum became legendary for the passionate, articulate, and sometimes outrageous debates that it facilitated on all things Pagan. The *Green Egg* ceased publication for a few years, thrived through the eighties and nineties, and has just stopped publishing again. We hope that it will resume soon and that the *GE* Forum will continue to provoke.

Culture-changing feminist magazines, like *Chrysalis*, of Los Angeles, and *Lady-Unique-Inclination-of-the-Night*, of Austin, Texas, also colored the Pagan tapestry in the early days. Then along came the Internet.

BUILDING THE LOOM: EARLY ELECTRONIC COMMUNICATION

I solicited stories from some Witches whose Craft lives developed in the old, intimate, often secret, working covens. Grey Cat is one of them:

> I subscribed to one of the early information services, Compuserve (known as CIS and CI$ by members), in 1988 or 1989, I believe. The deal was that your basic monthly fee (around ten dollars, as I remember) let you connect to news information and mail and certain other activities—probably the most important of which was the Practice Forum.
>
> The Practice Forum existed to help new CIS members learn to use the forums: reading messages, posting messages, replying to messages, and so on. Each message would have a header or subject line. For most of us, the Practice Forum was our first experience with the "magic" of being connected. For

myself, sending a message to someone in Europe or Australia and getting an answer back immediately seemed utterly amazing. Perhaps because I clearly remember the first transatlantic radio broadcast (Big Ben in London striking midnight), direct communication around the world seemed mind blowing.

Once out of these "free" areas of CIS, you paid so much per minute for your connection time, and most people used an application that allowed them to connect, get mail, and collect the titles of any new messages on the forums to which they belonged. After a minute or so of connect time, these applications signed off, and you could read through your mail and see what message "threads"—messages with the same subject—you wanted to read. The application could then be reconnected and would send your mail (primarily only to other people on CIS and, with some failures, to those on one of the other information services), and it would download all the message threads you'd selected. In this way, you could keep your connection time within a reasonable budget.

At that time, there were two forum areas of interest to Wiccans/Neopagans, the New Age Forum and the Religion Forum, both of which had Wiccan subforums. Here you could "talk" with Wiccans all over the U.S. (and, to a small extent, over the world—but at that time availability and high cost tended to prevent much activity from the rest of the world). Although it still seems as if the primary activity was defending our beliefs against an endless succession of Christians who wanted either to save our souls or inform us of our eventual destination, in detail, we also shared a good deal about our differing traditions and practices. We shared a great deal of our materials, and friendships were formed that continue to this day.

As well as the message boards, CIS offered what was called "conference rooms," which were, from a user's standpoint, like the chat rooms found everywhere today. The New Age Forum met every Sunday night in one of these chat rooms—visualized as a friendly bar with a hot tub in one corner—just to socialize for an hour. While this was a somewhat costly pastime, ten or fifteen of us managed to budget it in on a regular basis. At least at that time we were not hassled by drop-ins using unpleasant language or attempting to hit on any handle perceived as feminine. (I was Grandmother Owl in these forums.)

The software provided also for moderated chats with someone controlling who could "speak" when, and these were used for lectures, interviews, and rituals. Amber Wolfe, author of *In the Shadow of the Shaman* and several other books, visited with me and did an online interview, which was well attended, although the announcement was made only a couple days in advance . . . In the early nineties, a home-based network arose using applications called "bulletin boards." There were a number of these applications, most of which were used by businesses for internal communications or for online information sources. These were commercial programs and fairly costly.

However, an excellent program called WWIII (WW-3) was made available at no, or little, cost to individuals willing to host them on their home computers through their own telephone connection. Those who ran a WWIII BBS [bulletin board system] could join in a network of these **BBSs** and share forums worldwide. I "sysop'd" (system operator, what the BBS owner/operator was called) a Wiccan-focused BBS for more than a year, and, through the various forums, communicated with Wiccans and Neopagans throughout the U.S. and shared in many interesting discussions. No Witch-bashers here, as the sysops could, and did, keep them off the forums.

BBSs had the disadvantage of not allowing any direct interaction between the participants (the exception was that you could chat with the individual board's sysop if he/she wanted to). Messages essentially took a day or a half-day per exchange, which did have the advantage of cutting down flaming a bit. The sysop's control also tended to keep exchanges polite. Eventually, the WW-2 boards were able to offer e-mail through the Internet as well as just through its own net. I think the best things about the BBSs were that they let us get to know people in our own area in a way no modem-based system has done before or since. In fact, there are a very few BBSs still operating just for that reason, even though the job could be done as well with a mail list. Many boards got together every so often to increase this growth of community. And I went to a local sysops' supper and enjoyed myself greatly, although I was significantly older than any of the other operators. (SilverBird was my BBS handle.)

BULLETIN BOARD SYSTEM (BBS): A computer that can be reached by computer modem dialing (and, in some cases, by Telnet) for the purpose of sharing or exchanging messages or other files. Some BBSs are devoted to specific interests; others offer a more general service. The definitive BBS List says that there are forty thousand BBSs worldwide.

Bulletin board systems originated with, and generally operate independently of, the Internet. However, many BBSs have Web sites. And many Internet access providers have bulletin board systems from which new Internet users can download the necessary software to get connected.

BBSs have their own culture and jargon. A system operator is the person who runs the site (many BBSs are on small home computers that have simply added the necessary software to keep track of files and users). A lot of BBS users chat online.[5]

And so, at last, I come to *the Internet*—which contains all that was found at Compuserve and through the BBSs and an infinite amount more.

Grey Cat discovered, through the listserve I'd set up to discuss the ideas presented in this book, that among her past online acquaintances was another of my coconspirators, Jehana Silverwing.[6] So we follow the thread. When I asked my coconspirators if they'd made any lasting friendships via the Net, Jehana replied:

> I first got online on Compuserve in the late eighties, and over a period of time I have met many of these folks; and threads of friendship have been followed, have evolved, and have even stimulated my own spiritual directions to stretch out in other ways than what I might have taken. I'm now involved with the folks on the Summerlands (Celtic path reconstructionism); and I originally met Carol Maltby from this list, online . . . I've driven, two sprints in a row, down to Tennessee to meet up with the Summerlands crew. They've offered online classes (I participated twice), and we did spiritual/religious work, plus plain old getting to know each other, in person, down South.

So Jehana spins the thread to Carol Maltby,[7] another of my coconspirators. And, as Carol explains, her own cyberconnection has gradually taken on great importance for her:

> I've been a cyberwitch since 1993, when Jehana Silverwing suggested that, now that I had a Compuserve account, I might want to stop in and visit

the Pagan section at Compuserve. The Net is now an external nervous system for me, and it has been the major source of my growth in the Craft, complementing what I've learned from my coven, Wild Vine (a feral, eclectic, Wiccan/Quaker/whatever coven that probably has the most resonance with the values and practices of the Reclaiming and Proteus traditions).

While being totally hopeless as a geekette (and having the crappiest, clunkiest grasp of HTML around), I still manage to use the low-level technology enough to feel comfortable calling myself a technopagan, simply because as a priestess I do so much that is dependent on the computer. Sometimes being one step ahead of others can be enough to make them think you are far more adept than they are, but I'm not ready to be worshiped as Madame le Technomage yet.

Priestesses like Grey Cat, Jehana, and Carol were among those who helped set up the looms on which we spin our webs today.

STRINGING THE WARP: ESTABLISHING WEB SITES, CHAT ROOMS, AND E-LISTS

Many of the surviving groups and alliances that had been formed in the festival and zine cultures of the 1970s and 1980s were eager to establish an online presence. A surprising number of we Pagans earn our living in computer programming, Web design, and other computer-related professions. We spin Web sites and listserves from our minds and keyboards like spider silk.

Carol Maltby speaks about how she adapted, as a

mother, partner, and witchen priestess, to the new technology:

> I have never used online chat other than for rituals, but I find bulletin boards to be a superb method of human interaction, especially for me, as a parent of young children, since I'm not always able to get out or even make uninterrupted phone calls. I run four private bulletin boards at the moment and have three different Web sites in various states of disarray. While none of the Web sites are ostensibly about the Craft, I bring my values as a priestess to them in a way that may be more subtle than the preaching to the choir we do when we talk among ourselves. I make myself known as a Witch in some BBSs where there are few, if any, other known Witches, because that's where we are needed so badly. It's not all the warm fuzzy joy of being at home with Witches, but when you get to a certain point you know, as a priestess, that you have to go where you can be of the most use.

WEB RING: A way of interlinking related Web sites so that one can visit each in turn, eventually returning to the initial Web site. One can also elect to go backwards through the ring, skip certain sites, visit others at random, or view a list of all the sites on the ring. A Web ring is managed from one site equipped with a common gateway interface application that can select random sites and bypass sites that have dropped out or are unreachable.

Groups such as the Covenant of the Goddess (CoG), Circle Farm, EarthSpirit Community, Wiccan Pagan Press Alliance, Wiccan Anti-Defamation League, and Church of All Worlds have also set up Web sites. Many were rudimentary, at first—produced with volunteer talent and labor—but they soon grew into vast weavings, featuring **Web rings**, awards, and links to other sites.

THE WITCHES' VOICE

Perhaps the most influential Web site in all of Pagandom is The Witches' Voice, also referred to as TWV, or

Witchvox.[8] The Witches' Voice has set a standard of neutrality and inclusiveness. It has sought to celebrate the work, regardless of who's doing it. Rather than promote celebrity cults, TWV strives to give voice to all Witches who are contributing to our culture and community, regardless of their public status or name recognition.

TWV was founded by Wren Walker and Fritz Jung in Massachusetts in 1996. The pair mounted three pages on the Internet for Laurie Cabot's Witches League for Public Awareness (WLPA); their aim was "to promote tolerance" and to rectify "many of the misconceptions related to the modern Witch/Wiccan/Pagan movement." Wren and Fritz left WLPA, moved to Florida, and began creating the first version of TWV. Explains Fritz, "We acquired the domain name WitchVox.com and launched The Witches' Voice in cyberspace, on February 2, 1997, with fifty-six pages and some new technology for the links and contacts section."

The Witches' Voice, a legal nonprofit organization, was created for three essential reasons. First, its creators wanted to address what they saw as a need for "clear and well-developed educational materials for the Pagan and non-Pagan alike." Second, TWV was intended to serve as an antidote to discrimination against Pagans; it would assist individuals and groups working to eliminate discrimination by providing information and materials upon request. Third, TWV was conceived as a networking tool. "We created and evolved the state/country pages," says Fritz, "so that Pagans, Pagan groups, and Pagan shops could list their e-mail addresses, events, and workshops. They are listed by not only country and state, but now by city and town, as well. We have faithfully updated these 127 state/country pages and the five-thousand-plus listings therein on a daily basis, without fail, for the last year. We strongly encourage Pagans to become active at the local level, but we realize that you have to find one another first . . . The real fight for awareness and respect happens at a local level."

By the end of its first year, Witchvox was offering 385 pages, which were viewed on personal computers the world over. Within that time, the site had received 1,275,237 hits. It listed several thousand Witches, Wiccans, and Pagans on its state/country pages, 385 circles and events, 250 witchen and metaphysical shops (most submitted by customers), 976 Pagan Web sites (with complete contact info), and a site map.

In addition, TWV furnished the Pagan community with still other vital resources: informative essays; a White Pages section, outlining Witches' legal rights and the means to protect those rights; and a twenty-six-page commentary on inter-Craft conflict and conflict resolution, including suggestions on how to communicate better and unify our wonderful community.

Thanks to its sponsors and to its dedicated volunteer staff of seven, Witchvox managed to offer all of this to the community at no cost. Truly, TWV is something for us Witches to crow about.

The Witches' Voice Code of Ethics

We recognize that the global community is made up of many diverse cultures, each with its own set of inherent beliefs. Since those associated with The Witches' Voice seek to honor both the individual as an embodiment of the Divine and the healthy interaction of members of the greater society in which we all have a place, we have adopted this set of guidelines on ethical behavior.

The Witches' Voice is a people-oriented organization dedicated to fostering deeper understanding and cooperation amongst both the members of the Pagan community and society as a whole. We provide educational materials on the basic beliefs of the religion of Witchcraft/Wicca to dispel the stereotypical image perpetuated by the media and centuries of negative propaganda. We uphold the civil and religious freedom guaranteed to all citizens in the Constitution and Bill of Rights and will actively resist those who would seek to suppress or restrict these rights.

The Witches' Voice is dedicated to:

- *Truth and Goodwill:* An individual has the right to live out a life aligned with his/her personal beliefs. We encourage everyone to decide to what degree their participation will support the organization. By doing this, we hope that people will bring real passion into their efforts. Truth is important for an organization to enable it to have a clear vision statement and to operate from a firm set of values. Such an organization motivates its members to think and act as the leaders. The leaders "walk their talk," and all are valued for their contributions. When the organization becomes successful, everyone knows that they helped to make it so.
- *Civil Liberty:* Civil liberty encompasses the respect for, and the protection of, individual rights. While the exercise of these rights is dictated by the law of the land, in an "open society" it is largely dependent on what the people determine as valuable to their way of life. Multiculturalism has introduced an opportunity to learn new ways of dealing with beliefs different from our own. Conflicts arise when the aims of the differing parties include not only the validation of their position but also the neutralization or elimination of their opponent's position. We actively seek ways to preserve the unique cultural values of any group or tradition, while at the

same time promoting healthy interaction within an inclusive organizational structure.

- *Religious Freedom:* We recognize that spiritual belief is a very personal choice that each person is entitled to make based on what is in his/her own heart. The spirit is the true essence of who a person is and what he or she will become. No outside agency has the right to deprive a person of the free exercise of his/her religious practice or sincerely held beliefs without a real and compelling reason. "Compelling," in this country, has come to mean that society at large must be in real danger from the results of the religious practice for the government to interfere. Anything less than this "compelling reason" would be a violation of this right to religious freedom. We uphold religious liberty for all and shall actively resist any infringement on the right to free exercise of personal spiritual belief.
- *Freedom of Expression:* The Constitution of the United States guarantees a free press which allows for all to make public statements on their viewpoints. While we may not always agree with such statements and reserve the right to protest or offer rebuttal to articles that we find offensive or misleading, we uphold the concept of freedom of expression and will resist any and all attempts to censor opinions. The Witches' Voice will not remove any postings or articles printed under the submission guidelines. Articles will include the author's e-mail address or other contact information and all comments should be directed to the author. Postings to feedback forums will only be removed if the language is obscene or targets a particular person or group in such a manner as to cause emotional harm.
- *Integrity:* The Witches' Voice will always provide as much information as confidentiality or circumstances will allow about any action or decision we make so that our members

will be fully informed. We value your trust and we will never ask you to support that which conflicts with your personal sense of integrity. The Witches' Voice also expects members to respect the integrity of the organization and support this concept in word and action.

- *Personal Responsibility:* While not all Witches, Wiccans, and Pagans adhere to the Law of Three as an official tenet of their belief, most do believe that we should act in a responsible manner in our dealings with each other. None of us can profess to be perfect all of the time, and misunderstandings certainly can, and do, occur.
- Teamwork requires the proper use of communication, negotiation, and the ability to recognize and resolve conflicts as they occur.
- In real communication, each person is interested not in argument, but in seeking understanding of the other's point of view. All ideas receive an equal hearing. The real merit of any suggestion is allowed to emerge based on its value to the organization and not only on the passionate presentation of its proponent.
- Negotiation is used to change things that are not working. The offering of a well-thought-out alternative to a situation is a key element in the process. Once again, it is the greater good of the whole team or organization that is the ideal.
- Sometimes differences of opinion can become quite heated, and a situation evolves into a personal conflict. Recognize that the other person feels as strongly about his/her beliefs as you do about yours. Focusing on the overall mission statement and aligning yourself to the greater goal may be all that is needed to get things back on track. A cooling-off period may be a time to meditate on a new approach or solution.
- To accept responsibility for your part in any situation is a sign of maturity. To say that you were mistaken is not the

INTERNET SERVICE PROVIDER (ISP): A company that provides individuals and other companies access to the Internet and other related services, such as Web site building and virtual hosting. An ISP has the equipment and the telecommunication line access required to have POP [point of presence]; an Internet access point] on the Internet for the geographic area served... ISPs also include regional providers [and] thousands of local providers. In addition, Internet users can get access through online service providers (OSP), such as America Online and Compuserve. An ISP is also sometimes referred to as an IAP (Internet access provider). ISP is sometimes used as an abbreviation for *independent service provider* to distinguish a service provider that is an independent, separate company from a telephone company.[10]

same as stating that you are a bad person. It is simply acknowledging that you are human.

The paths to truth are indeed many. We at The Witches' Voice believe that this listing is broad enough to encompass everyone and at the same time allow the freedom for individuals or groups to practice their own moral codes.

"Those who walk in Love and Truth shall grow in Honor and Strength."

Blessèd be.

—Jeannette K. Waldie and Wren Walker (1997)

DRAKNET

When I first contemplated writing this book, I began casually asking my witchen friends if they thought the Net had influenced Craft, and vice versa. The reply was a resounding "Yes!" Several asked me if I knew of the Web host called DrakNet, owned by Lhiannon.[9] They advised me to check it out. At that point, I wasn't even sure what a Web host was, even though I had a small site of my own. My **Internet service provider** (ISP) had something called a server, where the data that comprised my Web site was stored; that, in fact, was my Web host, the place outside my computer where my data lived.

In the process of making this book a reality, I set up a listserve. A Texan friend, Rivercat, told me about another Texan named Jen who knew everything there was to know about Pagans on the Web—and she was fun, too. I should not proceed another step, insisted Rivercat, without first enlisting Jen's help. So, armed with Rivercat's "letter of introduction," I contacted this busy woman.

Jen and I joined our threads, mine spun from California and hers from Austin. We followed other threads, we tatted cyberlace. Then DrakNet emerged again—I learned that it hosted Witchvox in Florida as well as the sites of lots of my witchen friends. I was writing this book by this time, and one day I learned that my previously friendly and reliable ISP—and host of my Web site—had been bought out by a larger company. After that, service declined. When the ISP was sold yet again, service deteriorated to the point where my Web site host was down for more than a week. No explanation was given; I was merely told that getting it back up was a priority. I phoned every eight hours or so to see what was happening, but finally my frustration drove me to switch to DrakNet.

DrakNet is a great example of a culture-changing influence in the age of the Web. The good Pagan folk at DrakNet work hard to ensure that their business practices bespeak their values. They're proud to be a different kind of Web hosting company, a **virtual domain** where customers can store their Web data with confidence.

The company seeks "to make a positive and meaningful contribution to community activities and to behave in a socially and ecologically responsible manner." It's encouraging to find coreligionists who conduct themselves in such a constructive and ethical manner. DrakNet offers an example that we can all learn from. DrakNet's owners claim that "DrakNet sees the power of the Internet as great in the long-term scheme of the development of the Pagan community as a voice and a political power." They are committed to serving their community, despite DrakNet's "commercial nature," by providing free services to "nonprofit organizations, causes, and Pagans in

INTERNET PRESENCE PROVIDER (IPP): A company that provides the disk space, high-speed Internet connection, and possibly the Web site design and other services for companies, organizations, or individuals [who want] to have a visible presence (meaning Web site) on the Internet... Although one can maintain a Web site from a smaller computer if site traffic is very low, most moderate to high-traffic Web sites require a relatively expensive, higher-speed connection to the Internet. For this reason alone, most individuals and organizations put their sites on a server at an Internet presence provider.[11]

VIRTUAL DOMAIN: A virtual hosting provider is sometimes called a Web or Internet "space provider." Typically, virtual hosting provides a customer who wants a Web site with domain-name registration assistance, multiple domain names that map to the registered domain name, an allocation of file storage and directory setup for the Web site files (HTML and graphic image files), e-mail addresses, and, optionally, Web site creation services. The virtual-hosting user (the Web site owner) needs only to have a file transfer protocol (FTP) program for exchanging files with the virtual host.[12]

DRAKNET'S VALUES

• *Tolerance*: DrakNet maintains that tolerance towards the Pagan community can best be achieved by [demonstrating] tolerance within the Pagan community and tolerance from the community outward. Therefore, DrakNet will strive to demonstrate tolerance in all dealings within the Pagan community as well as with non-Pagans who may do business with us.

• *Charity*: DrakNet believes that any business that serves a religious community must have the concept of charity and philanthropy as one of its cornerstones. DrakNet will strive to serve the community in charity and philanthropy, in as much as it financially and technically can, without deliberately manipulating or exploiting those acts for self-gain.

need . . . DrakNet maintains a stated goal of giving away at least thirty-three percent of its services for this end at all times."

ONLINE ZINES

As computers have become ubiquitous, and as cyberculture has evolved, online zines have come into focus. These are not unique to Pagan culture, of course, but they have played an important part in our growing cohesion as a movement. Some are published online only, and others are produced in concert with print magazines. Of the latter, most issue some of their material online and invite their readers to subscribe to the print version, where they will find the full range of articles. The zine that comes from my own community, *Reclaiming Quarterly*,[14] does this, as do *PanGaia*, *SageWoman*, and the *Blessed Bee* (a Pagan children's magazine); these four are primarily print publications that employ the Net to enhance their visibility and increase circulation.

Two other online zines worth mentioning here are *Mystic Journeys Pagan Ezine*, the journal of Magickal Cauldron,[15] produced in Atlanta, Georgia; and the *Pomegranate: A New Journal of Neopagan Thought*, which comes out of the Pacific Northwest.[16] The *Pomegranate* is a serious journal whose contributors are primarily academics. *Mystic Journeys* is a general offering, packed with fiction, poetry, recipes, interviews, and book and movie reviews. *Mystic Journeys* is old and established as far as online zines go—it was started back in 1996. It is one of hundreds of online Pagan zines with myriad themes and emphases.

Then there is the resource called the *Wiccan/Pagan Times* (*TWPT*), an online zine that promotes the "Pagan community through art, literature, and music."[17] *TWPT* —which publishes author interviews, essays, book and music reviews, reading lists, ritual scripts, and news—was founded by Boudica and Imajicka, a wife-and-husband team who wanted to create a place where Pagans could share ideas, express opinions freely, and disseminate information, "in an atmosphere of cooperation, and with a positive spirit." *TWPT* will not endorse one particular spiritual path, but instead provides its readers with the tools to "learn more about the endless variations on a theme that exist in today's Wiccan/Pagan community." The zine's goal is to act as a source for links to Pagan information, wherever it may be found on the World Wide Web. Its founders believe that

> This, in turn, will create a Wiccan/Pagan who is educated as to the variety of paths that exist and the problems that confront them in our modern society.
>
> By the same token, we feel it is our right to express our feelings and opinions on and about those things we like or dislike about the current state of affairs within the Wiccan/Pagan community. We will do this in a positive and constructive manner, so that we are fostering growth and learning within our respective communities.[18]

When they started *TWPT*, in 1999, Boudica and Imajicka were living in Pennsylvania; they now reside in Ohio. Their project, like most Pagan Web sites, is a labor of love. Both hold down day jobs, and the money for Web hosting, software purchases, and postage comes right out of their pockets. Although *TWPT* is, technically, a for-profit entity, the only income it receives is small

- ***Honesty*: DrakNet will strive for honesty in all of its dealings with customers as well as the media. Any customer of any company deserves a forthright answer to a question or a forthright presentation of facts during any energy exchange, whether that energy is represented by money or not.**

- ***Integrity*: DrakNet maintains that it will strive to stand on these stated principles as well as upon the ethics and morality of our own individual Pagan paths.[13]**

commissions from its links to Amazon.com. Imajicka explains why they have chosen to operate this way:

> If what we do touches other lives . . . then we are grateful, but we will never send out pleas for money . . . We will run the site until such time that we can no longer afford it, or until it is no longer needed. Traffic to the site is a good indication of whether or not you have touched a nerve or uncovered a need in the community that needs to be met. Our traffic has shown a slow and steady rise over the past two years, and it shows no sign of slowing at this point.

Imajicka goes on to reflect on the zine's format:

> Each generation will be that much more familiar with looking for information on the Web, so, rather than spend time and money trying to publish a printed copy of *TWPT*, we learned the ins and outs of Web page creation and put our efforts into making the knowledge available on the Web, across the country and around the world. Since I had not seen author interviews done on a regular basis anywhere else on the Web, I also wanted to introduce the readers of Pagan books to the authors who created them—hence the Authors' Corner. We have developed such good relations with some of the authors we interviewed that they continue to be associated with *TWPT* by contributing articles to the site.

When I asked Imajicka to describe the inspiration behind the *Wiccan/Pagan Times*, he told me that he and Boudica were motivated by "the desire to pass our knowledge along to those who might just be starting out and not know where to turn. We would also like to think that we provide information that extends beyond the basics of Wicca/Witchcraft, that speaks to those further along the path." In that way, the zine has maintained its appeal for "a loyal group of readers who don't have to leave once they have a few years under their belts in search of more meat on other sites."

Nearly every Pagan site (including my own) features at least one bibliography of works that the site owners feel are important, or that have had the greatest influence on their own practice and understanding. But of all the Pagan online zines I've encountered, *TWPT* places the strongest emphasis on books and writers. Imajicka explains:

> I think that in many cases those new to the path will have had their first exposure to the Craft through a book or some other form of written material. This puts literature rather high on my list of things to expose our readers to. New books, new ideas, new authors that they might not know, old authors that they should know if they desire to understand where Wicca/Witchcraft has come from and where we might be heading in the next few years. I think that reading about how many of the authors found their way onto this path will show that the choices are infinite, and that no way is absolutely correct.

TWPT's Authors' Corner interviews are extensive. Interviewer and interviewee engage in long, far-reaching conversations, and these are faithfully recorded. Because of this, interviews are relatively complex and nuanced; they allow the reader to glimpse the personality behind a book title without the mediation of a publicist. In selecting interview subjects, *TWPT* considers a book's subject matter and its author's influence on the community, both currently and in its formative stage. But the zine also endeavors to feature new authors who have not been exposed to the community, and authors who present alternative perspectives on given issues.

I asked Imajicka whether *TWPT* felt the need to take a political stance, and he told me that since so many other Pagan sites have staked out their political positions, *TWPT* has generally declined to do so. They have no interest in duplicating efforts. He and Boudica also avoid airing disagreements on their site, preferring to settle disputes via private e-mails. Still, I wondered if there were any sites, projects, or people that *TWPT* might be tempted to oppose publicly, and Imajicka replied:

> We would not recommend sites that are carelessly thrown together, not maintained on a regular basis, those that promote any kind of derogatory approach to other religions and other paths, and, lastly, those who plagiarize the works of other writers. We would not publicly denounce them on our site; we would simply not list them on any of our links pages, nor recommend them if asked our opinions of the site. We have seen our share of behind-the-scenes, and there is much that you do not want

> discussed in an open forum where anyone can read it and, having read these opinions, then draw conclusions about the whole community based on opinions that rarely represent the majority of the community.

What Imajicka has observed in online Pagandom is true of the rest of the online world: opinions vary widely, and they are often expressed in unconstructive ways. And this is more prevalent in cybercommunication than in face-to-face discussions. *TWPT*'s policy in this regard, like the policies of Witchvox and DrakNet, is a strong indicator of the Pagan movement's increasing maturity. *TWPT* is but one of hundreds of sites set up by individuals, covens, traditions, and other groups to network and to shape Pagan culture, both in cyberspace and in terraspace.

ONLINE BROADCASTING

Yet another phenomenon to arise from the burgeoning Internet is online radio broadcasting. Among the many people who helped me write this book and achieve a better understanding of the Web are two witchen online broadcasters: Sandy Johnson and Mark Kelly.

Sandy, of Modesto, California's, Fellowship of the Earth, produces one of the newest witchen broadcasts, *The Talking Stick*.[19] Online broadcasting, Sandy explains, does not rely on airwaves, like AM and FM radio. It also requires much less equipment—all the online broadcaster needs are a computer, a connection to the Net, and some simple software. Add creativity plus content, and anyone can create her own live broadcast, providing listeners with a welcome alternative to corporate-dominated commercial radio.

Mark, the creator and host of Earth Radio International (ERI), broadcasts witchen news, talk, and information from a computer in Seattle.[20] His mission is "to recognize and celebrate the maturation of the Wiccan and Pagan communities in the world today, to provide a place not only to report on what's happening but also to help set the direction for Wicca and other Pagan religions in the future." He shares his thoughts on online radio and Net communications:

> Online broadcasting brings the human voice to the Internet, a world woven from text and images. The subtle shadings of conviction, the sound of a smile —none of these is possible with mere words on the computer screen. Hearing another human being strengthens the impact of the message. This is the real power of online broadcasting: the human voice.
>
> The Internet is sometimes referred to as "the people's press." The power of the press, no small influence in a democratic society, is suddenly available to anyone with access to a computer and a Net connection. If the Web page is the people's press, online broadcasting is the people's voice. With a fifteen-dollar microphone and free software, anybody with a mouth and even half an idea can be in at least the same ballpark as Edward R. Murrow, Walter Cronkite, or "Dr." Laura.

Yet, as Mark points out, online broadcasting is limited by the fact that it can only be received on another computer. It doesn't allow the mobility that regular broadcasting does. As Mark explains, you can listen to a traditional radio station "in your car, or just about anywhere with portable radios and headphones." But, while traditional radio is confined to broadcasting within a given geographical area, the only such restriction with online broadcasting is **bandwidth**. "Bandwidth is crucial to online broadcasting—the bigger the pipe, the more data you can stream and at faster rates. Someone who has a high-speed connection can broadcast much higher quality streams or stations than, say, someone who is limited to a dial-up connection. There are several services available, free and pay, that allow users to stream their stations off their servers and bandwidth."

BANDWIDTH: The amount of data that can be transmitted in a fixed amount of time. For digital devices, the bandwidth is usually expressed in bits per second (BPS), or bytes per second. For analog devices, the bandwidth is expressed in cycles per second, or hertz (Hz).[21]

Clearly, traditional radio broadcasting and online broadcasting have their advantages and disadvantages, but Sandy chooses to interact with the Pagan community beyond her immediate locale, a choice she considers positive.

> Being able to listen to a station that suits a person's interests or niche just adds another dimension to the online experience. A person in Denmark who likes a certain style of music or programming can tune in to the same program that someone in Akron, Ohio is listening to. This leads to (if the show or program is live) interaction between people who have been brought together from opposite sides of the globe out of the similar interest that has them tuning in to the online broadcast. It's another venue to offer entertainment or education that you can participate in while browsing the Internet. You can listen to online stations and do browsing, e-mail, or other Internet-related tasks and listen to unique and diverse programming from around the world. It's another way to bring people together and share

> information and celebrate diversity through aural stimuli.

Mark agrees. "For the first time in history, Wiccans and Pagans can be served by a media outlet, and broadcasters, in turn, have access to a worldwide audience." But he also adds that, "from a corporate media standpoint," Wiccans and Pagans make for "a lousy audience":

> We are spread all over the world, there are comparably few of us, and we have specialized interests not commonly shared with larger market segments. From the bottom-line perspective, it's impossible to reach us all with a "delivered one time" program, we're too picky, and there aren't enough of us to make us attractive to advertisers with big money.
>
> Internet radio, with its "on demand" nature, relatively small production and storage costs, and ability to target even small communities across the world, is an excellent fit for the Wiccan and Pagan community. Programs like Earth Radio International often seek only to recoup production and storage costs and thus can deliver a highly targeted audience to small Pagan companies at a price they can afford. Internet radio is an excellent example of self-sustenance in the Pagan world.

PAGAN MUSIC ONLINE

When it comes to music, the Net has also had a significant impact on Witches and on Pagan culture in general. There are all kinds of musicians, singers, and song-writers who draw their material from their Pagan lives. Many recreate ancient or traditional musical forms from all over the world, from Indian ragas to Irish keening. A Web-based company called Serpentine Music sells Pagan music, exclusively, from the entire spectrum of musical genres: bluegrass to madrigals, Goth to trance music.[22] Mark Kelly observes that, "if there's a form of music, it's likely that someone, somewhere, is playing it with a Pagan twist."

Mark also points out that "Internet radio has opened unprecedented listening opportunities for Pagan listeners and, just as importantly, new marketing opportunities for Pagan musicians." Musicians create their own Web sites, establish links to Witchvox and other resources, perform at festivals and conventions, and burn their own CDs. Pagan music is blossoming, and so, Mark tells us, it's not hard to track it down on the Internet:

> Probably the most visited Internet music site is MP3.COM, a site that allows would-be broadcasters to assemble their favorite independent music into "stations" that stream to the listener on demand. All kinds of music are represented, grouped by the "radio station" builder.
>
> One of the most widely listened-to Pagan MP3.COM stations is Above a Star.[23] Tony T., the site's owner and programmer, gives a tasty sampling of the best Pagan music available today.
>
> Many broadcasters are putting up streaming Pagan music stations on another free site, Live365.com.[24] WGDS, "Goddess Internet Radio," is another showcase for Pagan music.[25]
>
> Much of what makes the Internet the perfect marketplace for Pagan ideas applies to its role in the proliferation and commercial success of Pagan music.

> Unable to sign recording contracts with record labels, many Pagan artists are turning to self-production and promotion. These entrepreneurs write and record their music, make it available on the Internet, and join cooperative marketing plans that allow listeners to purchase pressed-on-demand CDs of the music.

PAGAN STUDENT ORGANIZATIONS

A few years ago, I met a hereditary Druid on a listserve. He was active in the Pagan Student Association at Cornell University in Ithaca, New York. That fall, I was planning to travel in the Northeast, presenting workshops, and my listserve acquaintance invited me to present to his association.

Shortly afterwards, I met some members of the Ohio State University Pagan Students Association at a festival in Ohio. Their association publishes a quarterly zine called *Paths Less Traveled*; it is edited by SilverPeace and is available both online and in hard copy. SilverPeace interviewed me for the quarterly, and one of the questions he asked was whether I had ever belonged to a Pagan student group. This question took me aback. It also pleased me because, as I explained, when I was in college these groups didn't exist. Back then, Pagans rarely referred to themselves as such. There were no Witches around. It seemed that everyone was either a Christian or a Jew, with the exception of a few foreign students—Buddhist, Muslim, or Hindu. While there were a few mainstream-religion student organizations, spirituality was not generally accorded much attention.

Then, in the early 1990s, Craft High Priestess Judy Harrow of New York City was approached by some students at the State University of New York at New Paltz, who asked if she would act as religious counsel for a group they wanted to start. The students cnvisioned Judy's role as similar to that of a Catholic priest with the Newman Society, or a rabbi with Hillel. The SUNY New Paltz group never got off the ground, but in recent years the Covenant of the Goddess has developed an associates' program that assists student Witches.[26]

Today, fellowships on hundreds of university and college campuses bring Pagans together. They hold meetings, lectures, workshops, discussion groups, and even sabbat and lunar rituals. Some groups are pan-Pagan, and others focus on a particular path—such as Witchcraft, ceremonial magic, or Druidism. To find a list of these fellowships, go to Witchvox. It is heartening to see so many young seekers exploring Pagan paths in an environment supported by their schools. This phenomenon strikes me, an older sort of Witch, as remarkable.

THE GODDESS 2000 PROJECT

During a full-moon ritual in early December of 1998, Abby Willowroot had a vision. She saw people all over the world creating large Goddess statues, paintings, labyrinths, and all kinds of Goddess imagery; she also envisioned them celebrating their creations together. Abby spun this idea into the Goddess 2000 Project.[27]

An artist who works in a range of media, Abby had also created the Spiral Goddess Grove, an online virtual Goddess temple, in 1997.[28] Websurfers visiting the grove's shrines—and their numbers were growing rapidly—signed the guestbook and inspired Abby to expand. The grove became a popular place for meditation, peace, and learning for Goddess folk of all levels of experience.

Abby began to design a Web site for the Goddess 2000 Project (G2K). Buoyed by her own enthusiasm and the enthusiasm generated by the Spiral Goddess Grove and its visitors, she issued press releases, obtained sponsors, designed T-shirts, mugs, and bumper stickers, created a Goddess art-postcard show, and scheduled a Winter Solstice 1999 celebration of G2K. The G2K mission statement describes the project as "a community event that seeks to include all branches of the Earth Spirit, Goddess, Pagan, Dianic, Wiccan, Asatru, Yoruba, Heathen, Indigenous Spirituality, and other related folk"; people will come together "to celebrate the return of the Goddess, focusing on our shared beliefs, not our differences." Abby claims that it was the Internet that made "this amazing tribute to the Goddess" possible. "The magic of electronic connection," she maintains, "has allowed me to easily communicate with Goddess folks instantly, and that makes coordination of this type of an international grassroots event feasible."

Cosponsors of G2K are The Witches' Voice—there's that singing again—Circle Sanctuary, and the Covenant of the Goddess. Follow the threads to chapter 7, which deals with online rituals, to find out how the Winter Solstice ritual was created by many contributors, designed by Abby and me, and performed throughout the world. G2K is ongoing, and it now has participants in every American state and in fifty-six countries.

INTERFAITH WORK

Along with so many other enriching developments that resulted from the Internet, interfaith work—locally, nationally, and internationally—emerged as an important societal force. During the Chicago World's Fair of 1893, an event called the Parliament of the World's Religions took place. Religious leaders from around the world participated. One of these participants was Vivekananda, founder of the Vendanta Society, a religious community based in India. Vivekananda's presence in Chicago opened a channel to the East, introducing Westerners to Eastern religious thought.

A century later, in 1993, a second parliament—now called Parliament of World Religions (PWR)—was held in Chicago. As befits our times, the 1993 PWR was even more diverse than the 1893 version. Representatives from virtually every known world religion, except those practiced by some (but not all) isolated tribes, attended. Among the participants were representatives of at least five Pagan organizations: Covenant of the Goddess, Circle Sanctuary, EarthSpirit Community, and the Fellowship of Isis. This marked a great shift in witchen culture. At that moment, we stepped from the shadows to walk in the sunshine and work amicably with other faith traditions. We were welcomed. We were not harassed. We Witches befriended the other participants. We learned about each other's religions with neither disdain nor distrust, but in friendship, with open minds and hearts.

A total of 7,500 people attended the parliament. A group of about 250 attendees held a series of closed meetings. They were dubbed the "Parliament Assembly," and among them were the Dalai Lama and the Pope (represented by a cardinal acting as papal nuncio). CoG, Circle, and EarthSpirit were represented in the assembly by Deborah Ann Light, an elder in all three groups. The assembly discussed and approved a document called "Towards a Global Ethic: An Initial Declaration," which stated that all of the world's faith traditions share certain norms of ethical behavior.[29]

The 1993 parliament was an unprecedented success for Pagans. From that point on, Neopaganism was recognized as a part of the American religious scene. We moved from being a fringe group to being a religious minority.

The assembly continued to meet after 1993, preparing for the next parliament. In 1998, Pagans Don Frew of CoG and Selena Fox of Circle Sanctuary were invited to join; the membership of the assembly grew to 350.

The next parliament was held in 1999 in Cape Town, South Africa, and it celebrated the end of apartheid.[30] Witches and Pagans representing CoG, Circle, EarthSpirit Community, and other organizations again participated. Much of the planning and discussion took place via e-mail, listserves, and Web sites.

The 1999 assembly discussed and approved a document entitled "A Call to Our Guiding Institutions," which put forward practical suggestions for implementing a global ethic.[31] Networking at the 1999 parliament resulted in the creation of hundreds of "gifts of service" around the world—projects drawing on interfaith resources to address societal and environmental ills.

The enthusiasm generated by the 1993 parliament also led to the creation of a new interfaith organization whose mission is to facilitate ongoing interfaith cooperation: the United Religions Initiative (URI).[32] Founded by Bishop William Swing of the Episcopal Diocese of San Francisco, URI came into official existence when its charter was signed in June of 2000. The organization already has over 150 member groups, or "cooperation circles," worldwide. Pagans are an active presence in the URI and the PWR, as well as in other regional interfaith bodies. Every one of these bodies has a strong Web presence and thrives using Net technology.

Picking up luminescent personal threads, Carol Maltby has experienced interfaith since her first days online. She has far more experience in online interfaith dialogue than most Pagans. She has been "out" as a Witch under her legal name almost everywhere—online and in the mundane world. "I have never had any problems with harassment coming out of this, even though I'm one of only two people with my name in the country, and thus easily findable, especially since I am often very bioregion-specific in my postings. The only exception to this policy concerns a couple of online places with some very hard-core fundamentalists who are well armed, where I am known by [a] more discreet handle . . . for security reasons."

Interfaith work, Carol feels, is one of the most important aspects of online action. She has at least two Christian ministers as friends and mentors. These people have become important enough to her life that she ranks them with her Pagan mentors: "While we may draw from different wells, there is a deep reservoir of wisdom we all draw upon that nourishes us and our communities."

Carol met these ministers years ago, through the Compuserve Religion Forum boards.

> One had come into the Pagan section out of curiosity, and the other I met in the Buddhism section, an interest we both share . . . One heads a traditional Midwestern congregation. The other had a first wife who had been a Witch, and out of an atheist, politico lifestyle in San Francisco followed an experiential vision of Jesus who appeared to him (he lost the atheism, kept his radical politics). I

> love these men as my brothers. I've met both of them, though each time it took one of us driving four hours out of the way when we were "in the neighborhood."

With these two friends, Carol feels a level of trust and honesty equal to that she feels with her most trusted Pagan companions, and she would be happy to include them in her private circle workings. Among the Christians Carol has met on the Net, she senses a willingness "to not just tolerate, but embrace our differences":

> They do understand that religion is a very personal matter, and that what works for one person may not be right for another. They also realize that in some ways the structures and frameworks of their religious life may not always serve their spiritual communities the way they used to, a realization the Pagan community also explores as we find ourselves becoming more accepted by the mainstream. Together, we explored what works in our spiritual communities and what could use improvement.

This openness Carol ascribes to "a willingness, on both sides, to explore the use of more inclusive vocabulary to describe our experience." This is the foundation upon which successful interfaith can be built. As Carol explains, "Knowing that Goddess is only one aspect of that unnameable Ground of Being, when I am on a mixed board and talking about spirituality I will often say the Divine as a more inclusive way of indicating God/dess. Yes, nuances of vocabulary matter when doing educational work and explaining terms, but we mustn't allow them to separate us from the people with whom we are trying to communicate."

Like Carol, I advocate being out of the broom closet online "in a way that doesn't make a big deal out of it." Ignorance of who we are and what we do is what leads others to fear us, so when they find out that we're their coworkers or their neighbors, that we inhabit the same world they do, we may counter the ignorance and dispel the fear. Carol expands on this:

> We still may be the only Witches most people will ever encounter, but hundreds of people who are "lurking" online may quietly form an opinion of Witches based on how we express ourselves online . . . Sometimes there is no hope of dialogue, and we find that the best we can hope for is two monologues gnawing away at each other. Some may enjoy this as a substitute for rugby or gladiatorial combat in the Colosseum, but I find it a waste of time and energy. When this happens in public, just remember that there are unseen others who are watching and forming their opinions of Pagans on the strength of this encounter, and try to keep good humor and grace present rather than anger and frustration.
>
> I've come away from some of these [encounters with Christians] shaky at the hatred and intolerance I've encountered, but I have also found them useful for introducing me to some of the seamier parts of the Bible that I hadn't run into before.
>
> Online sites have been a terrific source of textual criticism of biblical scholarship aimed at non-Christians, and they have offered a fascinating look

> at the inconsistencies in the Bible. Some of these can be useful for rebuttals when dealing with local conservative Christians who can't live and let live, such as the sites by those Christians who feel that Christians should not celebrate Easter or Christmas. I think that if there are Christians we have to defend ourselves from, the Internet offers valuable resources for us to better understand their worldview and use their own beliefs to influence their behavior.

If some Christian, Muslim, or other religious Web sites foster intolerance and hatred—or at least misunderstanding—then so do some Pagan Web sites and articles. They display a bigotry that is atypical of Pagans, in my experience, and they reflect poorly on the Pagan movement as a whole. Even though we may understand the experiences that bring these attitudes to the surface, they are unacceptable. Carol maintains that it is in the interest of every Pagan to foster a constructive dialogue: "Every positive association that allows respect for Pagans as individuals means a spreading of the idea that can benefit and protect us all, that we are not the 'other,' an unknown that is to be feared."

Spellweaver, a Massachusetts Witch, encountered an opportunity to do good interfaith work quite unexpectedly while she was on WidowNet, a chat group/bulletin board for widows and widowers.

> When it became apparent to some of the members on the list that I was not a Christian, they became curious about my beliefs. This put me in the position of explaining Wicca/Paganism. This, in

> turn, stirred a number of interesting threads about the differences between our faiths and, of course, how they relate to our beliefs about life after death —reincarnation versus heaven, and so on—and how our different beliefs helped to bring us comfort.
>
> In general, it was interesting and informative for all participants. I believe that many people came away from it with a better understanding of Paganism along with their own particular faith. Even when you think you know what it is that you believe in, there is something about having to write it down—taking time to formulate what those beliefs are, focusing the essence of them into a few sentences or a paragraph that can express it clearly to another—that helps to gel those beliefs within your own mind and heart.

Carol delivers this pithy summation to the interfaith question: "Cross-pollination can strengthen not only us, but also those we share these ideas with."

The experiences of Carol and Spellweaver demonstrate a few of the ways that threads connecting Pagans and non-Pagans can be spun. My coconspirator Lhiannon, owner of DrakNet, demonstrates yet another. She learned a profound lesson in religious tolerance from her Internet correspondence with a Christian rock star, a man with whom she shared what she describes as "the weirdest friendship on the face of the Earth . . . the Conservative Christian and the Witch Fan." Having developed a huge crush on the performer, Lhiannon visited his Web site, where she checked out the bulletin board. In his posts to his BBS, the rock star, a Mormon, had expressed a political opinion with which Lhiannon took issue. A debate ensued, says Lhiannon, that "went on for pages and days, finally culminating in a rather deep discussion of whether there was a universal reality of right and wrong that transcended religions. We both argued like seasoned politicians, tossing barbs and slight insults back at each other—it was a heck of a lot of fun."

Their conversation shifted over to private e-mail and continued for months. When the rock star discovered that Lhiannon owned a Web hosting business and had the technological expertise that running a successful Web-based business requires, he asked for her professional advice on what she would do to improve his Web site. A few weeks later, the rock star decided he wanted to do a fan chat. Lhiannon set up a chat room and moderated it for him, allowing him to interact with his fans. "After the chat," reports Lhiannon, "we were still on AOL [Instant Message] together, and we just began talking one-on-one. For about three hours we talked about religion, politics, and morality. He asked me about Wicca, and he talked about how he wanted to change rock and roll."

Lhiannon says that this postchat evening of online dialogue "was one of the more interesting and odd connections I've ever made on the Internet." But then she found herself growing mistrustful. The man's friendliness confused her, and she wondered why a conservative Christian rock star would be talking to someone like her. She suspected that he was trying to convert her. Unfortunately, Lhiannon's reaction isn't uncommon among Pagans.

Around that time, the rock star dropped out of the dialogue to focus on recording an album. Lhiannon was left to stew in her own prejudices. In his absence, she attempted to push him from her mind and put some distance between them. She had come to see him less as a person and more as a label. So, by the time the rock star recontacted her, Lhiannon had become standoffish, almost hostile. Soon afterwards, due to some ridiculous misunderstanding, she exploded at him and asked him not to write to her anymore. Later still, she scolded herself for her inability to get past her attitudes and enjoy their genuine liking for one another. She now ponders, "Are we so trained to expect discrimination that we brace ourselves for it? Possibly even provoke it? Do we mistake ignorance of our beliefs for disapproval, disagreement with our gods for a rejection of our path?"

Lhiannon wrote about this experience in an online forum called Themestream: "So many people urged me to contact him and apologize that I did, and he called me back and accepted, so we're actually speaking again."[33]

Over and over, we hear the sound of the plucked threads, the voice of Pagans on the Net. Fritz, of Witchvox, reminds us:

> Increased communication has been a wonderful thing for this community. With the advent of the Net, the power once held by the few was take back by the people of the community. It has been my observation that this doesn't [sit] well with some of the old guard. In contrast, many of the old guard are thrilled by the instant news, inspirational writing, and powerful networking of cyberspace. Fact is, you can't deny change—it's a constant.

Chapter 4

ENLIVENING THE FILAMENTS: DEITY AND "THEISMS"

The thread of deity has surfaced in many places throughout the weaving that is this book, beginning in chapter 1, where we spoke of the People of the Web. Pagans believe in various "theisms." We are pantheists, panentheists, polytheists, henotheists, monists, and even sometimes, though rarely, monotheists. And if that's not confusing enough, many of us speak of thealogy, the feminine form of theology.

Most of us experience the divine as being immanent rather than transcendent, although we can also experience divinity in ways that transcend and in ways that transform. We see divinity *within* the world and *as* the world; the world is not separate from the sacred. In his excellent book *Pagans and Christians: The Personal Spiritual Experience*, Gus diZerega notes that "The world is never completely separate from the Sacred, and therefore it possesses intrinsic value that we are obligated to respect, and which is quite independent of our own preferences." He further explains: "[W]hen we survey Pagan spirituality as a whole, we will find a range of emphasis along this point. Some people will emphasize Divinity's transcendental dimension . . . Others will emphasize more immanent spiritual dimensions . . . But nearly all Pagan traditions acknowledge the existence of both dimensions."[1]

Pantheists see the divine in everything, believing that God is omnipresent. They conceive of the physical universe as divine in its totality. Their view is one of immanence. Panentheists, however, conceive of the divine as both transcendent and immanent. I would describe myself as being a panentheist. I experience Goddess as suffusing and imbuing everything, including my own being. I see her in the vast view of the horizon from the summit, in sparkling brooks, in migrating geese, and in city sidewalks; she exists for me in garbage dumps, in scampering rats, and in shining red rubies; she's there in the aurora borealis, in redwood groves, and in a bag lady. I hear her in the roar of the freeway and the roar of the sea, in the squeal of the hawk's prey and the coo of the dove. Her scents arise from the dung heap and the rose garden, from the swamp and the lotus. I inhale her with every breath, and I step in time with her gait.

If panentheistic is an appropriate term to describe my belief and experience, then so is polytheistic. My name comes from Macha of Ireland. My writing is guided by Bridget, my computer is guarded by Ganesha, my car is Nuit Urania, I regularly attend Kali Pujas on the new moon. Hermes assists my Net connections. Sekhmet has spoken to me through rain, wind, thunder, and lightning. I am like many Witches in that I attend to the calls of many deities.

Most of the time, I experience deities as separate from myself, entities to be approached with reverence and treated with honor and dignity—except for those among them who want nothing to do with dignity. But sometimes circumstances arise that call for the divine to speak through me. So far, the divine, when manifested in my body, has been female; but I don't feel that it could never be male. My experience of immanent divinity within my body is merely limited to female. We Pagans of a more conventional gender identity can learn a great deal about aspecting and shape shifting from our edge-walking gay, lesbian, bisexual, and transgendered kin. When I experience the shift in consciousness that transforms me into whatever deity is manifesting in my body, I am ecstatic, in the sense that I am out of my stasis. The mortal Macha has receded in me and allowed the divine to speak. At such times, my experience of the divine is one of transcendence. I have transcended my human self and opened up to deity.

Let's look at one more "theism" while we're in this part of Spider Woman's web: henotheism. Henotheists work with a particular set of deities, while not denying the existence of others. I can happily work with a single set of deities, or a particular ethnic pantheon—in other words, walk a henotheist path—when I'm with people who do. I have two friends who, as dedicated Priestess of Hekate and Priest of Hermes, have set aside a temple where they perform a dark-moon ritual to both these deities. This is their regular religious practice. I would call it an example of henotheism.

Gus diZerega tells us that, because we see the world as a dimension of divinity rather than radically separate from it, we naturally look to sources other than texts for legitimate spiritual knowledge and insight.[2]

Some Pagans and Witches don't "believe in" any

deities, but they still find it beneficial to speak with, and for, them and to work with them in the context of group ritual. Reflecting on our attitudes towards deities, Erik Davis observes that "Most Pagans embrace these entities with a combination of conviction and levity, superstition, psychology, and hardcore materialism."[3] It is our shared practices, regardless of our individual beliefs, that bind our community(ies) together.

I want to explain how polytheism, in particular, interweaves so well with the Internet, and how certain deities have influenced computer culture. Polytheists believe in many deities. A different deity may preside over or influence a given activity or place. Aphrodite, for instance, is associated with sexual love. Her concern is not the running of a household, like Hestia, goddess of the hearth. By the same token, Aries, a war god, would be significant to a soldier, but the soldier might also honor Vulcan, the divine smith who fashions armor and weapons, and/or Asclepius, the healer. We are not restricted to the gods of ancient Greece, however, as we search for deities on the Internet.

INTERNET DEITIES

This book has been guided by the spirit of Spider Woman. A few spiders make their homes in the upper corners of the room I work in, and I don't disturb them, for I want Spider Woman to be with me as I travel her filaments. As this book's epigraph suggests, Spider Woman takes an interest in our web weaving in cyberspace. She is one of the deities that I, as a polytheist and a panentheist, have invoked to influence the development of my writing. She first emerged among a people far removed from my ancestors, in a place and time remote from my experience and the experiences of my forebears. Yet She has become a part of my culture, because I live on the continent, if not in the region, where She first arose, and because I embrace Spider Woman as one of many deities from whom I can seek blessing and inspiration, and from whom I can learn about myself and about life.

One Pagan has said that he sees the Hindu god Indra in the World Wide Web because that deity "holds in his possession a net stretching into infinity in all directions. A magnificent jewel is lodged in each eye of the net, and each jewel reflects the infinity of the other jewels."[4] Other Pagans associate Minoan Ariadne with the Internet and the World Wide Web. Ariadne gave Theseus a thread to follow when he entered the Cretan labyrinth so that he would not become lost.

I have dedicated the word-processing software with which I write to Bridget, mother of inspiration and she who oversees intellectual pursuits. Bridget has been deeply involved in the creation of this book. She has presided over its birth like the midwife She is. She has tempered it on Her divine forge, and She has brought it to health and vibrancy with Her cooling waters. She appears and reappears like a golden thread throughout this weaving. A candle, lit from Bridget's sacred fire at Kildare, Ireland, burns while I work. For a time, a beautiful leather mask of Bridget hung on the wall above my desk.

I have chosen Bridget for all She means to me. Another Pagan writer might well be inspired by another deity, or deities, and dedicate his tools accordingly. My computer hardware is one of my magical tools. So are my software programs. They are magical tools as much as athames, wands, cups, or pentacles are. Besides the word-processing program, I used an e-mail program, two Net **browsers**,

BROWSER: An application program that provides a way to look at, and interact with, all the information on the World Wide Web... Technically, a Web browser is a client program that uses the Hypertext Transfer Protocol to make requests of Web servers throughout the Internet on behalf of the browser user... The first widely used browser [was] Netscape Navigator. Microsoft followed with its Microsoft Internet Explorer. Today, these two browsers are highly competitive, and [they are] the only two browsers that the vast majority of Internet users are aware of.[5]

and listserves in the creation of this book.

My hard drive is named for Ganesha, the Hindu lord of obstacles. A small brass figure of an elephant-headed Lord Ganesha, with His broken tusk, sits on the shelf above my desk. I can look up and speak to Him if I find that I'm encountering obstacles. I can rub His shiny brass belly in appreciation. His presence reassures me. He keeps my spirits up and smoothes the way. May he remove all obstacles from within and without my working tool.

JEWITCH: A Witch of Jewish extraction who often incorporates Hebrew mythos and deities into his/her personal Craft practice.

Deities affect technology. Melissa is a technopagan and a **Jewitch** who is dedicated to the Kemetic (Egyptian) deity Ma'at, goddess of truth and order. Melissa has given Ma'at an honored place on her Web site,[6] in her professional life (she works in the computer industry), and in her personal life. Her site contains her writings about Ma'at and her encounters with Ma'at.

Another technopagan, the magus Sam Webster, is a dedicated priest of Hermes. Hermes—or Mercury, in his Latin form—rules communication, keen wit, swift thought, travel, and thievery—all aspects of the Internet. Erik Davis remarks that for thousands of years "alchemists, Kabbalists, and esoteric Christians developed a rich storehouse of mental tools, visual dataspaces, and virtual maps. It's no accident that these 'hermetic' arts are named for Hermes."[7] Hermes is almost palpably present in the mechanics of high-speed travel, including space travel, and in the workings of computers. Although He first emerged in human consciousness in ancient times—as Hermes Trismegiston ("thrice great") in the Mediterranean; as keeper of *The Emerald Tablets*, a compendium of arcane knowledge—He is still very much alive today. The essential hermetic maxim, "As above, so below," describes the cosmos as "a vast and resonating web of living symbolic correspondences between humans and earth and heaven." One day, while researching this book, I happened upon the Web site of a tattoo artist. There, in small type at the bottom of every page, I noticed the words "Thank you, Hermes."

Erik Davis sees that "The African religious impulse lends itself to a computer world much more than anything in the West." The complex, magical symbols called *veves*, Davis points out—which are drawn in white flour on the floor, or ground in Voudoun rituals, or painted in bright colors and sometimes beaded or sequined—resemble printed circuits. He also points to Legba, one of the West African *loa*, as ruler of "messages and gateways and tricks, and as the lord of the crossroads."[8]

I asked Adam if he associated specific deities with the Internet. He named Athena, then added, "and, of course, Eris." Adam explained that he "always saw Athena as the sort of goddess who would be really into technology—changing forms at will, digging out information, and so on. Especially the Athena of *The Odyssey*. The sort of cunning Athena . . . has always been my first thought when connecting deities with the Net."

Grey Cat, from Tennessee, on the other side of the globe from Adam in Australia, agrees: "It's that, I think, which has led me to associate Minerva as much with the Net as I do. She always seemed pretty cunning to me, and good at being invisible when the roaring lightning-type gods were around. As for gods, Hermes/Mercury is an inescapable connection."

Chaos magician Adam continues: "And **Eris** is self-evident, I think. The Internet is, to me, chaos. It is about all competing views shouting at once, in a structure that changes with every passing second. It is perhaps the

ERIS: Greek goddess who was "the embodiment of folly, moral blindness, infatuation, and mischief." Her toy, "the Apple of Discord, was the cause of the Trojan War."[9]

most organic and chaotic thing we have created, not to mention something that sows an awful lot of discord. The Internet *is* a Golden Apple."

Like most Pagans, I call upon any one or more of an abundance of deities when I feel the need. I have my favorites, and they have me. Some, like Sekhmet, have insisted that I pay attention to them. Others drew me to their worship in gentler, subtler ways.

The notion of Internet deities may seem strange to contemporary readers, but it is nothing new. In various times and places, spiritual traditions have identified gods and other entities as having special influence over certain activities. For example, Hestia presides over the hearth, White Tara is Mother of Compassion, and Saint Fiacre is believed to protect taxi drivers.

As I write this, I learn that Spanish Catholic bishops have advocated to the Pope that Saint Isidore, seventh-century Bishop of Seville, is the best candidate for patron saint of the Internet because he produced one of the world's first databases in the form of a twenty-volume encyclopedia called *The Etymologies*. In fact, the Vatican's own Web site, mounted in 1996, is powered by three computers that are apparently under the guardianship of archangels: they are called Raphael, Michael, and Gabriel.

NAV BAR: An area on a Web page or application that provides controls for browsing site content. The nav bar generally contains buttons (small graphics or words that, when clicked on, take the user to another part of a Web site) that let you advance, scroll, or search.[10]

TEMPLES, PERSONAL SHRINES, AND ALTARS

Pagans and Witches have been inspired to create Web sites dedicated to personal deities and pantheons. And some of us have created small online altars, dedications, and even temples within those Web sites. While my Web site does not have a shrine, evidence of my devotion to certain deities, as well as my regard for certain plant and bird species, abound. My **nav bar**, for instance, overlays a grove of redwoods, the spectacular and mighty trees that are native to the region where I live. Online shrines link to other sites in the fields of folklore, mythology, anthropology, and literature, among others.

One of the most beautiful and comprehensive Web sites I've found is a Canaanite-Phoenician temple called Qadash Kinahnu.[11] This site contains eighty-five rooms, some covering Canaanite and Phoenician history, mythology, and ritual, and it includes a Neopagan section, with a large subsection on "polytheology, that is, Neopagan theology." Qadash Kinahnu also contains sections titled "The Purple Book of Ancient Near Eastern Magic" and "The Priestess's Quarters." It is not strictly a witchen site, although the woman who created it considers herself to be a Witch and a Pagan, but it appeals to many Witches and other Pagans, who use it and its links for pleasure and research. The site's creator, Lilinah Biti-Anat, is a dedicant of the Canaanite goddess Anat. Her site reflects her unique, and very beautiful, approach to art, lore, study, practice, and personal reflection.

Abby Willowroot, whose thread has appeared several times in this book, was an early online Pagan presence. Her Spiral Goddess Grove site is filled with online shrines to different goddesses, different aspects of Goddess, a healing circle, a hearth, and even a Green Man Grove.[12] On this site, you can visit seasonal altars, historical altars, and ancestral altars. There are pages about making sacred Goddess wall art and Goddess masks. There are altars of Goddess jewels, the Ocean Mother, trees and glades, night and morning, stages of life, and several pages for children. What resonates most with me is the Grove of Remembrance, a memorial page for our **Beloved Dead**. Visitors can go to this shrine to reconnect with their grief

BELOVED DEAD: People whom we loved when they were alive and who have crossed over.

at the loss of a loved one. They can also post their own remembrances.

The Grove of Remembrance isn't the only site where Witches and Pagans can remember their loved ones online. Once again, we hear the song of Witchvox, which offers a place to post memories and photos of our Beloved Dead.

When my dear friend John Patrick McClimans died, his old comrades at Church of All Worlds set up an online memorial to him. NROOGD and Reclaiming priestess Judy Foster was remembered not only on special Samhain altars the year she died, but she is also commemorated on a beautiful page created by Melissa.[13] And other Pagan groups with a presence on the Net create memorial pages for their Beloved Dead.

Websurfers can find lots of online altars and shrines, but it's unlikely they'll discover anything as comprehensive as the Spiral Goddess Grove. On her site, Abby has even provided a page where you can create your own online altar. Choose from an array of candles, Goddess images, fairies, crystals, and ritual tools such as pentacles, incense burners, crystal balls, swords, chalices, brooms, wands, and **cauldrons**. When you are satisfied with the altar you've built, you can then save it to your desktop.

CAULDRON: A pot, often made of cast iron and having three or four legs, a handle, and a lid, which is used in various ways for magical work and rituals. In essence a cooking pot, it is also a tool for transformation. Objects may be passed through the fire burning within the cauldron to be purified; people may jump over the cauldron to be purified or healed. A cauldron may also be used over a fire, for brewing herbal drinks or making special soups to be eaten as part of a ritual. Filled with water, a cauldron may be used for scrying.

THE TEMPLE OF SEKHMET

In a remote desert area north of Las Vegas, Nevada, near a nuclear test site, on ancient Western Shoshone land, sits a sacred temple to the Egyptian goddess Sekhmet. In 1992, Genevieve Vaughan and her daughters built this small, environmentally appropriate temple in honor of the lion-headed Egyptian goddess of birth, fertility, and rage. Staffed by Crone Priestess Patricia Pearlman, whose life is dedicated to Sekhmet, the temple "provides a calm space of refuge for opponents of nuclear weapons tests of any sort." The land on which the temple is constructed, a twenty-acre expanse, was returned to the Western Shoshone to whom the area originally belonged.[14]

I'd heard of this temple through e-mails from friends, and I had visited its Web site. In the summer of 1998, the annual Grand Council of Covenant of the Goddess was scheduled to meet near Las Vegas, and, as national first officer that year, I was going to conduct the meetings. Since the Sekhmet temple would be so near, it occurred to me that a pilgrimage was in order. Here is the story of that pilgrimage.

On Monday, August 31, 1998, in the second quarter of the autumn lunation, four other Witches and I visited the Temple of Sekhmet in Cactus Springs, Nevada. My companions shared a lineage, and we all shared Goddess worship and Witchcraft. This greatly increased our compatibility and our willingness, even eagerness, to share our work.

We drove a long way out into the increasingly desolate desert. None of us had any experience with such an environment, but we had been advised to bring food, water, sunscreen, and a hat, since there was nowhere to get anything to eat and no water source for miles around; also, the desert sun is most often oppressively hot, relentless, and unforgiving. The farther we retreated from Las Vegas, the fewer signs of human habitation we saw. The last structure we spotted was an abandoned military installation some miles from the temple.

A little later, we caught sight of a pale-colored, circular structure standing some distance off the highway. It had large arched openings that faced the four quarters, and an open dome of curved metal bars.

We pulled our two cars into the barren parking lot (which was equipped with a lone portable toilet), got out, stretched our legs, and slowly approached the path leading to the temple. That path, as well as the three others extending from each of the temple doorways, was bordered with rocks. A sign reading "Quiet Area" was posted at the head of the path. Small to medium-sized sculptures, figures of deities such as Ganesha, Lord of Obstacles, and carefully placed geodes, fossils, and other stone formations stood in the quadrants between the paths.

We entered the temple through the west doorway. To our left was a large, black, human-sized statue of Sekhmet, with beautiful hanging dugs and a wise cat face.

One member of our party, Marilee, a magical aromatherapist, incense maker, and herbalist with many years of experience in several Craft and other magical methods, began by spreading the ritual tools she'd brought with her out on the floor in front of Sekhmet. She placed jewelry—her own and that of others who had requested that she consecrate their jewelry at the temple—in Sekhmet's lap. She lit incense. Then she placed a spot of lotus oil on each of our third eyes.

There were half a dozen small potted plants inside the temple, and they looked very dry and wilted. Starting at Sekhmet's left and walking deosil (sunrise, clockwise), I poured a bit of water from my spring water bottle into each pot. Looking around the temple, I saw little shelves and alcoves, plus a few small altar tables, upon which sat figures of other goddesses and some magical tchotchkes: a triple Hekate; a bare-breasted Cretan goddess, arms extended and entwined with snakes; a fat, dreaming Anatolian goddess; Diana the Huntress; and my own personal matron, Kali Ma.

Returning to Sekhmet, I placed the scarab ring that I've worn for thirty years in Her lap. Each of us, in turn, proffered what we could to the Lady Sekhmet. I kneeled and placed my head and hands on the floor in front of me in honor of Her. I asked for Her blessings on my work. We had as much time as we needed to do our individual work, but, as it turned out, none of us took very long.

All this time, Marilee's incense burned. In 1964, an ancient Egyptian tomb dating from approximately 2400 B.C.E. was opened. Among the other artifacts found inside was a large jar of incense. Marilee holds such a prominent position in the world of incense makers that she came into possession of a small quantity of this very incense, which was about 4,500 years old. She had saved it for just such a special use. Since its discovery, the Egyptian incense has been analyzed, and the recipe for it has been published in trade journals. Marilee brought with her to Nevada both the original incense and some she had made using the recipe. At the desert temple, she burned a little of each at Sekhmet's feet.

As we took our turns in front of Sekhmet, we passed our jewelry through the incense, speaking what words we felt moved to say. My ring moved from Sekhmet's lap through the incense and back onto my right hand.

As all of this was happening, the light from the sky had been changing, and it continued to change. When we arrived, the sky had been slightly overcast. The desert stretched as far as the eye could see, filled with tenacious, efficient, low-growing flora and surrounded by mountains, with more mountains beyond in every direction. There were no signs of tree or river or stream anywhere, and no other buildings were within sight; only the occasional roar of a truck going by on the highway that cut through the landscape a short distance from the shrine disturbed the healing, pristine—and very welcome—desert silence. As we looked, our perception of distance shifted. The mountains sometimes appeared closer than they had a moment before. Sometimes, sections of the mountains, or entire sides of them, were illuminated by the waning sunlight, and at other times their colors changed with the movement of clouds between the sun and the mountains.

As the five of us proceeded with our impromptu ritual, designing it as we performed it, we chanted together. At one point, we chanted, "The river is flowing down to the sea," which I thought rather odd in such a harsh, arid place.

Early in our rite, I noticed fork lightning striking the ground several miles to the southwest.

We had come to a quiet, contemplative time. I sat meditating on a cushion on the temple's stone floor as the sunlight came piercing through the curved bars of the dome. Soon, drops of water the size of quarters began plopping on my lap, head, and shoulders. They were warm and friendly raindrops, carrying no threat or chill. I felt as though the Goddess were washing me with her tears, washing me clean of the unhealthy casino energy I had been immersed in for the preceding five days. I smiled and welcomed her soothing bath. Soon I was soaked, my flimsy summer dress sticking to my skin.

Then, as subtly as the rain came upon us, it withdrew. A strong, dry wind came up, brisk and refreshing. I stood and walked out of the temple. Heading along the southbound path, I passed an amethyst geode and a toy dinosaur. Wind blew my hair and dress about until I was completely dry. I circumambulated the temple three or four times, observing both the temple grounds within the circle I inscribed and the vast landscape surrounding us.

Soon, the lightning moved in closer, and thunder boomed all around us. It began raining again, becoming heavier and more lightning-and-thunder-laden than before. Fork lightning struck the Earth within yards of the temple. As we Witches stood inside the temple, we were jolted by the loud sound of a lightning bolt striking the structure's open copper-tube dome. Sekhmet had commanded our undivided attention.

We decided that since there was no other shelter from the rain and the increasingly intense lightning, which was by this time striking every minute or so, we should head for the safety of our cars. We took shelter in the cars for the rest of the storm—it lasted about forty minutes. By this time, we'd met Patricia, Crone Priestess and caretaker of the temple. "It *never* rains out here!" she insisted. The annual rainfall in those parts is less than seven inches.

What does it all mean? Besides being a bonding experience for us, this unusual encounter, and its attendant meteorological phenomena, undoubtedly had profound personal meaning for each of us. For me, the cleansing rain, followed by a refreshing wind, was restorative and healing. And the experience was also about encountering Sekhmet. I know that She was intent on riveting my attention by striking the temple with lightning while we were in it. I don't know exactly what She has planned for me next, but I have no doubt that my pursuits will be blessed by Her presence.

Sekhmet is not a goddess I know much about, nor have I had much connection with Her over my years of practice. In fact, I do not resonate strongly with the Egyptian pantheon except Queen Isis, who, in any case, extends far beyond Egypt. I do love cats, however, which is the main form that Sekhmet takes. For eighteen years, I had a black familiar named Cybele. I welcome Sekhmet's presence in my life now, and I open myself to Her influence. I believe it would be sacrilege to make light of, or disregard, Her messages.

When I encountered Sekhmet, I had reached a point in my life (beginning my second Saturn return, for one thing) when I found myself much freer to devote myself to being a priestess of the Goddess. Until then, I had been a struggling single parent in an unsupportive cultural environment. By the time I arrived in the Nevada desert, doors had opened before me. I only needed to step across the threshold.

It's interesting to note that, had I not been active on the Web, chances are that I would not have heard of the wonderful Temple of Sekhmet. The fact that the temple has an electronic presence as well as a physical one makes it accessible for virtual pilgrimages as well as terraspace visits.

ORD BRIGHIDEACH

Bridget is a goddess who has always spoken to me. She is dear and close. She is part of my heritage as an American of Irish descent. I often turn to Her for help in one endeavor or another. I light a candle to Her and say a brief prayer when starting a creative project, particularly a writing. Now I can join with other Brigidians the world over in worship. We are all members of the Ord Brighideach, an online sisterhood and brotherhood of people who honor Bridget.

We came together as a devotional order through a Web site created by two women in Oregon. We are a cyberproject. We met online; we share poetry, writings, thoughts, and experiences online. We are worshipers bonded together by the act of keeping a small flame burning on our individual altars—in our homes and workplaces and hearths around the globe.

The site invites those who hear Bridget's call to join together in devotionals. "If she speaks to you—as a poet, healer, smith, storyteller, musician, craftsperson, midwife, mother, hearth keeper, land steward, tender of herds, seer, woman of fire, lawgiver, deity of the home, lady of the sun, or simply as goddess or saint—you are welcome to walk among us."[15]

I had known of the order for a few years, visited the site, and reflected on whether I wanted to join before I actually did. My reservation about joining was that I travel erratically, and I wondered how I could maintain my watch in airports, buses, cars, or wherever I was lodging. I knew that I was expected to tend Her flame once every twenty days, for as long as possible, taking safety into consideration. The principle is that the longer we are able to tend the flame, the more energy we will generate. We are making an offering to this world and the otherworld, as well as to Bridget, "She Who Gives Energy."

Ord Brighideach is comprised of nineteen cells—the number reflects the nineteen priestesses of Bridget at Kildare—with nineteen people in each. Each cell is named for a tree, and every day one of the nineteen tends the flame; on the twentieth day, as of old, Bridget Herself tends it. So I continued to contemplate joining, returning to the site from time to time and listening for Her call.

Bridget is a goddess of power and brilliance, tenderness

and compassion. As bright as She is, She's easy to approach. To the strong woman, She exemplifies righteous strength. The independent woman sees Her as someone who needs no partner to make Her whole. Bridget displays strength, skill, industry, and artistry in ways that don't threaten men and don't restrict women. People all over the world can hear Her lovely voice. We call Her Brighid, Breda, Bhride, Brigantis, Bridey, Brigit, Brigid, Brigantia, Bride, Brigantu, Brid, Briga, Bridgid, Briginda, Brigdu, Brigittina, Cailleach Bearra, Minerva, Maman Brigitte, and She answers. (I use Bridget, Brigid, Brigit, Bridey, and Brighde interchangeably.) She calls across barriers and brings diverse people together in Her honor.

When this book was in its conceptual stage, I finally joined the Ord Brighideach. At the time we join, we can choose to be in a women's cell, a men's cell, or a mixed cell. I chose an all-women cell and thus became a sister of the Laurel, a member of *Cill Labhras*. I take the fourteenth shift. Once every twentieth day, I join in tending Bridget's sacred flame with others who hold Bridget dear. Beginning at sundown, in accord with the Celtic counting of nights and days, each of us lights our candle. My cell sisters are Witches, Pagans, Christians, liberal and conservative, conventional and unconventional. What we share is our dedication to maintain the sacred flame of Brighde throughout the world. One member of our cell, Tiffany Lavendar, designed a Laurel Cell Web site to help establish our group identity.[16] Some of the other cells also maintain a Web presence, and all are linked to the main order. Laurel Cell, like the other cells, has set up a listserve to help members share experiences, insights, recipes, and stories. There's also a listserve for the entire order; subscription is optional.

One of the first things I did upon joining Ord Brighideach was to print out the calendar I found on the order's Web site that indicated the dates on which my flame watch fell. I noted those dates on my personal calendar. Then I set up a big, fresh white pillar candle on a shelf above my work space. Having the flame there before me as I work not only helps me to maintain my watch, but it also lends its holiness to my work.

The flames we tend are lit from Bridey's sacred fire at Kildare (the energy of the flame is carried in the wick, not the burning candle). This fire had been extinguished for four hundred years when the sisters of the order relit it in 1993. Even before I became a member of Ord Brighideach, I had a candle lit from that flame, which I used to light other candles for special purposes—usually healings. I relight the candle every year from Her sacred flame at an annual Brigit ritual held in early February. So I already had the flame I needed to begin my watches. The process is that, when a person joins the order, she or he sends a small donation to the keepers of the flame—that is, the people in Oregon who created the Web site and set up the order. In return, the new member receives a candle lit from the Kildare flame with which to start her flame keeping, a prayer, and a blessing for flame keepers.

Like everyone who applies to join the order, I was asked to swear an oath to Brighde the first time I tended Her flame. That oath includes a statement of our dedication to Brigid and of our commitment to tend Her flame faithfully.

Often, I feel that my knowledge of what Bridget has to offer me comes from the time I spend in Her forge. She heats me to the point of dissolution, melts me, and refines me. She guides the smithy's hands and powers the blows that shape me. She is the annealer of my soul. Yet I see Her in the greening Earth after winter's dark, I seek to be pierced by Her fiery arrow of inspiration, and I listen for Her song. She pours the waters of healing, She stirs the cauldron of compassion, She knows the secrets of herbcraft, She changes honey to mead. She is balm to my soul. These are the things I spoke when I first pledged myself to Ord Brighideach.

The members of the order—all three hundred of us—dedicate ourselves to our Irish goddess and tend Her flame in twelve countries: Australia, Brazil, Canada, Finland, Greece, Ireland, the Netherlands, New Zealand, South Africa, Spain, the United Kingdom, and the United States. We honor our heritage as we take it into the age of the Internet. We carry Bridget's light of consciousness through the darkness and into the future.

Chapter 5

WHO HOLDS THE SHUTTLE?

Notions of Authority, Authenticity, Hierarchy, and Institutionalization Online

Just as Christianity has its sects—Protestant, Roman Catholic, Greek Orthodox, Russian Orthodox—so does Paganism; these are often referred to as traditions or denominations. Similarly, there are many Muslim groups that purport to represent the one true Islam, yet they diverge in many ways. In his book *Virtually Islamic: Computer-Mediated Communication and Cyber Islamic Environments*, Gary Bunt notes many Web sites even within particular Islamic sects that claim authority and authenticity. I mention this example because it's often easier for non-Muslims to see the phenomenon of sectarianism versus standardization in another religion—in this case Islam—than it is to see it among ourselves.

Yet, as we saw in chapter 3, attempts at standardization have been made within the Pagan movement in the past. Some, such as the 1974 Council of American Witches' Principles of Wiccan Belief, have been broad and inclusive. Such approaches have helped us, as American

Witches, to define ourselves. Other approaches have merely involved patterning ourselves on mainstream corporate or judicial models.

BOOKS OF SHADOWS

FAMTRADS: Family tradition; a Craft tradition that is kept within a family and passed down, generation after generation.

BOOK OF SHADOWS: A compendium of rituals, spells, liturgies, invocations, songs, chants, recipes, pathworkings, deity names and attributes, and instructions in certain sacred technologies, which is kept by an individual, a coven, or a tradition.

While the notion of a standardized authority within Witchcraft remains the subject of debate, few would argue that there are many valid claims of authenticity within individual traditions. Some traditions, British traditional Wiccans, **famtrads**, and eclectic Witches, keep what's known in the Craft as a **Book of Shadows**. This is a compendium of things sacred and specific to a particular tradition. A tradition may possess a single Book of Shadows, which is kept at the **covenstead** by the high priestess or priest.

Books of Shadows, sometimes called by a term used in Western ceremonial magic—"Grimoires"—contain ritual scripts for esbat, sabbat, initiation, elevation, and other rites of passage; invocations and poetry; recipes for incense, oils, and spells; written instructions about specific sacred technologies, such as drawing down the moon; pathworkings; chants; names of deities specific to a given tradition and a description of their attributes; whatever else the upholders of that tradition have deemed necessary for inclusion.

Most initiates or coveners who have attained a certain level of skill and experience are given a Book of Shadows; at one time, they would have been asked to copy the book in their own hand, but with advances in print and reproduction technology, people began to photocopy their Books of Shadows instead. Loose-leaf binders replaced handwritten books. One Witch of my acquaintance collected, and continues to collect, many useful writings in file folders that live in what she calls her Cabinet of Shadows. Nowadays, however, many covens keep their Books of Shadows on disk, prompting the name Disk of Shadows.

There are online publications, marketed as Books of Shadows, that are nothing more than patchwork collections of rituals, poetry, and such—material that has been widely circulated elsewhere, or that has been taken from published books. These may hold some archival interest, but they are not to be confused with private-coven Books of Shadows. In addition to tradition and coven Books of Shadows, many of us keep personal books filled not only with invocations, spells, and recipes, but also with dreams, personal visions, and records of divinatory readings.

COVENSTEAD: The place where most coven rituals are held. A covenstead can be situated in the country, but more frequently it is a temple room of some kind in a coven member's home, or perhaps a circle marked with stones in a backyard. One coven I know used a combination of tools and methods, including trance, maps, pendulums, and reconnaissance work, to find an outdoor covenstead suitable for their coven workings. When they finally found a good site, they contacted the Park Service people responsible for overseeing and maintaining the park where the site was located. They explained why they wished to meet there in the moonlight, assured the Park Service that the site would be kept clean and undisturbed, and received permission to circle on parkland.

LINEAGES

Many Craft traditions, especially those established before the 1980s, derive their teachings from their lineage and point to lineage when making claims for the authenticity of their practice. By lineage, I mean a line of descent from an individual or a group ancestor. The most well-known lineage-based Craft tradition originated with British civil servant Gerald Brosseau Gardner. Gardner's writings, and those of his former covener and high priestess Doreen Valiente, comprise one of our primary literary heritages. Witches who descend directly from Gardner's coven in England, and who may be found throughout the United Kingdom, North America, Australia, and New Zealand—and even in non-English-speaking countries, like Brazil—are called Gardnerians.

Britain may have spawned Gardnerians, Alexandrians, and 1734s, but there are countless eclectic traditions of the Craft worldwide, especially in the United States. Adding to the texture of our tapestry, some of us circle exclusively with women, invoking only Goddess energy in our workings. We are loosely referred to as Dianic Witches, although our particular lineage may have a different name. Dianics may or may not be lesbians. There are both female and male Dianic Witches.

My first coven, Holy Terrors, was made up of nine women. We represented a narrow age range—from mid-twenties to late thirties—and five of us were mothers; there were seven coven children among us. Our sexuality covered the spectrum. To a great extent, we were Dianic in that we usually didn't invite a god into our circles. Yet when we did, we welcomed him with all our hearts. We sometimes invited our husbands, boyfriends, and girlfriends to join us. God was always invoked on these occasions.

At that time, we weren't aware of how many different traditions were part of Craft—at least I wasn't. I did know that there were Witches called Dianic because they only worked with Goddess and women. One of my coven sisters, Cerridwen, had trained with Z Budapest in the Susan B. Anthony Coven Number 1 in Los Angeles, and the tradition they belonged to Cerridwen termed Dianic. But she also consorted with Witches in the Church of All Worlds (CAW), which is a mixed-gender group. I knew, as well, that there was a tradition called NROOGD (New Reformed Orthodox Order of the Golden Dawn), because I had done some training with them ten years earlier. I knew that Starhawk had been initiated into the Faery Tradition, and that there was a famtrad south of where I lived called Tower Family. But, despite my knowledge of these Craft variations, I continued to think of us all as just being Witches.

During the years that Holy Terrors existed, we each underwent an initiatory rite of passage. I was the first to experience this. The secret part of my initiation was performed by my teachers from Coven Raving and my sponsor, who was one of my coven sisters and a self-initiate. The internal and external transformations begun the night I took my vows before my sister Witches, the Mighty Ones of the Craft, and the Goddess and God included the sense—knowledge, even—of this kinship with all Witches everywhere. It also included an appreciation for our shared heritage and the bonding that comes with the sharing.

The shuttle that guides this thread through the warp of Pagan traditions—traditions that I recognized yet did not recognize—picks up a new fiber: the eclectic thread of the Reclaiming tradition. There was no Reclaiming tradition when I was in Holy Terrors, but there was a Reclaiming collective, to which I belonged. We put on public sabbat rituals, taught classes, met on the beach on the solstices, organized and supported antinuclear demonstrations, and generally enlivened our city. We were not yet aware that what we were doing was developing a tradition.

My experiences in Holy Terrors helped me to attain a better understanding of the sensibilities of my lesbian and gay Witch kin. Around the time that Reclaiming was spinning fibers connecting Faery Craft with Dianic Craft with British traditional Craft, there emerged the thread of Radical Fairy Witches. Radical Fairies are not all Witches, though many identify themselves as such. They established fairy zines, purchased communal retreat lands, formed urban groups, created rituals, and pursued political and social goals in keeping with their Fairy identity. Another gay male Craft tradition proudly and lovingly call themselves Faggot Witches.

These days, Radical Fairies are a strong presence in America and on the World Wide Web. They are both active and visible; they own and maintain rural retreat land in several states. Radical Fairies are a spiritual movement, but they are not exclusively Pagan. Nor are all Radical Fairy circles now composed exclusively of gay men, a fact that is still energetically debated within the community.

I, like many others, was under the impression that the Radical Fairies were Pagan for three reasons: one, all the Radical Fairies I know are Witches; two, specifically witchen retreats have been held on Radical Fairy land; and three, there is often a strong Radical Fairy presence at Pagan festivals. During the course of researching this book, I was "set straight," so to speak. It was explained to me that the Radical Fairies are a gay *spiritual* group that embraces Buddhists and practitioners of other faith traditions. Furthermore, gay sexuality is a key spiritual component of Faggot Witchcraft, and it is one of the key distinctions between Faggot Witches and Radical Fairies. There are gay Pagans who don't define their spirituality in terms of their sexuality.

One of the first gay male Craft traditions was the Minoan Brotherhood, originally founded in New York City in the 1970s, as a gay male coven. It continues to thrive.[1] The brotherhood's rituals and tools are based on traditional British Craft forms, adapted by their founder, the late Lord Gwydion (Edmund Michael Buczynski), who was Gardnerian-trained. Rituals were reconfigured to accommodate a different ritual custom and a different core mythology, which was drawn from ancient Crete and Mycenae. Worship centers on the Great Mother of All Living, as well as Her divine son, the Starry One, and His consort, the Earth-Shaker.

Simultaneous with the formation of the Minoan Brotherhood, Lady Rhea and Lady Miw established the Minoan Sisterhood. Then, in 1998, a group of mixed-gender covens came together and called themselves The Minoan Temple (TMT).[2] They base their practice on the traditions (rituals, mythos, deities) of the Minoan Brotherhood and Sisterhood. The core mythology of TMT is drawn from the legends of King Minos, son of Queen Europa, and "upon distinct but related legends of Ariadne, Dionysus, and others." The temple articulates its reconstructionist approach: "TMT considers aspects of the Minoan belief system gained from relevant material obtained as Minoan civilization sites and materials continue to be discovered, reconstructed, and assessed." TMT practice also incorporates elements of Shamanic, Celtic, Greek, Roman, Egyptian, Hindu, and Native American practices, "as well as Irish, Welsh, and Scottish traditions of Wicca as developed by Raymond and Rosemary Buckland and Janet and Stewart Farrar."[3]

Witchcraft is a living religion. That's one reason its practitioners have so readily accepted the wealth of new technologies associated with the Internet. Minoans believe that each person must actively take responsibility for her or his own spiritual development. Few Witches would disagree with that approach. These three traditions—the Minoan Brotherhood, the Minoan Sisterhood, and The Minoan Temple—all contribute to the living religion; they clearly demonstrate eclecticism and evolution in action.

They do this in a couple of ways. First, the brotherhood was founded in the United States by a man with a Polish surname who used a Welsh magical name, adapted British rituals, tools, and forms to Minoan-inspired reconstructionist mythos, and tied them all together using a pantheon that was deeply meaningful to gay practitioners. Second, two related Craft traditions were originally created to work in sexually segregated covens. Upon the foundations laid down by the brotherhood and sisterhood, TMT evolved into a kinship of mostly mixed-gender covens. Now there are three related Minoan traditions, each serving the needs of its congregation, and each a part of the ancient/future faith tradition that is contemporary Witchcraft.

I am no authority on the Minoan tradition. I have friends who are Minoan, but I've never circled with them. Some Minoans may feel that I've misrepresented them here. To them I offer the explanation that I drew my conclusions from the Minoan Web presence, and I was intrigued by the notion that this tradition could stand as a fine example of some of the many ways Craft has unfolded in the past quarter-century, and most especially in the past digital decade.

Faggot Witchcraft is another tradition—though not large in numbers—that places gay sexuality at the center of its theology and ritual. Faggot Witch Sparky Rabbit reflects on the interrelationships among the phenomena of Witchcraft, Queers, and the Web, and in the process he provides us with some valuable insight.

Queer Witches and the World Wide Web: Breaking the Spell of Invisibility

One of the biggest obstacles faced by Queer women and men is the cloak of invisibility put on us by the dominant culture's heterosexism. Sometimes consciously and sometimes unconsciously, straight women and men participate in patterns of behavior that ignore or trivialize or tokenize the lives and realities of lesbians, gay men, bisexual and transgendered folks. Sometimes Queer people do the same things.

One of the worst experiences many Queer people share is the feeling, from childhood on, that "I am the only one of my kind in the world." One need only look at the amount of Queer youth suicide and the huge percentage of drug and alcohol abuse in Queer communities to see that this emotional isolation has had devastating effects on many Queer lives.

So when the Web became available—*bam!!*—Queers were all over it from the git-go. When I was first learning about computers and the Internet, in the mid-nineties, a friend of mine said, "The Internet is made up of Pagans and Queers." I don't believe that statement was statistically correct, but it definitely was an accurate expression of what many Queer Pagans I know were experiencing on the Web: there were a Hel of a lot more of us out there than any of us had ever guessed.

Well, imagine what a revelation *that* was! Suddenly, I could go into a chat room at http://gay.com and other sites, and I could talk to other gay men from, literally, all over the world! And of course the same was true for Queer Pagans—we could find each other a lot more easily.

So I think the existence of the Web has done a lot to break the spell of invisibility that so many Queer men and women have suffered under for so long. It doesn't mean that everyone's physical isolation is lessened; but it does mean that the forty-something gay guy in Wyoming who is just coming out can get on a computer and find lots of gay resources and even other men to talk to online. And that is an amazing change from just a few years ago.

I think this new Queer Pagan visibility on the Web has had several effects on the Craft. One is the simple fact that straight Pagans may be even more aware of a Queer Pagan presence on the Web and in their spiritual lives than they were before.

Perhaps, more importantly, as Queer Pagans gain emotional strength and confidence from our new Web visibility, we may also break other cultural spells we have suffered under: for instance, an unconscious yet pervasive feeling that we, as Queers, are indeed inferior to straight people, and that we need to cajole and cater to heterosexuals lest they withdraw their favor or even punish us.

In my experience, breaking this spell can cause a real dilemma for straight Pagans on the Web. When faced with a Faggot Witch who acts as an equal, some straight Pagans—especially the liberal ones—find themselves shocked to encounter a Queer who states that there are big differences between his reality and theirs, and doesn't assume that straight Pagans automatically have the correct one-and-only interpretation of experience in the world, any more than Christians have the one-and-only truth about spiritual realities.

Another factor that comes into play here is the safety that physical distance can provide. It may be a lot easier for a lesbian or gay Witch to stand up to a bunch of straight Pagans online than it is to do so face to face. Cyber name-calling may hurt emotionally, but it's often seen as preferable to a physical beating.

Change often encounters resistance, of course. So sometimes the liberal straight Pagans feel hurt and attacked by the Queer Pagans, saying versions of, "But some of my best friends are Queer!" and, "What more do I have to do before you'll be satisfied?" (The liberal Queer Pagans who are upset say things like, "*I* don't have any problems with straight Pagans! Those people are a bunch of radicals!")

The gift these straight Pagans are being offered is a chance to see into Queer worlds they weren't aware of, and a chance to let go of some of their leftover, unconscious feelings of heterosexual superiority. The gift the Queer Pagans are being offered is a chance to wake up to the richness their own sexuality can bring to their spirituality, as well as a chance to fully feel more of their own equality and to see the truth that we deserve a place in the world.

Some straight Pagans accept those gifts, and others resist them. Some Queer Pagans welcome the gifts, and others reject them. Like everything else, it's an ongoing process.

The Web can empower Queer Pagans to realize that we have unique, rich spiritual lives, which are worthy of exploration—both in spite of and *because* of the fact that our spiritual realities are often quite different from those of our straight Pagan sisters and brothers.[4]

Some of us find greater comfort, and thus a deeper level of intimacy, among people with whom we share a status that is imposed on us by the mundane world. By this I mean that if we are gay, we may wish to work exclusively with other gay Witches because of the bond created by our shared experiences in society. For similar reasons, lesbians may choose to work in a circle where there is no male energy. And women, regardless of their sexuality, may feel safer working within a women-only congregation. Such covens can be a tremendous source of healing, reintegration, growth, and strength.

All of these colorful strands of Craft have vital online presences in the form of Web sites, listserves, and the like. Some sites, in addition to presenting other witchen material, trace lineages by coven rather than by individuals, further authenticating those traditions.

Now, after a decade or so of exploring the magical new media of electronic communication and the World Wide Web, we are witnessing the emergence of **cybertraditions**. Like more conventional terraspace Craft traditions, cybertraditions develop ways of working together, tradition deities, common symbology, Books of

CYBERTRADITIONS: Witchen traditions that exist exclusively in Cyberspace, in the terraspace.

Shadows, systems of training and elevation, and methods of passing on power. They thereby establish a traditional way of doing things, a style and system that makes them unique. (See chapter 6, where the online magic thread reemerges.)

ACCOUNTABILITY AND ETHICS

As we learned when we looked at spellwork and prayer, most, but not all, Witches have a sense of karmic accountability. That is, we believe that what we put out into the world returns to us threefold. This is called the Law of Threefold Return, and it means that, if a Witch were to perform a spell towards a negative end, something to cause harm to someone else, she would then reap that negativity three times over.

This concept has been borne out in cyberspace. For so many subtle, and not so subtle, reasons, e-communication often prompts people to launch tactless, undiplomatic, ill-considered, hurtful, disdainful, dismissive, or inflammatory attacks on one another. (This behavior is not, of course, limited to Pagans; it's a common phenomenon.) This may be partly explained by the fact that conversing in cyberspace means typing on a keyboard and looking at a monitor instead of speaking with our voice and breath and looking into someone's eyes; speaking from our heads without compassion in our hearts; missing the tone and timbre of someone's voice and being; not seeing people's body language; not modulating our words for print.

When it comes to witchen folk, in particular, it's as though gunpowder is being tossed on a bonfire. Curses beget curses. Fires erupt violently and burn out quickly. Before the Internet, disagreement would simmer for weeks or months or even years before it reached the boiling point. Now, a dispute will flare up in cyberspace, scorch everything in its path, and die for lack of fuel when everyone pulls away from the conflict—all at magical Internet speed. Fritz Jung confirms this: "These days, gossip/emotional situations in the community play out in just a few days instead of months."

Wiccans may debate issues of mutual concern fiercely at times, but, while we do not have an established set of laws or rules, many of us do share certain ethics. One source of these is known as the Rede, or the Wiccan Rede. It states, "An it harm none, do as you will" (or, "Do as thou wilt"). (Here, "an" means "if," not "and.") The Covenant of the Goddess uses this phrase in its code of ethics: "An ye harm none, do as ye will."[5] The phrase is very likely based on the words of the English ceremonial magician Aleister Crowley: "Do what thou wilt shall be the whole of the law. Love is the law. Love under will."[6] Many see the Rede as a guide for right conduct. Others think that it's too loose and open to too many, possibly conflicting, interpretations in any given circumstance—so the debate continues.

All of this sets Witchcraft apart from other faith traditions. While many witchen traditions have instituted rules—and some, particularly the British-derived traditions, swear by the **ardanes**, or **ordains**—we have no universal code of behavior, mission statement, or principles of unity. When the Covenant of the Goddess was first formed in 1975, it declared itself bound by Craft law, although, as CoG pointed out, that law was not necessarily identical in all traditions.

ARDANES OR ORDAINS: A set of laws or rules pertaining to the practice, technology, and beliefs of a particular tradition of the Craft.

This is one of the reasons Craft is so diverse. While one coven or tradition may have a stringent set of criteria and a rigorous training regimen that a candidate must complete in order to be initiated or elevated, another's approach may be far more casual. Therefore, what it means to be initiated into one tradition may be quite different from what it means in the case of another. Some traditions require initiates to memorize liturgy and entire rituals; others merely ask them to read from a book. Members of still other traditions may reject the idea of performing scripted rituals and instead work spontaneously, as the spirit moves them. And some traditions or covens may insist that initiates demonstrate certain magical skills, and perhaps take up a magical specialty—such as herb craft, poetry, metal smithing, candle making, dance, or a divinatory art.

We've seen how some of us have Books of Shadows, and some don't; some take oaths to adhere to a certain set of rules, and some don't; some work only with family members; some circle only with other Witches of their own gender. In addition, we may work **skyclad**, robed, or in street clothes.

SKYCLAD: Nude, clad in the sky.

What, then, besides the Rede (which still remains for some a source of debate), do we absolutely hold in common? Three things: the eight-spoked Wheel of the Year; a professed love of Nature, which includes a commitment to live in harmony with our world rather than embracing domination and exploitation and despoliation; and The Charge of the Goddess. This charge, this unique piece of liturgy, is the chord that rings true in all our hearts and minds. There are many variations of the charge, but an essence permeates all. So powerful is this writing that it has traveled around the globe. People who represent our presence in the world of international interfaith have befriended Indians from a Hindu goddess sect who revere Doreen Valiente's version of The Charge of the Goddess.

The recitation of the charge, either by a priestess or priest or a group speaking in one voice, sends shivers up and down the spine, makes the hair on the arms, neck, and head stand on end, brings tears to the eyes. Every time I've had the experience of hearing this precious liturgy spoken, I have reacted this way, and so has everyone else present.

The Charge of the Goddess

Listen to the words of the Great Mother, Who of old was called Artemis, Astarte, Dione, Melusine, Aphrodite, Cerridwen, Diana, Arionrhod, Brigid, and many other names:

Whenever you have need of anything, once a month, and better it be when the moon is full, you shall assemble in some secret place and adore the spirit of Me Who is Queen of all the Wise.

You shall be free from slavery, and as a sign that you be free you shall be naked in your rites.

Sing, feast, dance, make music and love, all in My presence, for Mine is the ecstasy of the spirit and Mine also is joy on Earth.

For My law is love unto all beings. Mine is the secret that opens the door of youth, and Mine is the cup of wine of life that is the cauldron of Cerridwen, that is the holy grail of immortality.

I give the knowledge of the spirit eternal, and beyond death I give peace and freedom and reunion with those who have gone before.

Nor do I demand aught of sacrifice, for behold, I am the Mother of all things and My love is poured out upon the Earth.

Hear the words of the Star Goddess, the dust of Whose feet are the hosts of heaven, Whose body encircles the universe:

I Who am the beauty of the green Earth and the white moon among the stars and the mysteries of the waters, I call upon your soul to arise and come unto Me.

For I am the soul of Nature that gives life to the universe.

From Me all things proceed and unto Me they must return.

Let My worship be in the heart that rejoices, for behold, all acts of love and pleasure are My rituals.

Let there be beauty and strength, power and compassion, honor and humility, mirth and reverence within you.

And you who seek to know Me, know that the seeking and yearning will avail you not unless you know the Mystery: for if that which you seek you find not within yourself, you will never find it without.

For behold, I have been with you from the beginning, and I am That which is attained at the end of desire.

—Doreen Valiente, adapted by Starhawk

LEADERSHIP AND "CLERGY"

Pagans don't have "clergy" in the Christian sense of the word. We have no one to assist us in interpreting law or scripture, since we possess neither of these things. (The clergy and priestess threads reemerge in chapter 7.) But this is not to say that our coreligionists—our coveners, high priestesses, and high priests—do not provide comfort, aid, and advice to those who find themselves on the horns of an ethical dilemma. They do, indeed, help us in such ways. (I have also found a tool to help me if I am ever confused about a course of action: a book called *When, Why . . . If: An Ethics Workbook*, by Robin Wood.) Finally, however, as individuals we are responsible for our own behavior, for making our own decisions, for choosing our own courses of action. We are ultimately self-determining and self-reliant.

Pagan scholar Gus diZerega explains that, "because we see the world as one dimension of Divinity, rather than being radically separate from It, we naturally look to sources other than texts for legitimate spiritual knowledge and insight . . . When Divinity is seen as manifesting within and throughout the world, it is absurd to argue that ultimate authority is within a text, especially one 're-vealed' in only one language to only one person, people, or tribe."[7] Consequently, to a far greater extent than transcendental religions, Paganism emphasizes personal experience of the divine through ritual, meditation, contemplation, trance, spirit incorporation, vision quests, and the like. Furthermore, many Pagan traditions also stress the importance of having a lineage of practitioners who are able to train others and who can incorporate the experience of countless generations within a living tradition.

This brings us to the topic of pastoral counseling: that is, counseling an otherwise mentally and emotionally healthy person, usually a covener, when he encounters a crisis in his life. Pastoral counseling is for the short term. It should not be employed as a substitute for long-term, ongoing therapy, which is designed to address deep, long-standing personal issues.

It's natural for a person in crisis to call a friend. Such a person could also decide to consult with his high priestess, or someone else in his coven—someone he trusts and whose life experience and judgment he respects. Speaking with another Witch is a good option for an individual who believes that his dilemma might have a basis in magic, or that magical practices such as divination or trance work might afford him some insight or even a resolution. He might feel that he could be aided or relieved by the application of magical practices.

The Pagan in crisis may well feel that a secular

counselor would not understand his worldview and thealogy, might not "speak his language." We Pagans share certain assumptions, skills, imagery, and symbology; this allows us to use a kind of psychic shorthand when we're talking with our coreligionists. To someone unfamiliar with our spiritual path, these images and symbols that we share might seem meaningless, or their meanings might be different.

In mainstream religions, members of a church congregation turn to their priests or ministers to help them move through their grief over the death of a loved one. Coveners, too, will turn to their high priestesses or priests (or fellow coveners) for grief counseling.

However, there is a distinction to be drawn between those with the wisdom to offer guidance in times of trouble and those who authorize. I believe that one of the sustaining strengths of Pagan paths is the lack of a central authority. Witchcraft has no charismatic leader. On the contrary, there are many charismatic Witches who possess the skill, training, temperament, and inclination to assume leadership roles. There are also leaders within small coven groups, and there are other leaders in secular areas of witchen culture. For instance, a priestess who manifests personal power, charm, and magical adeptness within her coven may be considered a leader in that context; but this would not necessarily mean that she has the social and political acumen to strategize with other Pagans, devising means and methods to ensure our safety and freedom of worship. By the same token, a good Pagan civil rights activist might be capable of performing priestly roles, yet he may not do it with the level of skill he brings to freedom fighting.

The same is true of Roman Catholic priests, nuns, and

monks. Some serve as parish priests, some as organizers and administrators, some as teachers, nurses, attorneys, or accountants, some as stewards and housekeepers, some as interfaith representatives. The most motivational preacher may not be the best person to comfort an injured child or a dying grandfather.

The "cult of personality," which has been so prevalent in American religious history, is largely absent from contemporary Witchcraft. As I've mentioned, there are charismatic priestesses and priests. There are articulate authors and compelling thealogians. There are, as well, particular groups that arise and glow with creativity and power. And these groups and influences have life cycles, like everything else in the world. They are born, they grow and flourish, they mature, they fade, and eventually most of them die. Some are reborn in a new form.

A coven may last for years, even generations, but most have shorter lives. I know of few covens much older than thirty years. Many are fifteen or ten years old. Most thrive for three to ten years before they either dissolve or reconfigure themselves with enough changes in personnel to be virtually new entities. A tradition, which is ideally passed on to succeeding generations of Witches, will generally survive much longer than a coven.

Now that we have cybertraditions and cybercovens, perhaps we will soon witness an acceleration in the life cycles of our traditions and covens. And those Pagans who seek to codify our beliefs and practices, to institutionalize them, may find their aspirations undermined by the Internet's accelerated, fluctuating nature.

In the meantime, we Witches continue to have no ultimate authority, no central organization that maintains political and social cohesion. Instead, we have our solitaries. We have our small, bonded covens. We have traditions. We have guilds and leagues, special-interest groups, cultural, educational, legal, and civil rights organizations—many of which overlap. We have the World Wide Web.

Our authority is within each of us. This shared democratic conviction assures our diversity, a diversity that is essential to any viable ecosystem. Our authenticity shows in our actions. We have the vitality and durability of the spider's web. We move along the shimmering filaments of her web, we glisten as dewdrop jewels.

Chapter 6

GATHERING AND WEAVING MANY THREADS

Witchcraft, a long-misunderstood spiritual and magical practice, expanded and became more visible beginning in the 1970s. Some of the bolder and more public Witches formed groups around mutual interests, common traditions, or civil rights and legal defense. More recently, a spate of Witchcraft-themed Hollywood films and TV series further stimulated the interest of the general public. Negative stereotypes and public ignorance about Witches began to dissolve with the expansion of the Internet in the 1990s. Witches and Pagans have now become visible fibers in the webs that are our neighborhoods.

One of the few ways I'm conservative about Craft relates to how we find the training we seek. I don't subscribe to the marketing approach that many mainstream religions tend to use. We haven't been out on street corners handing out tracts. We have no preachers bidding us. We have no buildings to go to where we'll find other Witches. But if we really want to find good training and to form close relationships with other Witches, we can. We may need to search, and it may take patience, but when we find the right situation it'll be all the sweeter for the effort and wait. One of our strengths has been that people who wanted to find us, to be with us, to join us, had to seek us out. I believe we're stronger, both individually and collectively, for the effort that it takes.

With greater visibility and more people seeking to learn Pagan ways came a need for teachers and training. The demand for training exceeded what existing covens could provide. Some teaching began to take place in classes rather than covens. Those attending classes did not necessarily know one another beforehand, nor were they selected for suitability and compatibility, as they would have been if they were training in a more conventional coven setting. But, even with classes opening the doors for more people, seekers who lived in rural areas or in socially conservative communities were left with no one to train them. They had the Internet, though. They had their computers. They discovered that they had that amazing tool of communication, ruled by the god Mercury. So these isolated seekers began to follow their paths in cyberspace.

At this point, before we look more closely at online teaching, I want to say caveat emptor ("Let the buyer beware"). This is a good general rule to adhere to when contemplating any purchase. The same applies to learning magic, whether in terraspace or in cyberspace. Discerning what's authentic and who's sincere is not necessarily easy in every situation. We are often blinded by our deep desire to *believe*. We can be very gullible, especially when we're hearing something that we *want* to hear. When I was first exposed to Second Wave Feminism, there were a lot of "goddess" books in the stores, telling tales of goddesses, of their characteristics and personalities and the areas of life they ruled. There were books telling of a golden age of matriarchy. I didn't know any better, and I really wanted the things spoken of in these books to be true, so I believed them. I and thousands of other women. Later, as archeology evolved as a science and more scholarly research was funded and published, some of the more simplistic and sweeping pronouncements made in those early goddess books were disproven. Those of us who followed the literature learned that some of the assumptions we'd carried about goddess cultures and matriarchies were not founded in fact. So I lost my innocence, but I gained a keener sense of what constitutes authentic research and criticism.

Such naïveté can also be present in spiritual pursuits. You find something that strongly appeals to you, and you want to believe it. Maybe you find a charismatic teacher and begin training with her. For those of you embarking on a path of spiritual learning, I recommend looking at the frequently cited Advanced Bonewits' Cult Danger Evaluation Frame 2.5.[1] It's a good set of guidelines to help you decide whether the person you want to train with is effective and trustworthy. It's good for people to have guidelines to help them evaluate ventures that they're contemplating. It is with this in mind that we explore the mysterious realms of magic in cyberspace.

ONLINE TEACHING

When the demand for Craft training burgeoned, many people stepped forward to fill it. Some seem to have successfully adapted their teaching methods to the Net, providing their material in a format similar to that of an instructional video. This works well for content- and text-based learning, but I'm not convinced that it is effective for the kind of teaching that relies on the experiential dimension more than the intellectual. Much of what we teach and do is subtle. In other words, it's easy to teach *about* Witchcraft on the Net, but it's not so easy to teach the art of magic. With this in mind, I asked my coconspirator Adam for his thoughts on online teaching:

> As to teaching, it is much the same on a MOO as in a chat—we just have a few bonus tools. One of which is the lecture theater—many people can attend, but only one person can be heard. Another of which is the tutorial room—like a chat, but with potentially more control over how the tutorial is run. And the third is the use of virtual teaching tools. For example, an old MOO . . . called "DynaMOO," used to have a representation of the assassination of Lincoln . . . You could look at the room, examine the objects and people, see where they were seated, and watch the shooting unfold. On InfoMOO one of the students created a virtual car engine, which you could fix by examining the parts and working out what was wrong. Both might be better done in full graphical VR, but this way we can experiment now, and we can get results much quicker—to do the same as those two would take many months graphically, but only a week or so on a MOO.

Here I should point out that I am writing this from the perspective of a terraspace Witch, by which I mean a person who was trained and continues to practice ritual in person, in a physical space with others, and in real time. Unlike Adam, I have never done online teaching, but I have been an online student. (The thread of my experiences with online learning reappears in chapter 7.)

THE ONLINE SEMINARY EXPERIENCE: Cherry Hill Seminary teaches pastoral-counseling courses in an academic format, with online "lectures" to download and read, and assigned student discussions and papers sent out on a listserve for the whole class. But the addition of a chat "classroom" where students can interact in real time gives students a strong sense of each other as people. And since a lot of what pastoral counseling is all about is learning to be open and real with people as we listen to them, that is very important.

Not everyone deals well with the rapid-fire nature of online chat, where four or five "speakers" can be sharing their ideas at once. As a teacher, I have learned it's good to share the excitement of open chat with "rounds," where I ask a question and then give each student a chance to share his or her ideas in turn. This is the best use of chat; it slows the pace enough so that even slower-typing students have a chance to be heard, and everyone's ideas can be better appreciated.

—Cat Chapin-Bishop

ONLINE RITUAL, MAGIC, AND SPELLS

In the early 1990s, as more people logged on to the Web, and as technological developments created more possibilities for electronic communication, Witches and Pagans began to experiment with online ritual. What are online rituals, and do they work? Jehana Silverwing, who is a longtime terraspace practitioner, did a lot of online rituals when she was on Compuserve, and she was surprised to discover that they do indeed work, "if one remembers not to be over-wordy in real-time typing."

Jehana tells of a spontaneous Compuserve ritual she conducted as part of a small group back in 1987. It was a healing for a member of that group. None of them had met each other before, but they were still able to tap into and focus on their joint will and intent, and they pulled off a successful healing. After that, they continued to do circles together, for both healings and celebrations.

As I've said, I'm a more traditional Witch—if you can say that of a radical feminist eclectic—and I've had almost no experience with online ritual. To be honest, I haven't been drawn to try it. For that reason, this chapter about online teaching, rituals, magic, and spellwork has been one of the most challenging for me to write. I took on the task, however, because I want to do justice to those who perform online ritual as a regular part of their practice. My own ignorance or inclination is no reason for dismissing online ritual out of hand. Many Witches I know and respect claim that it is a powerful tool, and I'm in no position to refute them; also, I know how important and meaningful it is for isolated or differently abled people to have such a venue to share their practice. I questioned several Witches experienced in online ritual, hoping that I would be able to weave their threads into our web.

When we followed the ways of learning threads, we discussed energetics and sacred technologies. Here we take those notions into the vast realm of cyberspace. Technopagan Mark Pesce claims that "the Craft is nothing less than applied cybernetics."

Since 1994, my coconspirator Moose has been creating online rituals, sometimes for large numbers of people. He's presented a workshop called "The Care and Feeding of Online Rituals" at Pagan festivals. To the argument that Pagans as practitioners of a Nature-based religion cannot worship their gods online, Moose responds:

> Would any of you deny that legitimate worship services occur via television? I dare say a paradigm shift had to occur when worship services moved from the realm of radio to television. A similar paradigm shift probably occurred when worship moved from the pulpit to broadcast radio . . . and when it moved from hand-written word to the printing press . . . and when it moved from oral history to the written word . . . Meaningful worship is independent of the technological level of the worshiper. Online rituals are, in my experience, as powerful and transformational as any ritual in the face-to-face world.

Adam explains online energy working from his perspective as a chaos magician: "It is at most a different kind of energy. When you talk to a lot of those working specifically online magic, such as many chaos magicians, they argue that the different energy requires different paradigms, but that it is still compatible with the basic principles of magic in Wicca or ceremonial magic."

Let's look at some of the ways online rituals might be less effective or less satisfying than terraspace ritual. Let's identify elements or qualities that might be diminished. At the same time, let's identify ways in which magic can be enhanced by online rituals. If some things are lost in this new medium, perhaps others are gained. There are beneficial aspects to cybermagic.

In Reclaiming, we tried to work with the "different type of energy" that Adam refers to; most of us concluded that something was lost and something was gained in the paradigm shift. When we first formed our **e-cell**, the small group responsible for maintaining Reclaiming's online presence, we attempted to create a sacred space by casting a virtual circle. Before we did this, we introduced ourselves and explained a bit about our magical practice, our passions, devotions, and dedications, our personal deities, animals, plants, and so forth. We didn't do anything to **purify** the space, other than deliver some opening remarks. We did a ritual that wasn't in real time—instead, it was sequential. Each person said something about what influence she sought from each element. So, in a sense, each of us cast a circle, one after the other. There was a delay, because we were working via e-mail. We weren't all together at the same time. We contributed our part to the ritual when we logged on and sent a post. We then built on each other's messages. Each of us called upon deities to ask for their blessings on our work. We spoke about what the work meant to us, what we felt we

E-CELL: Reclaiming operates in small working cells, each of which focuses on a particular area of interest and endeavor. Examples of some cells are teachers' cell, public rituals cell(s), Quarterly cell, and administrative cell. The e-cell maintains Reclaiming's electronic presence, and it involves design and maintenance of the Web site and maintenance of many listserves within the tradition.

PURIFY: To cleanse spiritually and mentally; to get rid of any thoughts or feelings that might interfere with participation in the ritual or the ability to focus and do magical work. Among the techniques used for purifying are a preritual bath, possibly in scented water, Epsom salts, or herbs; asperging the space with incense; and sprinkling the space and participants with salt water.

wanted to do and could do, described our plans for the cell/circle. Our primary purpose was to become better acquainted with each other, since the e-cell was the only Reclaiming cell whose members weren't required to live in the Bay Area—we could meet in cyberspace.

I can't say that I *felt* anything from the ritual. No shiver of magical recognition, or anything like that (it's so thrilling when it happens). But we did develop a better sense of each other. We tried to remain aware of the sacred nature of the work we were doing, even though most of that work was rather mundane. We reminded ourselves that we were all building the same community. (The e-cell thread is picked up again later in this chapter.)

THE GODDESS 2000 RITUAL

I also want to tell you about another kind of online ritual (which I spoke about in chapter 3), that I was involved in: the ritual initiating the Goddess 2000 Project created by artist Abby Willowroot. Abby wanted to launch Goddess 2000 with an opening ritual performed on the 1999 Winter Solstice. It was to be called "Dancing the Goddess Home," and it was published on the G2K Web site.[2] Abby's plan was to have everyone do a ritual at the same time: 8:00 P.M. in whatever time zone they inhabited. This way, the energy of the ritual would be carried around the Earth, passing from one time zone to the next, all night long.

During the year, Abby had solicited written pieces for the ritual from prominent authors, ritualists, Pagans, people involved with Goddess spirituality, visitors to her Spiral Goddess Grove shrines, and people who had responded to her early announcements about the Goddess 2000 Project. In addition to Abby herself, a total of sixteen people contributed poetry, chants, prayers, blessings, or other writings to the opening ritual.

Abby and I then crafted a ritual script out of all the submissions. The script included detailed instructions for performing every ritual act, from the setting up of altars and the purifying of the space to the raising of energy through chanting; we also put in a technical description of exactly how to dance a spiral. The ritual began with a welcoming message, followed by a blessing by author Merlin Stone and a meditation by Hallie Austin Iglehart. We offered two alternative wordings for the casting of a circle. Lunaea Weatherstone wrote the quarter callings. After the circle was set up and the quarters called, Goddess was brought into the circle in tripart invocation: we began by speaking of her in the third person, progressed to speaking directly to her, and then speaking in her voice.

Next, we performed a powerful Great Goddess chant-dance, contributed by Selena Fox. Beautiful poetry that praised Goddess appeared throughout the ritual. We chanted and danced a spiral to raise energy to dedicate all the Goddess art we'd brought with us and that we and everyone who participated in G2K would be making throughout the year. Following that, we offered a prayer for a happy, safe millennium, written by Marian Weinstein. We blessed the beverages and food that were to be shared in the sacred circle and spoke a final blessing before releasing all that we had called into the circle and uncasting it.

In addition to the script itself, we also published a complete set of instructions for those with no ritual experience, or for those who simply felt more confident having that information. We included an addendum to the ritual called "Wisdom Words from Elders," which was designed to be read aloud right after the ritual or taken home and read alone.

The script could be used in its entirety or in bits and pieces. We encouraged participants to adapt it to their personal magical practices and ritual styles or to take inspiration from it in creating their personal rituals. We took care to be specific so that people who were inexperienced in ritual could be guided, yet we left it loose enough for experienced ritualists to use as they wanted.

At the appointed time, I performed this ritual in a group of ten, which I convened. Most of us were friends who'd done rituals of various kinds together over the years, but a few knew only one other member at the start of the ritual. We decided to use the ritual just as it was written, because I cowrote it and convened our group, and we all wanted to see how it would work. It turned out that we had just the right number of people to allow each to speak one part of the script. So we met in terraspace, prepared to perform a ritual that had been distributed in cyberspace, and completed the rite. Afterwards, we ate, drank, and socialized. We all left feeling happy and connected. We'd been part of something big, beautiful, and beneficial to everyone.

RITUAL PREPARATION: PURIFICATION AND ALTARS

There are certain things that help me shift my consciousness into what Starhawk calls "starlight vision." (I love that term.) They are things that one *could* do in an online ritual, but they would have to be done separately by each participant, wherever she was working. To begin with, ensure that your working space remains private. Moose recommends turning off sources of outside distraction—such as the telephone—just as you'd do for a ritual in terraspace. One of the first things I do to prepare for ritual is to take a ritual bath or purify myself in some other way. Of course, you can do that alone ahead of time, but I really like it when a priest/ess does a purification ritually with everyone, one at a time. You could purify for an online ritual with words, but using words alone doesn't involve the physical sensations of warm water on your skin, scents, steam, anointing oils. I love inhaling the incense that wafts on the air of the sacred space. I love the act of waving the smoke around. I like feeling the refreshment of salt water sprinkled on my face. All of these aspects of ritual are lost in cyberrituals.

Yet there are people with environmental sensitivities who cannot tolerate incense or oils, and when they participate online they are safe from exposure to substances that are toxic to them. If they're allergic to cats, and their fellow coveners have cats, it's not a problem online.

It's common to begin a ritual with a brief grounding and centering exercise, such as a guided meditation on the Tree of Life. This is easily adapted to online ritual. Reading a meditation on a Web site (on the temple wall?) or on a screen as it's typed can help move us into an altered consciousness. It can also be said that the very act of reading, and the translation that goes on in your brain when you're reading, shift you out of a magical state of mind and into a more linear consciousness.

Messy spaces can impede magical progress. Having a lot of junk around can interfere with your ritual. Working in an uncluttered space helps us make the transition from a busy, mundane life to a more serene, centered state of mind. Moose advises us to keep the area in which we're working free of clutter and to incorporate our computers into the same area, or decorate our computers as we would any altar.

Building altars is a first step in the collaborative, interactive, collective act that is a ritual. In our tradition, altars are usually created by several people, and there is no formula for what needs to be placed on an altar, beyond the fact that if you're doing a West altar you might want seashells on it; in the North you might use bones and rocks, and in the East feathers. I think creating an altar can be the beginning of the shift in consciousness that one presumably cultivates when creating sacred space. Preparing the space (cleaning the room, sweeping, and so forth) is part of this process for me.

To prepare for any ritual, we must also build an altar in a serene, uncluttered space. In online rituals, do participants create altars around their computers or in the room where they're working? Or do they create altars onscreen? Do all participants see the same altars? Who creates them? Are they provided by the person or people convening and conducting the ritual? Are they animated? Do different people create altars for the different directions? Does each participant have four quarter altars on four monitors in his room? Does each person have actual (as opposed to virtual) tools to use manually during the rite? Do participants burn incense? Do they tap out rhythms? Hum? Chant? Speak aloud? Wear special garments?

Erik Davis writes in *Wired* magazine that Mark Pesce, a Pagan systems operator, introduced him to a cyberritual by explaining that "Without the sacred there is no differentiation in space; everything is flat and gray. If we are about to enter cyberspace, the first thing we have

GUIDES FOR CHOOSING AN ONLINE TEACHER: **How would online teachers show they were the right teachers for you?**

• Her formal and informal speech online show a certain congruence, and she models the characteristics you would like to have someday yourself. Her publicly visible essays, research, and counsel should be of a high caliber, yet in her private e-mail she should display the same values she displays when everyone is watching.

• He models a respectful manner of dialogue online.

• His style of leadership is one that sits well with you.

• He is aware that in his public interactions he must not only consider the known audience but also the invisible one, and thus subtly let lurkers feel that they are included in the process.

• He can answer the most basic of questions from newcomers with as much attention as he pays to more sophisticated posters.

• He is as knowledgeable about Internet teaching methods as he is of face-to-face methods, and he is able to understand the differences in technique that are needed.

—Carol Maltby

to do is plant the divine in it." Erik describes an online ritual performed in 1995 in which the quarters, the watchtowers of ceremony, usually symbolized by colored candles or statues, were monitors instead of altars: "Tonight's watchtowers are four 486 PCs networked through an Ethernet and linked to a SPARCstation with an Internet connection." This reflects "the degree to which our society has replaced air, earth, fire, and water with silicon, plastic, wire, and glass."[3]

Maybe the altars used in online rituals are housed in vast virtual temples. The Healing Circle, an online ritual space, gives a beautiful narrative description of its sacred space as a welcoming, a purification, a grounding, and a centering, all in one.[4] It offers a lovely transition from mundane reality to sacred space. It works in my head. It serves as a portal through which I may enter sacred space, a gate leading into another reality. The same site also gives advice on circle etiquette that would be second nature to a trained Witch, but which is helpful and reassuring to someone new.[5] Most of the advice amounts to common sense and good manners when applied to any kind of ritual in any religion, though it does bear repeating.

SOUND, VOICE, RHYTHM

I'm big on using voice and chanting for bonding and energy raising. It's one of the most efficacious means I know of to change consciousness, raise energy, heal, invoke deity, and sing praises. But how is it done online?

Do participants listen to recorded music? If so, do they all listen to the same selection? Does the music come from a single source and play on their computers? Jehana explains how her online ritual group coordinated things by having everyone play the same recorded music in the background as they performed the ritual. (Recorded music has the advantage of drowning out any distracting household or outside noises that may invade your ritual space.)

RHYTHM AND DRUMMING: Drums and the beat they keep can be the skeleton upon which the rest of a ritual can be built. When rhythm is employed in a ritual, the sensitivity and skill on the part of the drummer(s) are essential to the overall effectiveness of the rite. The drummer can accelerate and intensify the energy of the circle when that is called for, and when it's appropriate to soften and decelerate, the drummer can moderate his speed, volume, and intensity accordingly.

And do participants tap out rhythms? Moose includes drumming in his online rituals by describing it to the group. He'll say something like "The HP begins to drum. Slow at first, a heavy, steady beat. The beat is speeding up. A counterbeat: thump-thump, thump-thump. Can you hear it? Like a heart. Thump-thump, thump-thump. Faster. Faster. Now the drum is speeding, and your blood is matching the beat. Faster, faster, wilder and wilder . . ." Yet, as evocative as this is, it's not real drumming. It's all in our heads. When I asked Moose how participants harmonized or became attuned with one another, he replied, "The participants use all their usual ritual skills in raising the cone. They are empowered to do it by themselves, but in concert with others. The words (typed by the facilitator, not en masse) on the screen mark the progress of the raising and signal the release of energy."

Moose claims that raising energy, shaping it in online rituals, is "exactly the same as offline—all the usual methods and precautions are in play. The only significant difference is that you may be physically alone, and that in some cases the energy raised can affect the modem. If you're the kind of person who can occasionally stop watches, you may not want to choose online ritual as your first option."

I asked Moose how he perceives energy raising and other people during online ritual.

> In the midst of raising and guiding a cone of

> power online, I can't honestly say I see the movements of others. I do get a sense of movement, but it's more like being in a fog, seeing more or less dense areas moving this way and that (and I'm using "seeing" here very loosely). I don't know that what movements I sense are directly related to the timing and tone on the keyboard, but I've had enough confirmation by e-mail postritual to know that something more than chance is going on.

I like breathing together. I like hearing us inhale and exhale together. I like hyperventilating in preparation for magic. Online, everyone may breathe in unison, but we can't hear each other breathing. I like joining hands in a circle and feeling the energy run from hand to hand. I cannot feel the pulses of my companions over the Net.

SCRIPTS

When we first learn to do ritual, most of us rely on some sort of script. There are few exceptions to this method of magical training. Book-taught Pagans, especially, tend to use scripts. Without a teacher or a guide, we have only books and our personal experience to help us find the way. Scripts may be read or memorized. An entire script may be spoken by one or two or a few officiants, leaving little for other participants to do except watch and become absorbed in the experience that is being created for them. As we become more adept at ritual, more familiar with the material, more confident of our abilities, we may dispense with scripts and move on to perform spontaneous, unscripted rituals. This is the way I learned; I know how to attune myself to the energies of the moment, be they the energies of an element or of a

SPIRIT: The spirit is the center of the circle: it is life, which is created by the elements of Air, Fire, Water, and Earth; some Witches consider spirit itself to be an element. Witches sing "Air I am, Fire I am, Water, Earth, and Spirit I am." Many Witches believe that spirit is the external individual consciousness that exists independently of our bodies and is eternal, and most believe that all life forms (animals, plants, rocks, mountains, rivers) have a spirit. Some believe that the spirit of an individual enters into another being after death.

LURK: To eavesdrop on a chat room or conference. In most online areas, lurking is perfectly acceptable behavior and is, in fact, encouraged so that you get the feel of the area before posting your own comments. However, some online areas, particularly ones where participants are discussing personal issues, frown on lurking. One who lurks is known as a lurker.[6]

deity, and to speak as **spirit** moves me. Some of us can do this with ease, while others perform better with more structure and control.

Moose keeps a hard copy of his ritual script in plain view of his monitor. He works with a leadership team who all have copies of the script and are prepared to take over the ritual should an officiant get bounced from the ritual space. Both Jehana and Moose caution against rituals that are too long-winded, because they lack inflection and can become boring, thus losing the participants' attention. Jehana also warns us not to scroll the script too fast.

On the Net, I've seen some online rituals that are essentially lovely scripts, with a different person "reading" or "performing" each of the parts. I still don't understand how these rituals can work magically. Anyone can type "Hail, Guardians of the Watchtowers of . . ."—but how is it anything more than just typing? Does it become something more when it's read by others? How is it different from reading instructions on a site and filling in the blanks? Does retyping the words of a script within the context of an online ritual replace speaking those words? As beautiful and as lyrical as the writing may be, how is retyping or rereading or respeaking the words within the context of an online ritual significantly different from simply reading them and enjoying them yourself? For Jehana, "There is something about putting oneself in that space and *experiencing* that does the trick. It is the active, not passive, act of connection that stirs energies—and while close proximity, all other things being equal, helps, it is not entirely essential, as we have discovered to our delight."

Moose and Jehana have conducted online rituals

together. Moose describes the dynamic that makes these rituals work for him: "The words are infused with energy and intent by the person typing them. Kind of like magically empowering your vote just before you actually go to the polls." Does the typing of the ritual script require a special skill? Moose explains that the high priest/ess or anyone else conducting a ritual can manipulate the energy of the rite: "Anyone who can type and has the script *can* perform the role, but it would not necessarily be magic. I have found that putting words on the screen a phrase at a time, and actively deciding how long to wait for each phrase to appear, is part of the HP/S online skill set."

Ceffyl is another experienced online ritualist. She speaks of the vulnerability she and others sometimes experience online, a vulnerability that seems to sharpen their intuitive sensitivity:

> Seems like the depth you allow yourself to participate in a ritual online is the same as it is in person. You mentioned before about people assuming identities online, playing a part or having a mask . . . having a false intimacy. There's the flip side to that—that same sense of intimacy creates an interesting effect in online circle. If you are in circle online and tell everyone to visualize holding hands, it can have a much more powerful effect than being in person. You're establishing an immediate energy link with the other people. You're more open doing that than in regular circle, where you can just let the energy ride over your shoulders if you want to participate but not necessarily contribute much (say you had a bad day or something, for whatever reason).

> So, how I approach circle online is a little different from how I do ritual in person. I'm much pickier online, which probably doesn't make much sense. But it's the intimacy or energy work that makes me very cautious. There are very few people I would consider doing circle with online; in person is something completely different.

From where I stand, it's hard to comprehend how a cyberspace circle can have a more powerful effect than a terraspace one. Perhaps it does for some and not for others. Even when all participants are in the same physical place, their experiences of the shared ritual can vary widely. But I wonder how you tell, online, when someone's shielding or just being a blockhead. Do you experience a break in the energy link? How do you determine if that's what has happened?

Moose and Jehana both emphasize the importance of involving all participants in the ritual by allowing space for others to "speak." "You need these responses," insists Moose, "because otherwise it's hard to know anyone's there." Moose's rituals are done in a performance ritual format, with a "leadership team" and "players" and "audience participation" and "readers." He says that "the ritual should include something that makes the participant physically move"—she could, for example, point her athame or finger or wand and trace a circle around herself. Furthermore, Moose suggests, each participant could have on hand some small item, like a stone, to infuse with the energy raised in the ritual.

ENERGY FLOW

I've been attending class in a chat room for a few weeks now. It's a first-time experience for me. I find, however, that the cohesion and flow of the class is compromised by our tendency—brought on by delays in electronic communication—to stumble over each other's threads. Shawn Arthur expresses a similar frustration:

> As one who has performed many cyberrituals (with many years of other ritual experience under my belt first), I can definitely say that it can be really hard to concentrate in a meditative state: while reading from a well-lit screen, while concentrating on typing legibly, if you want to write ("say") something and other people are changing the subject, if the chat room you are in is causing problems, if you are communicating through instant messenger, if you are trying to lead the ritual and take part in it as well, and so on. When one loses one's meditative state, IBM and AOL cease to be sacred very quickly!

If this method of communication is challenging in the context of a class, then how much more challenging must it be in the context of a ritual, when you want your powers of visualization and focus to be clear and sharp? Moose admits that this constitutes one disadvantage to online rituals—but "Flaky modems, noisy phone lines, and intervening thunderstorms are simply part of the landscape in cyberspace." Since these irritants can cause members of the "ritual team" to disappear during a ritual, he recommends having a contingency plan.

SACRED SPACE/CIRCLE

When we talked about ways of learning, we discussed ways of consecrating space and focusing on it as sacred. We cast circles with gestures, words, tools, sounds, and scents. We used tools and techniques to effectuate the changes in consciousness that would allow us to feel the intensity and protection from outside interference that sacred space provides. How do we create sacred space online? If we do it live in a chat room, we sanctify the chat room in cyberspace rather than a private living room or a meeting room in a hotel or a hall. Do we cast a circle online? If so, how do we walk around the space? Ceffyl says:

> Creating sacred space online is pretty much the same as creating sacred space in person. It has the same kind of steps. The difference is where you are casting. I recently did an Imbolc ritual online with my best friend, who was in Japan at the time. We cast circle between us, so that circle went around my computer desk and where she was sitting. Oddly enough, we didn't do circle in a chat room, we did it sending messages. We agreed upon what we wanted to do, basic format, and did it. No script, nothing prewritten. It worked very well.
>
> Another time I did a student's online dedication ritual in a MUD environment I wrote. I created a virtual (text-based) environment complete with altars at all quarters, elements and their representative items, main altar, candles, and so on. You could even light the candles. (Emotes are useful things.) That created a very strong sense of space. That ritual was scripted.

BETWEEN THE WORLDS AND CYBERSPACE

Are there similarities between what Witches know as the place "between the worlds" and that place known as cyberspace? Opinion on this question diverges in the Pagan world. Shawn Arthur says:

> I think that for many Wiccans, cyberspace and the realm between the worlds have large areas of intersection. The largest of these areas is in the mind of the meditator.
>
> Cognitively, these two realms can be very similar if one chooses to explore both comparatively. The "realm between the worlds," which is a phrase often related to sacred space, can be theoretically transplanted into the realm of cyberspace, especially if one's use of cyberspace is for the same reasons. In other words, the realm between the worlds in a Wiccan ritual is the same whether or not one is in a physical circle with physical friends, in a physical circle with cyberfriends, or in a cybercircle with cyberfriends.
>
> The instantaneous qualities of cyberspace, along with the availability of virtuality (much like well-honed visualization skills—the typed word "cup" in the practitioner's mind becomes a cup, and therefore part of the practitioner's reality, yet without a physical representation), provide a growing number of Pagans with an alternative "space" for their practices. I do, however, think that the practitioners who have extensive physical circle practice benefit much more from cyberrituals than do those who have little or no other experience (since the analogous aspects of cyberspace and sacred space can

> only be realized if one knows both—of course, those who have only done cyberrituals may have a completely different concept of sacred space than others) . . . I experience rituals (physical and cyber) in many of the same ways. I think of cyberspace and "the space between the worlds" as places of extremely complex webs of interconnections. Tapping into different aspects of the webs allows the work in these realms to be accomplished (much like a shaman learns to work with the many varied aspects of the underworld).

To this, Moose adds, "The Internet is good practice for going between the worlds. It teaches you to think of people as personalities rather than bodies, and places as centers of synergy rather than destinations. It is a real-world parallel, in many respects, to the inner landscape of being between the worlds." Moose thinks that we can go between the worlds in cyberspace, but he's not convinced that cyberspace itself is necessarily that magical intermediate place. "Cyberspace is a place from which one can travel between the worlds. Ritual is the doorway. The door just happens to sit in cyberspace." And Moose suggests another way of looking at rituals that take place in cyberspace: "If all paths lead to the truth, that includes online ritual."

Here are a couple of provocative questions that have arisen about the parallels between cyberspace and "between the worlds" space. I propose no answers here. I offer the questions as food for thought as our cyberwitchen future unfolds.

> • In neoshamanic terms, does cyberspace equate

with the Upper or Lower World rather than the Middle World?[7]

- How does a move towards a virtual medium for ritual reconcile with what we often claim is Paganism's admirable emphasis on immanence, on the body, on the actual Earth?[8]

And of those Witches who have performed powerful and satisfying cyberrituals with people they first knew personally in the mundane world, I ask

- Do you think it worked well because you were already bonded in terraspace?
- Do you think it could have worked as well with someone you'd never met?

ONLINE COVENS

The word *coven* can mean various things to different people. For the purposes of this discussion, I am using the term to mean a small congregation of Witches who meet regularly to perform ritual, worship, and/or do magical workings. A coven is an intimate group, closely bonded; each member is familiar with, and sensitive to, the special gifts, talents, and strengths of the other coveners.

How do online covens compare to face-to-face covens? Some descriptions of early online rituals refer to those in attendance as coveners. In that sense of the word, a covener can be anyone who logs on to the space in the cyberworld where a ritual is taking place. All participants may be strangers to one another—except the facilitators who design and execute the ritual. Compare this to a face-to-face ritual within an established coven, where participants have developed a deep level of love and trust.

Websurfers looking for cybercovens can find an array of them. Books are beginning to be published about cybercovens and cybermagic and how to practice the Craft online. Do cybercovens have the same genuine intimacy that good, healthy covens do? Or might any sense of intimacy felt by online coveners be illusory? The result of wishful thinking? Do cyberspace covens experience the occasional internal conflict, like terraspace covens do? If so, how are they resolved? If someone is hurt, can the others truly sense her pain? Can they see her tears? How do cybercovens share hugs? Do they break bread together at the end of the ritual? Do they need to reground the way we do after terraspace rituals?

By posing these questions, I may seem to be challenging the validity of cybercovens. I am not. Instead, I am attempting to understand a relatively unfamiliar yet wondrous technology. When I was a child, few homes contained a television set. No earthbound metal container had been launched beyond Earth's gravity. No human had set foot on the moon. My religion and spirituality are inspired by visions brought by the four winds; energized by the heat of the sun; carried by my coursing blood; and grounded in my flesh and bones.

INTIMACY

There is something strange about Web communication: it seems to prompt people who maintain healthy boundaries in all other aspects of their lives to dissolve those precautions. The Net has a seductive quality that can make us relax our inhibitions. In other words, the Net fosters an instant intimacy.

When you aspect, you prepare, you have a working partner, you move your personality out of the way so the deity can speak through you. In shape shifting, you "put on a glamour" and appear in a different form from the one you inhabit in "ordinary reality." When you wear a mask, you present a different face to the world, and you may move and act in ways that you wouldn't consider were you not "acting out" behind the mask.

Can these things be done online? I think they can. As I have suggested, people can be seduced into relaxing their normal inhibitions online, especially in private e-mails and closed discussions or closed chats. This enables them to drop their everyday personalities and allow deity to dominate. At the same time, many people do this intentionally to accomplish other ends—like the adult male cop who pretends to be an adolescent girl while working on an online sting. Or the pedophiliac predator who attempts to lure young victims on the Web. Or anyone who tries to attract others by posing online as someone he's not—an athlete, a body builder, a model. Some people can readily identify a phony person through online contact alone. Others are more gullible, less sensitive, perhaps more innocent. They can be duped. I tend to believe whatever a person puts out to me—I'm only a little suspicious by nature.

From my limited experience with online ritual, I can say that so far I haven't experienced shivers up my spine the way I often do in terraspace rituals. However, there are Witches I know and respect who claim that online rituals work, so I don't feel I can dismiss these rituals just because I haven't experienced them with the intensity and transformative potential that others have enjoyed. How can I say what they do for someone else? I value the immediacy of breathing together with my circle mates, of looking one another in the eye, of running our energy hand-to-hand. What substitute is there for that online? I don't believe that there is one, but that leaves me wondering what kinds of magical experience people can have in cyberspace that aren't possible in terraspace.

Moose says, "I do agree that a terraspace Nature religionist will probably never use cyberspace as more than an adjunct ritual setting." And Fritz adds, "To me, the Net will never hold a candle to the impact of eye-to-eye. This is one of the reasons that we've worked so hard to develop our networking section. To us it happens best at the local/physical level."

INFORMING AND MOBILIZING FOR SAFETY AND CHANGE

I tend to think of Paganism as a movement rather than a community. We are many diverse communities. Picking up the newspun thread of witchen online networking (which first appeared in chapter 3), let's look at what's linking Pagan communities into a movement these days.

For about four years now, I've been working with an ad hoc group of Pagans, not just Witches, on a few projects. We began as an informal group of about fifteen people who had been asked to provide feedback and opinions on a dictionary project coordinated by PEN (Pagan Educational Network). Later, we came together in a more formalized sense as a listserve called OurFreedom. OurFreedom arose in response to the attacks on Craft by Georgia congressman Bob Barr in the wake of the Fort Hood Spring Equinox ritual of 1999. We wrote a press release emphasizing our First Amendment rights and the freedom of religion guaranteed by the U.S. Constitution.[9] We collected enough money (seven hundred dollars) on a grassroots level (that is, among ourselves) to hire a distribution company to circulate the press release. On July 4, 1999, it was sent to President Clinton, all senators, congresspeople, wire services, television and radio networks, and several major metropolitan newspapers. This was the first time such a diversity of Pagans had come together to address a common concern.

Participants in this project—that is, the signatories representing the various Pagan groups—were in turn encouraged to distribute the press release to their local and state legislators as well as their local media, and to provide contact people for the press. The release was truly a historical document, signed by people from groups who had, in the past, for whatever reasons, mistrusted each other. Even five years earlier, some of the participating Pagan groups would never have endorsed the same document. Yet, in the summer of 1999, these people were wise and prudent enough to set aside their smaller differences in order to address a large common concern. This, to me, is an unmistakable indication of the maturation of the Pagan movement.

Furthermore, the movement's more recent responses to President Bush's proposed faith-based charities were built on the solidarity we achieved in our earlier collaborations. I'm proud to be a signatory of the letter we sent to the president reminding him of the guarantees laid out in our Constitution and Bill of Rights and the importance of maintaining the separation of church and state. Once there is a chink in the wall that divides church and state, this crucial barrier will be breached. We must not allow it to happen. We must remain active and vigilant. Those who retreat from efforts to ensure our rights put us all in danger of losing them. We are of the world; we need to keep it safe and clean.

The Internet has been a powerful tool for Witches working to communicate, organize, and mobilize. We can now do this with unprecedented speed. In my own community, Reclaiming, which is far more politically active than most Craft traditions, we've successfully mounted actions and generated support for them on the Net. In 1998, I joined my community in protesting the harvesting of the precious, primeval, old-growth redwood forests in the Headwaters National Forest in Humboldt County, California. We were part of a large and impassioned action organized by Earth First! and other groups. My partner, Corby, our friend Cary the Fairy, and I drove to a campsite in the redwoods to join a support team for others who were doing direct action. Before we left home, we'd all been in touch via e-mail to be sure we had all the supplies we needed and everyone knew who was responsible for stoves, food, dry clothing, and other such necessities. We knew where to rendezvous with our group. By the time our activists returned, in the early hours of the morning, cold, wet, and weary, we had set up a tarp-covered kitchen and prepared coffee, eggs, and fresh fruit.

Many of the supplies were donated by merchants in our home cities and towns. One friend, Tami, solicited fresh produce from the merchants at our weekly downtown farmer's market. The growers sent their gratitude and support along with their fruits and vegetables. Tami had learned via e-mail that the protesters would be needing support. Even though neither she nor the farmers were able to go to the redwoods, Tami loaded cars with the donated produce she'd collected and sent us on our way.

Later, after we'd returned from the action, when full-time activists were still blocking lumber trucks and Julia Butterfly began her two years of living up in Luna, we were able to keep abreast of what kind of support—emotional, financial, spiritual—the protesters needed, and we provided whatever we could.

In December 2000, many Pagan activists I know and love went to Seattle to protest the World Trade Organization (WTO) meetings. We supported the protesters, jailed or not, via the networks we share with other Witches throughout the country and the world, and we were able to distribute news of loved ones quickly. This action went far beyond my Reclaiming community, as reports from students, teachers, reporters, nurses, and activists of all sorts were exchanged from list to list. Lots of Pagans had been unaware before the action took place of the existence of the WTO, much less its potential to do great social, environmental, and economic ill. It was an exciting time. Those of us who couldn't be at the site of the action still felt connected to it in a very immediate way. Witchen supporters throughout the e-connected world had immediate energy exchange with our kin in the streets of Seattle. Having those reports and connections sustained us in ways we'd never felt sustained before. For many of us, it was a source of hope.

CONSENSUS DECISION MAKING ONLINE

My tradition, Reclaiming, is loosely organized into working groups, which we call "cells." Some may see this as a legacy of the Communist Party, but I see it as an organic patterning on the dwellings of bees. In any case, each Reclaiming cell is autonomous, yet accountable to a wheel. I won't try to explain the mysterious organizational structure of Reclaiming here, but I will describe one particular cell: the e-cell, in which I worked for several years. The e-cell maintains Reclaiming's electronic presence. All Reclaiming cells operate by consensus; consensus is the name of a broad category of processes that evolved from the meeting practices of the Religious Society of Friends (Quakers).

> [Consensus is] a nonviolent way for people to relate to each other as a group. Consensus allows us to recognize our areas of agreement and to act together without coercing one another. Under consensus, the group takes no action that is not consented to by all members. The fundamental right of consensus is for all persons to be able to express themselves in their own words and of their own will; the fundamental responsibility of consensus is to assure others of their right to speak and to be heard.[10]

You can find a small library of articles on the consensus process at the Reclaiming Web site. I believe that consensus processes are especially well suited to Pagan organizations. Our e-cell adapted consensus process for use in cyberspace. When the cell began, it was comprised of people living in the San Francisco Bay Area who were connected with the Reclaiming Collective, so we all knew each other personally. We shared the common goal of establishing and maintaining Reclaiming's electronic presence, and we were confident that we could work together comfortably. When the collective dissolved itself and metamorphosed into a larger entity, this allowed the e-cell to expand beyond the limits of Northern California.

Working cells may have a limited life span because they are formed for a project that will eventually be completed. The e-cell is an ongoing cell, so from time to time people leave. They may wish to pursue other interests, or they may feel that they've contributed as much as they can, or they may have personal priorities that preclude their active involvement. A good, strong cell has enough people to perform the necessary work while still allowing individual members to have a lighter load once in a while. Sometimes, cell members will even take sabbaticals, planning to return in due course.

Cells expand when they feel the need to—when they have become too small to do all of their work, when members need a break, or when they want to take on related projects. In the e-cell, this might mean that the cell wants to add more pages to the site and needs someone to set them up and maintain them. This is usually someone who has helped out on a particular cell project (if it's a project-oriented cell), like assisting a public ritual cell in putting on a sabbat, and who has expressed an interest in doing more work with the cell. Because she has already worked with them, cell members have had a chance to get to know her and to evaluate her skills and commitment. Having special skills is not the main prerequisite for joining a cell—many cells are happy to train new people who are eager to take on different tasks. It is important, however, that the current cell members know and trust those they will be working with.

Before we expanded the Reclaiming e-cell to include people who lived beyond our immediate area, we thought carefully. The prospect of working consensually with people we didn't know and who lived great distances from where most of us lived concerned us, so we decided that one criterion for new members would be that they had to be personally known by at least one current cell member. Because so many of the WitchCamp teachers were from the original San Francisco-based collective, several local people knew Witches from the various regions of the country where WitchCamps had been held. I was also traveling a lot when I still worked in the e-cell, and so I had a chance to become acquainted with potential volunteers.

We in the e-cell had articulated on the Web site what our requirements were, as far as new members were concerned, so interested people could visit the site to see if our needs fit their interests. We encouraged potential volunteers to ask us questions—both about how the cell works and about ourselves as individual people—and we asked them about themselves. We didn't rush things. Even after we had invited someone to join, we allowed for a brief probationary period during which we all adjusted to each other and thought about whether we really wanted to work together.

When it comes to doing the actual work of the cell—that is, working on the Web site, listserves, e-correspondence, calendars, policies, new projects—we present a topic to the cell at large via e-mail and enter a response date in the subject line. Sometimes the topic is an issue we want to discuss; other times it is something that needs to be done or a request (from another cell or from people in the community) that has to be addressed. Friday is our response date for any action proposed during the preceding week. This means that, if something is actively on the cell agenda, we respond and generate discussion by Friday. Every agenda item has at least seven days from the date the topic is introduced for the cell to reach consensus on it. If, by Friday, we still haven't reached consensus or resolution, we can arrange for more time.

At some point during the discussion, if someone senses agreement, she rewords the matter in the form of a proposal. Those who don't respond one way or another by the response date are assumed to have no opinion or objection. In other words, those who choose not to express themselves cannot block the progress of an action. And each member is responsible for keeping herself informed about what is going on in the cell in any given week. During my involvement with Reclaiming's e-cell, I found this method of operating efficient and satisfying. I offer it here for those who would try it.

Chapter 7

ADDING COLOR AND TEXTURE

The Witch and Pagan communities that grew during the outdoor festivals of the 1970s and 1980s enabled magical folk of all kinds to find others who believed and practiced as we did. Within such communities, we talked about our individual skills, techniques, training, and special magical pursuits. We joined with others to create **sacred space**—liturgy, ritual implements, invocation, song, and rhythm—together. We shared meals, deep conversation, tales, recipes, art, music, and humor. So we danced. We drummed. Some of us made love.

SACRED SPACE: A place, usually a circle, in which a ritual or any kind of magical work is done, either by an individual or a group. Often, people will stand in a circle to begin a ritual, but during the ritual they may move about in any configuration and are still said to be "in circle" or "in sacred space."

As the Internet expanded, we Pagan folk joined the rest of the population in exploring its wonders. We found even more colleagues online than we had met at festivals and gatherings. Some of us even found ourselves; we had been Witches at heart, with no community. We'd had no sense that there were others like us. Our elders and those with mobility or health problems that prevented them from attending camping events could now communicate with us on the same level as everyone else. Our web expanded. New webs were spun, overlapping and interweaving with yet more webs.

We created listserves for tradition-specific discussions, permitting isolated, widely dispersed initiates to maintain easy communication, and reinforcing our ties to our extended witchen families. Listserves are often connected to one or more Web sites; a Web site may generate several listserves. Reclaiming's e-cell creates and maintains listserves for other Reclaiming cells (regional teachers cells, *Quarterly* cells, regional public-ritual cells); the RIDL (Reclaiming International Discussion) list; the BARD list (Bay Area Reclaiming Discussion); and a single e-addy for class, workshop, and event announcements. These announcements are delivered to the *Quarterly* for print publication, to the e-cell for posting on the online calendar, and to the events line for recording on a telephone calendar.

LISTSERVE: **A small program that automatically redistributes e-mail to names on a mailing list. Users can subscribe to a mailing list by sending an e-mail note to a mailing list they learn about; listserve will automatically add the name and distribute future e-mail postings to every subscriber.**[1]

Many **listserves** foster the divinatory arts. There are lists about Tarot, about specific uses of Tarot, about particular Tarot decks, and about particular schools of Tarot thought. Organizations, listserves, and chats allow priest/esses to discuss and experience matters of common concern. We Pagans grow and deepen as a result of these networks.

Search any site that hosts free listserves and you'll find hundreds of these e-mail mailing lists, both open and private, relating to Paganism, Neopaganism, Witchcraft, Wicca, magic, and Goddess spirituality. There is a list for every possible special interest. I subscribe to several Pagan listserves. Of course, there's a limit to the amount of time a person can beneficially spend online, so rather than clutter up our lives and our e-mail programs with countless messages from a single busy listserve, we can choose to have our listserve messages delivered in a daily digest form; or we can go online and read the messages in the archive instead of having them come to us as mail. These technologies give us greater access to one another and increase peer support and sharing.

The World Wide Web connects us to sources of advanced skills and gives us access to special resources. Some areas of pursuit in which we have much to share and learn are

- Herb cultivation, lore, and use; herb schools; seed sources; recipes
- Shamanic skills
- Voice training
- Dance, movement, yoga, ethnic dance
- Smith craft, jewelry making, glass blowing
- Tattooing with spiritual and/or magical significance
- Psychic skills training
- Theater arts—acting, staging, lighting, sets, makeup, pyrotechnics

BUILDING AN INTERNET PROJECT

My own online exploration began in the mid-1990s with the easy access offered by the ubiquitous America Online. At that time, AOL was overselling its services, and it took forever to establish a connection. It didn't take me long to find another ISP, one that could give me the uninterrupted services I was paying for. The first thing I did was search the words *Pagan* and *Witch*. I checked out several lists and began expounding my own ideas about the topics that were being discussed. At one point, on a message board that had nothing to do with Paganism—it concerned motherhood and birth mothers and adoption —I found myself detailing my entire reproductive history! To strangers! I was utterly amazed at how seductive this medium was, how tempting it was to reveal my personal life in cyberspace.

Not long after that, I began work on a book called *Crossing Over: A Pagan Manual on Death and Dying*. It was a collaborative project of the Reclaiming Collective. Starhawk had come up with the idea that we Witches and Pagans needed a resource to help us meet the challenges presented by **death**, to help us through the various crises that arise when someone we love is dying or has just died. She knew me to be a woman with a long-established interest in writing, editing, and publishing, and that I was not deeply involved in other collective work at that time. So she handed me a sheaf of papers containing some thoughts, poems, prayers, and other writings that she'd produced over the previous six months or so, and she asked me to begin working these pieces into a book along with contributions from others.

DEATH: The state that we enter after "life," as it is commonly defined by Western biology, ends. Death is understood as part of the circle. Many Witches believe that the dead continue to exist on another plane and that it is possible to contact them, especially at Samhain, through a psychic connection. We are all aware of our connections with our ancestors and of the fact that, in some sense, we will live on in our descendants. We sing "What is remembered lives."

From her assistant, I got Starhawk's writings on disk, and I began the process of soliciting pieces from others whom I believed had worthwhile things to say on the topic. The creative and editorial processes that culminated in *Crossing Over* were conducted almost entirely online. Another local witchen writer collaborated with me in the early stages. Then I designed and produced the book on my word-processing program. The cover was done the old-fashioned way: artist Laura Kemp drew it with pen and ink. It's the only thing that was done by hand.

The Reclaiming Collective paid for printing and binding, which were expensive because we were working against a tight deadline. The original idea was presented to me at a retreat in January of 1995, Starhawk gave me her sheaf of papers in mid-February, the printing and binding were done in late October 1995, and the books went on sale at the big annual Spiral Dance Samhain ritual the day after they were picked up from the printer.

In 1996, Starhawk showed a copy of *Crossing Over* to her publisher. The publisher wanted to put out an edition of the book to be on store shelves by Samhain 1997. So we got to work rearranging articles and liturgy, soliciting more pieces, and writing. The expanded edition, called *The Pagan Book of Living and Dying: Practical Rituals, Prayers, Blessings, and Meditations on Crossing Over*, contains the writings of thirty-six Pagans, not all of them Witches. Some were people I knew, either personally or professionally; some were people Starhawk knew; some we both knew.

Some of the new contributions were unsolicited, and they delved into subjects that we hadn't even considered. For instance, we received a query from Dennis and Beth in Massachusetts; they'd done research, meditation, and other work on the question of organ donation, and they wondered if we'd be interested in seeing their writings. Naturally, we were. Their essay, which eventually found its way into *The Pagan Book of Living and Dying*, included a prayer for releasing a donor's essence from his organs and another for people who use cadavers to gain knowledge in the healing arts. The piece was based on the writers' investigation of the theme of the dying god in Robert Graves's *The White Goddess*. In the book, we don't assume that organ donation is right for everyone; we leave that up to the individual and the family. We accepted Dennis and Beth's essay because we wanted to make our book relevant to contemporary readers. We see Craft as a living, evolving spiritual path that continuously adapts to the times.

Of the articles that we did solicit in order to fill the

gaps, one was a piece on the death of a child. Another offered rituals and practical suggestions on how to help children who must deal with the death of a loved one or a pet. Once these articles were in place, however, I realized that we had nothing about losing a child, one of the most difficult passages to accept. Death is a part of the cycle of Nature. It comes to everyone sooner or later, no matter what some people may propound about avoiding or transcending death. Death just *is*. But the death of a child is out of the natural order. Children are supposed to survive their parents. So when a child dies, especially a very young child, it knocks us off balance emotionally. We needed someone to address that in *The Pagan Book of Living and Dying*.

So I asked around. One collective member told me of a woman in her community who'd lost her very young son and had written about it. I asked whether this woman was a writer or just using writing as therapy. My friend assured me that the woman's writing was good, so I sent her an e-mail. She sent me her article within a few hours of my request. Such is the magic of online communication!

The piece, called "A Scent of Grace," was so moving that I sat there at my computer screen weeping as I read it. I e-mailed the author to tell her what a priceless gift she would be making to our project and to our growing culture, and asked her permission to publish her article. She e-mailed me right away that it was a gift to *her* to be given a chance to share her experience with the public. That's how "A Scent of Grace" made it into *The Pagan Book of Living and Dying*. As it turned out, the author, Lady Bachu, and I have several friends in common, although we had never met. It was not until the first release event for the book, which was held in Berkeley, California, that the two of us finally met face-to-face. By expressing her grief to others in the context of our publishing project, Lady Bachu moved closer to accepting the tragic death of her child.

Thanks to the Internet, we established this connection, exchanged the article, edited it, and put it into the book in a matter of days. Were it not for the Net, I probably wouldn't have known that such a work existed. I would never have phoned everyone I could think of who might know a Pagan whose child had died and could write about it. But because I could write a general message and send it to either an e-list or a group of individuals in my personal address book, this wonderful contribution manifested.

PRIEST/ESSCRAFT, SPECIAL-INTEREST MINISTRIES

Movies, television, books—Witches are turning up everywhere in pop culture. And, as more and more people seek a religion that meets their spiritual needs, that addresses their everyday concerns and the bigger questions in life, they are finding their way onto Pagan paths. Discouraged by the rape of Nature, by the declining quality of air and water, agriculture and animal husbandry, we find hope in Paganism. We create rituals of commitment and renewal in the face of ecological perils. We rejoice in our diversity. We encourage creativity and self-expression.

As more people find themselves drawn to Pagan practices, they seek information and connection on the Web. Priest/esses have rallied to meet that challenge. Together, we have created ways of teaching and learning online. In many ways, the World Wide Web has supplemented, and in some cases even enhanced, the passing on of the Craft of the wise. People search on the Internet for Pagans to conduct their rites of passage or to counsel them in crisis. In response to this need, priestesses and priests, individually or as a dyad, perform services that we might recognize as being similar to those that mainstream clergy perform.

Pagans, more than ever, are seeking the support of other Pagans: for instance, some Pagan expectant parents are more comfortable having a witchen midwife attending the birth of their offspring. I sometimes receive phone calls from distraught people who are witnessing a loved one go through the process of dying. Because of my work on *The Pagan Book of Living and Dying*, they believe that I might have a special understanding of their situation, and they seek my counsel. I suggest ways of coping. These people also reach me through e-mail, and through the Web I spin out all the words of comfort I can.

My colleagues and I have created memorials and funerals. To hospital chaplains, hospice workers, and funeral professionals who ask for advice on how to serve their Pagan clients, I have spoken about our beliefs and practices. I have also lectured to college classes on Pagan views of death. This is one part of my ministry.

Laura Spellweaver, of Massachusetts, is a priestess who performs rites of commitment. Most of these rituals are marriage ceremonies, legal in the eyes of the state. Laura, like many others who conduct weddings, conducts premarital counseling sessions. She also keeps a collection of liturgical writings from which those who seek her services may choose selections to weave into their own unique ceremonies. Laura is one of many Witches across the continent who have responded to a calling and developed a specialized ministry.

Pagan counselors who have secular training in therapy may specialize in such areas as working with victims of domestic violence or child abuse. As with any human being in any profession, their spirituality can enhance and enrich their professional practice.

As a Priest of Bridghe, Patrick McCollum is a remarkably skilled and gifted goldsmith. He is the Wiccan chaplain for the State of California Department of Corrections, the first Pagan chaplain in any state to be appointed to serve Pagan inmates. Patrick also serves on the Prison Issue Task Force of Lady Liberty League,[2] as well as being a consultant to prison administrations in seven other states and to the Federal Bureau of Prisons. Patrick's ministry, called Our Lady of the Wells, is now one of several throughout the country. They exist in a number of states among them, Washington, Arizona, Missouri, Tennessee, and Florida.

Pagans, myself included, who are doing prison ministries are beginning to find colleagues on the Internet. We are sharing information that helps other prison ministries. Witchen "clergy" working in the prisons also enjoy professional relationships with other prison clergy and with prison staff. We also work in concert with adult-literacy teachers, who offer social services within the prison system. We have formed alliances that benefit prisoners, their families, and ourselves.

Ordained interfaith ministers now have training in Pagan beliefs and practices. In addition, some Pagans are called to the interfaith ministry; they train at interfaith seminaries such as the Golden Gate Interfaith Institute in the San Francisco Bay Area. With such training, these witchen folk join with interfaith ministerial colleagues to serve in schools, hospitals, and prisons, to officiate at weddings and funerals, and to assist at other meaningful events in the lives of their coreligionists. On the peninsula south of San Francisco, there is a Witch who serves as a hospital chaplain. More and more frequently, hospices and hospitals have patients who request the ministrations of Pagan clergy. I'm encouraged when these chaplains, nurses, and other caregivers seek me out upon hearing that I'm conducting a workshop or when they come across *The Pagan Book of Living and Dying*. They are motivated by their desire to serve their clients in a way that is respectful of their faith tradition. I'm similarly encouraged when my coreligionists train to provide chaplaincy services to people of all faiths.

Some Pagans use the term "clergy" in defining their community responsibilities, but there are parallels between the roles of the Judeo-Christian clergy and Pagan priest/esses that cannot be fairly drawn. For one thing, Witches do not have a sacred text—we obtain spiritual guidance from spirit and spiritual encounters. Gus diZerega provides us with a clear explanation of the differences.

> In most instances the Christian titles are descriptions of a person's relationship to an organized body . . . [A]n ordained priest is a qualified intermediary between God and the people . . . Every Protestant stands in a completely personal relationship with God. The minister is therefore in no sense an intermediary. However, he or she is charged with leading the congregation, teaching its members, preaching God's word, and generally being the primary human authority for interpreting Scripture within the Church. Ministerial authority largely

derives from the freely given recognition by members of the congregation of his or her abilities as a preacher, in interpreting Scripture, and in living by Christian precepts . . . A traditional Wiccan priestess or priest does not preach . . . Neopagan priestesses and priests are often teachers, but what they teach is not primarily doctrine. Rather, it is how to act within a small group that, as a coven, works with the world of spirits and Spirit. In Traditional Wicca, the high priestess is usually the most skilled and experienced female member of the group, and the high priest is the male member she chooses to perform in that role. Oftentimes their authority is greater than a minister in a Protestant church because they can expel members unilaterally. On the other hand, they do not possess anything like the institutionalized authority of a Catholic priest or a minister appointed by one of the more institutionalized Protestant churches. Nor are they paid for their services.

While the high priestess or high priest possess only minimal institutional authority (other coveners may well possess as high a formal initiation as they) they are expected to be the most adept or at least the most experienced at working with the world of spirits and of Spirit . . . they are primarily judged by their ability to work with spiritual powers . . . These abilities link traditional Wiccan priestesses and priests with healers, diviners, mediums, and shamans in many other Pagan traditions . . . Next in importance (and for sensible people just as important) is their personal spiritual maturity. Last, and often distantly so, is their institutional affiliation.[3]

PAGAN SEMINARIES AND OVARIA

As the Web grows larger more webs intersect and intertwine, our communities expand, our religions evolve. There are, and have always been, those among us who seek to deepen our practice, to hone our skills, to explore unfamiliar territory, to push boundaries beyond the known.

Beginning in the late 1990s, particularly, Pagans began to perceive the need for more advanced training. We saw that we had much to learn from one another. Some of us wanted to pursue knowledge and experience in a more structured way. People who'd been in the movement for years wanted to engage in deeper work than much of what could be found at festivals, where people of all levels of experience gathered. (See chapter 5 to pick up the thread of authority and institutionalization.)

Some of these people attempted to fulfill this goal by pursuing advanced studies in conventional seminaries. An example of such an institution is the Starr King School for the Ministry,[4] a Unitarian Universalist member of the Graduate Theological Union, in Berkeley, California. I know several people who have obtained Master of Divinity degrees from Starr King. Another formal institution whose program harmonizes with a witchen worldview and that grants degrees and ordination is the University of Creation Spirituality (UCS) in Oakland, California. Founded by former Dominican priest Matthew Fox, UCS articulates Ten Principles of Creation Spirituality, the last three of which are especially applicable to Nature religions.

- We are all sons and daughters of God; therefore, we have divine blood in our veins, the divine breath in our lungs; and the basic work of God is: Compassion.

- Divinity is as much Mother as Father, as much Child as Parent, as much Godhead (mystery) as God (history), as much beyond all beings as in all beings.
- We experience that the Divine is in all things and all things are in the Divine (Panentheism) and that this mystical intuition supplants theism (and its child, atheism) as an appropriate way to name our relation to the Divine and experience the Sacred.[5]

Throughout this book, I've tried to convey a sense of the vastness and diversity of witchen thought, belief, and politics. Some Pagans claim to be apolitical; we demonstrate our politics by making that very claim: that our politics are irrelevant to our spirituality. But many other Pagans involve themselves directly in society; we are active in the PTA, in neighborhood actions, in state, national, or global efforts. UCS's mission statement reads the way some Crafters talk:

> The Creation Spirituality movement seeks to integrate the wisdom of western spirituality and global indigenous cultures with the emerging scientific understanding of the universe and the passionate creativity of art . . . Creation Spirituality provides a solid foundation and holistic perspective from which to address the critical issues of our times, including the revitalization of religion and culture, the honoring of women's wisdom, the reinvention of work, the celebration of hope in today's youth, and the promotion of social and ecological justice, and the remaking of models of education.[6]

The UCS program that grants the degree of Doctor of Ministry (D.Min) is the very first of its kind. Students pursuing this credential come from all walks of life and from a range of faith traditions; there are social workers, doctors, lawyers, artists, therapists, clergy, and social activists. There are also Witches. Most UCS students are working adults who come from all over the nation and the world. One of their areas of study is the indigenous mind. They examine the spiritual outlooks of diverse peoples. Such an endeavor comes naturally to many Witches—those of us who have already heard the call to investigate our biological and ethnic roots, to learn the ways of our ancestors, to explore and understand the wisdom of the indigenous mind.

UCS is but one of a number of panspiritual learning environments where we Witches can deepen our knowledge. Yet other Pagans have begun establishing their own Pagan seminaries, what I call "ovaria." We have also organized retreats for deeper workings. Among these ovaria is the Reformed Congregation of the Goddess-International, Inc. (RCGI),[7] which has set up an ongoing priestess training program called Cella (the term refers to "the inner mysteries"). Cella is open to women only, and it requires a minimum commitment of one year, including attendance at three weekend intensives. At the completion of the first year, students must decide whether they wish to continue in the program, which, in its entirety, requires a commitment of six years and eighteen weekend residencies.

Cella training provides each student with a basic program structure and an advisor. The student herself defines her own activities and sets her own pace within that structure. Cella has six areas of specialization, called paths: Creatrix, for art, dance, writing, music, and theater;

Earthwalker, for service combining practical mundane activities with self-understanding; Scholar/Teacher, for study and teaching; Ritualist, for sharing celebration with others; Healer, for achieving maximum personal wellness and assisting others to achieve the same goal; and Organizer, for organizing events and activities that allow others to share Goddess energy.

RCGI originated in Madison, Wisconsin, in 1983, and it now has communities of practitioners in six states—California, Texas, Virginia, Wisconsin, Colorado, and New Jersey. RCGI established The Women's Thealogical Institute Cella Training Program in 1991, and to date it has ordained sixteen priestesses in all six types of ministry.

A related program provided by an affiliate of RCGI is the Matrix Program, sponsored by the Circle of Aradia, based in Los Angeles. The invitation to join explains that "Matrix is a Dianic four-year program within the Circle of Aradia community, whereby we as women engage in an ongoing relationship with one another towards the goals of: (1) empowering each woman on her path of spiritual service; and (2) teaching each woman new ways of leadership through the recognition and practice that we are always teaching and learning at the same time."[8]

For many years, New Mexico's Ardantane Project (*"Ardh an teinne"* means "the light of the fire") had been the dream of the members and friends of a coven called Our Lady of the Woods. It is now an independent nonprofit corporation with a governing board composed of representatives from several Craft traditions. The project started in 1996 by presenting short workshops in various cities and at Pagan festivals. In 1999, it took on its current form and started offering evening lectures, festival workshops, and one-day seminars. In that it serves all traditions of the Craft and opens most of its programs to other Pagan traditions, as well, The Ardantane Project is non-denominational. Its curriculum covers coven leadership (counseling, ritual design and presentation, administration and group process), advanced magic (divination, spell casting, ceremonial systems), environmental sustainability (ecology, organic gardening, alternative energy, Earth-friendly housing), and alternative healing (herbalism, energy work), along with other topics. The project is not intended to replace traditional coven training; rather, it provides its students with an opportunity to benefit from advanced training and peer sharing.

Currently, most Ardantane classes are one-day intensive workshops, although project staff are planning to launch weeklong programs in the near future. They are also preparing to launch a Web site—at ardantane.org—and they are exploring the possibility of running certain classes on the Internet. The founders hope eventually to establish a permanent campus retreat near Santa Fe, New Mexico, with straw-bale and passive-solar structures, outdoor shrines, gardens, and a stone circle. There, they intend to offer longer residency programs, but their plan is to continue outreach, as well. The Internet will play a large role in this effort.

Another more formal institution of learning is the Woolston-Steen Theological Seminary, an adjunct of the Aquarian Tabernacle Church International, based in Washington State.[9] The seminary is a highly structured "postsecondary school for the training and preparation for ordination of Wiccan and Pagan clergy." It offers Associate of Ministry, Bachelor of Ministry, Master of Ministry, and Doctor of Ministry degrees. Because its founders believe that "there is no replacement for face-to-face interaction, discussion, and learning in the critical thinking process," the seminary's program is residential.[10] While the seminary does not conduct classes online, many of its students found out about it online, researched it online, and registered online before traveling to Washington to study.

The California Institute of Integral Studies (CIIS) in San Francisco offers a Ph.D. in Women's Spirituality.[11] Other schools on the West Coast offering studies and degrees in women's spirituality, parapsychology, East/West psychology, and ecology are New College of California,[12] and John F. Kennedy University.

Reclaiming has taught at weeklong summer retreats called WitchCamps. There are WitchCamp communities throughout the United States, and in Canada, England, and Germany. Communities of folks who have sponsored WitchCamps have taken on the challenge of teaching in their own cities and towns. Groups exist in Los Angeles; Portland, Oregon; Seattle; British Columbia; Missouri; Michigan; Austin, Texas; Florida; Charlotte, North Carolina; West Virginia; Virginia; Georgia; Pennsylvania; Vermont; and Toronto.

There are WitchCampers of all levels of training and experience—from neophyte on up. Reclaiming WitchCamps are an example of a tradition-specific learning environment. Between camp sessions, WitchCamp teachers and organizers maintain discussions about their teachings and the organization of the camps. They choose and develop themes, select teachers and teaching teams, plan teacher and organizer retreats, book sites and accommodations, arrange catering, and conduct registration. For all of this, they rely on listserves, e-mail, and Web sites. Though the actual training takes place in the intense retreat environment of the camps, the growth and development of the phenomenon of WitchCamps have been accelerated and made more efficient by electronic communication.

There are other tradition-specific training programs available. For instance, the Foxwood Temple in Maryland runs retreats and workshops through which they teach Witchcraft and magic in the Foxwood tradition.[13]

The Pagan "graduate school" that I have personal experience with is Cherry Hill Seminary, located in Vermont.[14] Like The Ardantane Project, Cherry Hill Seminary is open to walkers on all Pagan paths. I recently audited a thirteen-week course called Boundaries and Ethics for Pagan Pastoral Counselors. Although the seminary, which is seeking accreditation from the State of Vermont as an institution of higher learning, conducts many of its more basic courses at its Bethel campus during weekend and weeklong retreat sessions, Boundaries and Ethics took place in cyberspace. The teacher was in western Massachusetts, and the students logged on from New York, Ohio, Florida, Texas, New Jersey, and California. We all had standard psychology textbooks, and we were given assignments supplemented by additional readings posted on our private Yahoogroups site. We discussed our readings via an e-list and read an online weekly lecture. Then we met in real time in a chat room for a class discussion. With classes such as this, Cherry Hill Seminary has begun the process of deepening and broadening our work and defining ourselves and our movement.

One of the assignments for the Cherry Hill Seminary course Boundaries and Ethics for Pagan Pastoral Counselors is to read the codes of ethics from several professional organizations, such as the

National Association of Social Workers, the American Association of Pastoral Counselors, the Association of Professional Chaplains, and the Council of Spiritual Practices. Using these codes and our witchen spirituality as our guides, we students are asked to write our own personal code of ethics. Here is one I think many Witches will feel speaks well for them.

The Charge of the Counselor: A Statement of Ethics

Thus spoke She who is the guardian of the heart, the speaker of the words of life, singer of Earth and Time, dancer of wholeness, She who weaves breath:

As My priestess, you are charged with the care of hearts and the guardianship of life-roads. To you I give the gift of the steady foot, to walk the path of life with those who ask you to accompany them. I give the gift of legs strong enough for the journey, and wise enough to know when to halt and suggest that they reconsider their way, asking one another, their own hearts, and the path itself for direction. I give you the gift of a sturdy back, for the bearing of your own burdens and for when you need to carry someone else or give others a boost up to a high branch along the way, for two together can reach what one cannot reach alone. I give you keen senses, to be aware of the dangers and the opportunities that arise on life's road, to look and listen and smell and touch them for yourself and for those others who trust you to walk their path with them. I give you a sharp mind and a soft heart, and a mouth that only opens to give good counsel, not to insist, manipulate or condemn. Finally, I give you ears and a heart that will listen ten times more than your mouth will speak. With all these gifts given you, oh counselor, I ask only that you use them wisely, with compassion and understanding, and in the service of Life and Love.

—Margaret Hammit-McDonald (© 2001)

All of these emerging programs, which help us deepen and broaden our experience and practice, have been fostered by the World Wide Web. They might have flowered without the Internet, but it would have taken years. Due to the speed of electronic communication and its ability to reach so many people so readily, Pagan learning has expanded far beyond what any of us could have imagined in the days before the Net.

Each Pagan training approach mentioned here is one aspect of a broad spectrum. Each reflects a different view of contemporary Witchcraft—from Dianic, to anarchic, to conventional, to academic. And each deals with ongoing training in a distinct way. They all have something unique to offer. But every one—the RCGI Cella Program, the Ardantane Project, the Woolston-Steen Theological Seminary, Reclaiming WitchCamps, Cherry Hill Seminary, and many more that are not named here—has been profoundly affected by the Internet.

CONCLUSION: BROADENING AND COLORING THE TAPESTRY

Throughout these pages, I have tried to formulate questions that will help us navigate the intricacies of Spider Woman's web. My hope is that these questions will stimulate witchen thought and suggest new, unexplored ways of interweaving spirituality and technology. The possibilities are limitless.

The first major challenge I faced in writing this book was to focus on a moving target: the ever-changing world of electronic communications and the World Wide Web. I don't claim to speak the last word on Witchcraft and the Web. No one can. This book, and our faith traditions, are works in progress.

The second challenge was to represent accurately our considerable diversity of thought, belief, and practice. We are a *living* religion. And we are a pragmatic one, too. We adapt and change with the times and places in which we find ourselves, while revering Nature and our places in Nature's web.

We humans, regardless of our individual faith traditions, have reached a critical point in terms of how we exist on our planet. We have treated Mother Nature as though she were an inexhaustible resource. And so, in many ways, she is. But even if we view her as boundless, we urgently need to recognize that, unless our habits and expectations—our collective attitudes—change, we will damage our world and the life it sustains irreparably.

Many mainstream faith traditions have come to this realization, as well. They are also seeking to address the important issues surrounding our natural resources. Many of these people view themselves as stewards of the Earth. Unfortunately, the notion of sacred stewardship got lost somewhere on the road to manifest destiny, and the attitude of "man" having dominion over all the birds of the air, the beasts of the field, desert, and woodland, the fishes of the seas, the trees and vegetation, the waters, and the minerals that form Nature's body has taken precedence over the notion of caring for and managing the Earth's bounty.

We have the hope and the tools to devise new ways to steward Earth's resources for the good of all life forms. We may follow a Pagan path, or we may not. As a species, we have the capability to readjust our lives to minimize, and in some cases even eliminate, our disturbance of the natural rhythms of life. The Internet has rapidly become an important tool for helping to resolve ecological crises, and many Web sites devoted to conservation efforts show evidence of Paganism's vital presence on the Web. Many dedicated Earth activists are Witches and Pagans. Our beliefs reinforce our commitment to activism. We may use magic to strengthen our actions. We may also use it for restoration, renewal, and rededication in the face of seemingly overwhelming odds. The work that our eco-activists do in the field is demanding, and it can take its toll on those of us who ceaselessly engage in it. We may find strength and solace in ritual—not simply in faith or belief, but in ritualizing our work and our lives. Envisioned in our uninhibited imaginations; fueled by our commitment; shaped by our magical activities, spells, and rituals; informed by scientific thought and new developments in technology, we can change our reality.

As we learn to harmonize with the natural rhythms of life, as we grasp how to tread more lightly on the body of our Mother, let us dance the web, traveling along her lacy filaments from node to node, open to every possibility.

NOTES

CHAPTER 1

1. Gary Snyder, *No Nature: New and Selected Poems* (New York: Pantheon, 1992).
2. <www.whatis.com>.
3. Steven Posch, personal communication with the author.
4. <www.magusbooks.com/newalexandria/>.
5. *American Heritage Dictionary* online.
6. Graham Harvey, <www.uni-marburg.de/fb03/religionswissenschaft/journal/diskus/harvey2.html>.
7. J. Gordon Melton, personal communication, 21 Nov. 1995. Qtd. in Chas S. Clifton, "The Significance of Aradia," in *Aradia; Or, The Gospel of the Witches: A New Translation,* trans. Mario Pazzaglini and Dina Pazzaglini. (Blaine, WA: Phoenix, 1998).
8. More of Richard Ely's writings about sacred geology can be found at <www.enlightenment.com>.
9. <http://maeshowe.mypage.org/>.
10. <www.whatis.com>.
11. <http://www.kodak.com/US/en/corp/features/birdcam2001/index.shtml.>.
12. <http://birdcam.backyardwildlife.com/>.
13. <www.arborday.org>.
14. <www.rainewalker.com>.
15. <www.nps.gov/havo/pele.htm>.
16. <http://alohaweb.com/Pele/>.
17. <www.mbari.org>.
18. <www.csulb.edu/%7Ewgriffin/>.
19. <www.nccn.net/~tarot/welcome.html>.
20. <www.webcom.com/gimbutas/belili/movie.html>.

21. One of many sites is <http://catal.arch.cam.ac.uk/catal/catal.html>.
22. <http://catal.arch.cam.ac.uk/catal/goddess.html>.
23. <www.mistress-of-folklore.com/>.
24. <www.uni-marburg.de/fb03/religionswissenschaft/journal/diskus/harvey2.html>.
25. Ibid.
26. Ibid.
27. See Margot Adler, *Drawing down the Moon: Witches, Druids, Goddess-Worshippers, and Other Pagans in America Today* (Boston: Beacon, 1979, 1986).
28. <www.uni-marburg.de/fb03/religionswissenschaft/journal/diskus/harvey2.html>.
29. Erik Davis, "Technopagans," at <www.techgnosis.com/figment/technopagans.html>.
30. <www.horsegoddess.net>.
31. Erik Davis, "Technopagans," at <www.techgnosis.com/figment/technopagans.html>.
32. Ibid.
33. <http://www.flindersclub.asn.au/pagan/>.
34. <www.cynsmoon.com/>.
35. <www.bloomington.in.us/~pen/>.
36. <www.caw.org>.
37. <www.milpagan.org/>.
38. <www.cuups.org>.
39. <www.witchvox.com>.

Chapter 2

1. Erik Davis, "Technopagans," at <www.techgnosis.com/figment/technopagans.html>.
2. Gaetan Delaforgem, "The Templar Tradition: Yesterday and Today," *Gnosis,* <www.chaosmatrix.com/lib/chaos/texts/gegregor.html>.
3. From the Council on Spiritual Practices, at <www.csp.org>.
4. *Encarta World English Dictionary,* 1999 ed.

5. <www.ozarkavalon.org>.
6. <www.beliefnet.com>.
7. Mary Louise Schumacher and Tom Heinen, "Praying on the Web," *Milwaukee Journal Sentinel* 13 Dec. 2000.
8. <www.whatis.com>.
9. Ibid.
10. <www.techgnosis.com/figment/technopagans.html>.

Chapter 3

1. <www.stepchild.org>.
2. <http://users.ids.net/~theitic/nectw.html>.
3. <www.cog.org>.
4. <www.nroogd.org>.
5. <www.whatis.com>.
6. Pour down like Silver <www.candledark.net/silver/>.
7. <www.stonecircles.com>.
8. <www.witchvox.com>.
9. <www.drak.net>.
10. <www.whatis.com>.
11. Ibid.
12. Ibid.
13. <www.drak.net>.
14. <www.reclaiming.org/newsletter/>.
15. <www.magickalcauldron.com/>.
16. <www.interchg.ubc.ca/fmuntean/>.
17. <www.twpt.com/>.
18. "*Wiccan/Pagan Times* Mission Statement."
19. <www.fote.org/>.
20. <www.witchradio.com>.
21. <www.webopedia.com>.
22. <www.serpentinemusic.com>.
23. <http://stations.mp3s.com/stations/91/above_a_star_earth_spirit.html>.

24. <www.live365.com>.
25. <www.witchwayisup.com/wgds.htm>.
26. <www.cog.org>.
27. <www.goddess2000.org>.
28. <www.spiralgoddess.com>.
29. <www.cpwr.org/calldocs/ethictoc.html>.
30. <www.pwrsa.co.za/>.
31. <www.cpwr.org/calldoc.html>.
32. <www.uri.org>.
33. <www.themestream.com/>.

Chapter 4

1. Gus diZerega, *Pagans and Christians: The Personal Spiritual Experience* (St. Paul, MN: Llewellyn, 2001).
2. Ibid.
3. <www.techgnosis.com/figment/technopagans.html>.
4. Ibid.
5. <www.whatis.com>.
6. <www.bbzzz.com>.
7. <www.techgnosis.com/figment/technopagans.html>.
8. Ibid.
9. Patricia Monaghan, *The New Book of Goddesses and Heroines* (St. Paul, MN: Llewellyn, 1998).
10. Definition provided by my coconspirator Ceffyl.
11. <www.geocities.com/SoHo/Lofts/2938/>.
12. <www.spiralgoddess.com>.
13. <www.bbzzz.com/judy/>.
14. <www.sekhmettemple.com/>.
15. <ordbrighideach.org>.
16. <http://www.laurels.uni.cc>.

Chapter 5

1. <www.geocities.com/SoHo/5756/minbtrad.html>.
2. <www.minoantemple.org>.
3. Ibid.
4. © 2001, Sparky T. Rabbit, used by permission.
5. Covenant of the Goddess bylaws, art. 9, sect. B.1, rev. Jan. 2001.
6. Aleister Crowley, *The Book of the Law* (York Beach, ME: Samuel Weiser, 1997). There are unpublished studies indicating that the phrasing of the Rede goes back as far as 1535.
7. Gus diZerega, *Pagans and Christians: The Personal Spiritual Experience* (St. Paul, MN: Llewellyn, 2001).

Chapter 6

1. <www.neopagan.net/abcdef.html>.
2. <www.goddess2000.org/G2000Ritual.html>.
3. Erik Davis, "Technopagans," at <www.techgnosis.com/figment/technopagans.html>.
4. <thedance.com/rituals/guestbooksamp.html>.
5. <thedance.com/rituals/circetsamp.html>.
6. <webopedia.com>.
7. Chas S. Clifton, personal communication with the author.
8. Grant H. Potts, personal communication with the author.
9. <http://www.bloomington.in.us/~pen/military.html>.
10. From INVERT, RFD 1, Newport ME 04953, at <www.reclaiming.org./about/consensus/index.html>.

Chapter 7

1. <www.whatis.com>.
2. <www.circlesanctuary.org/liberty/>.
3. Gus diZerega, *Pagans and Christians: The Personal Spiritual Experience* (St. Paul, MN: Llewellyn, 2001).
4. <www.sksm.edu>.
5. <www.creationspirituality.org>.

6. Ibid.
7. <www.goddesswomen.com/>.
8. <www.coa.org>.
9. <www.atc.org>.
10. Ibid.
11. <www.ciis.edu>.
12. <www.newcollege.edu>.
13. <www.foxwood-temple.net>.
14. <http://sites.netscape.net/laurelinkirk/CherryHill.htm>.

GLOSSARY OF WITCHEN TERMINOLOGY

This glossary defines words as they would generally be used and understood within the Reclaiming tradition. Variations on, or additions to, these meanings may be found in the lexicons of other Witches and Pagans. I have added to the glossary several other common Pagan terms that appear in this book. (The definition of Chaos Magic was written by Adam Jenkins; the definition of Egregore is by Gaetan Delaforgem.)

ARDANES/ORDAINS A set of laws or rules pertaining to the practice, technology, and beliefs of a particular tradition of the Craft.

ASPECT, ASPECTING A magical technique whereby deity is summoned, or drawn down, into an individual. That individual, working with a partner in whom she has complete trust, allows her ego to be released, or diminishes her mundane, mortal personality, to a point sufficient to allow the divine to enter, speak, and act. If the aspecting is truly deep, the subject will be unlikely to remember anything that she has said or done while in that state, which can last for several hours. She will be exhausted and hungry afterwards, and it is critical that her working partner attend to her needs so that she can return fully to ordinary consciousness. Also known as "drawing down the moon," particularly among the British traditions of the Craft.

ASPERGE To purify ritually by sprinkling with salt water; often, this is done by dipping a fragrant branch, such as rosemary, into the water and sprinkling it over the participant in a ritual.

ATHAME Pronounced ah-thah'-may (also, ah'-thame, or ah-tham-may'), this is a blade or knife used as a ritual tool; usually, it is a knife with two sharp edges. It is also a tool associated with the East, symbolizing and enhancing the power to choose, to analyze, to define, to separate one thing from another. In some traditions, an athame is used as a phallic symbol. When a Witch chooses not to use the blade because, for example, of its association with weaponry, she or he may substitute a feather, bone, or like object, or use her own hand.

BELOVED DEAD People whom we loved when they were alive and who have crossed over.

BOOK OF SHADOWS A compendium of rituals, spells, liturgies, invocations, songs, chants, recipes, pathworkings, deity names and attributes, and instructions in certain sacred technologies, which is kept by an individual, a coven, or a tradition.

CAST To "cast the circle" is to define the boundaries of the sacred space, usually a circle in which a ritual is about to take place. (See Circle.)

CAULDRON A pot, often made of cast iron and having three or four legs, a handle, and a lid, which is used in various ways for magical work and rituals. In essence a cooking pot, it is also a tool for transformation. Objects may be passed through the fire burning within the cauldron to be purified; people may jump over the cauldron to be purified or healed. A cauldron may also be used over a fire, for brewing herbal drinks or making special soups to be eaten as part of a ritual. Filled with water, a cauldron may be used for scrying. (See Scrying.)

CENSE To purify, using incense or the smoke of a smudge stick. (See Asperge and Smudge.)

CHAKRA Literally, "wheels." The term derives from Hindu beliefs. A chakra is one of seven energy vortices located throughout the human body, beginning at the base of the spine and ending just above the crown of the head. These can be "opened" or stimulated through certain physical movements and psychic/mental/spiritual techniques, so that the energy can be released and utilized.

CHAOS MAGIC In essence, chaos magic is concerned with throwing out what its practitioners see as the unnecessary paraphernalia and rigid structures of magic and getting down to the core. Those who practice it move away from the complex beliefs and symbolism of other magical systems and instead employ a basic magical framework that produces results through methods unique to each practitioner. This framework provides a set of tools and techniques that often involve sigils, gnosis (or altered states of consciousness, achieved through a variety of methods), ritual, humor, and rigorous self-assessment.

The most interesting thing about chaos magic is neither its forms nor its flexibility: it is the attitude of the chaos magician. Practitioners use techniques, not because they were taught to use them, but because they work. In the end, a chaos magician uses what feels right, being far more interested in the performance of magic than in the theory.

CHARGE To infuse with energy that is directed towards a particular purpose. A charged object holds magical energy and releases it to work the magic.

CHARM A small object, often a bag or other container containing herbs, stones, or other materials, charged with the energy of a specific spell, and usually carried or worn by the person for whom it was created. Or such an object charged more generally and used by anyone needing/desiring the effect of such energy—for example, a charm for protection, or for love. It may also be called a "charm bag," a "mojo bag," or a "gris gris."

CIRCLE A sacred space in which a ritual, or any kind of magical work, is done, either by an individual or a group. Often, people stand in a circle to begin a ritual, but during the ritual they may move about in any configuration and are still said to be "in circle." A circle is also a concept fundamental to the thealogy of modern Witchcraft, generally referring to the cycle of life, death, and rebirth, and to the interconnectedness of everything in the universe. The word "circle" is also a synonym for "coven"; used as a verb, it means to join others in a sacred space.

COVEN An autonomous group of Witches who meet regularly to do magic. Traditionally, a coven had thirteen members and met under a full moon. Today, a coven may be any size, and its members may be women or men. In some traditions, there is an accepted set of coven leadership and membership requirements. In the Reclaiming tradition, covens set their own rules. Most covens meet privately and are not open to visitors; occasionally, however, a coven may declare an open ritual and invite outsiders to join in for that ritual only. Coven membership is gained through personal contact. Often, coveners become very close and consider each other as family. Covens are also known as "circles" or "groves."

COVENSTEAD The place where most coven rituals are held. A covenstead can be a place in the country, but more frequently it is a temple room of some kind in a coven member's home, or perhaps a circle marked with stones in a backyard.

COWAN A person who is not a Witch, just as a Gentile is a person who is not a Jew.

CUP Tool of the West; used to hold salt water, water, or any drink used in a ritual. In some traditions, the cup is symbolic of the female. It may be a goblet, chalice, bowl, or other vessel capable of holding liquid.

CURSE To work a spell, usually on a person or people, directing energy intended to affect the object of the curse in a way she or he would perceive as negative—for example, causing pain or failure. Most traditions discourage the use of curses, but some say a Witch who cannot curse cannot cure.

CUT To cast a circle, or to ritually leave or enter a circle after it has been cast by carefully opening a space to pass through and closing it after crossing the boundary.

DEATH The state that we enter after "life," as it is commonly defined by Western biology, ends. Death is understood as part of the circle. Many Witches believe that the dead continue to exist on another plane and that it is possible to contact them, especially at Samhain, through a psychic connection. We are all aware of our connections with our ancestors and of the fact that, in some sense, we will live on in our descendants. We sing "What is remembered lives." (See Reincarnation.)

DEITY Most modern Witches believe in a pantheon of Gods and Goddesses who are associated with many religious traditions around the world, both modern and ancient. Most commonly, Witches call on the deities of Celtic, Greek, and Roman cultures, but many also call on Egyptian, African, Scandinavian, Native American, Chinese, and Indian gods and goddesses. Most Witches are careful not to appropriate other people's spiritual practices or beliefs; but, since we also recognize that different cultures affect each other when they come in contact, we are open to the influence of religions that are harmonious with Craft.

DEVOKE To thank the deity or deities that have been invoked for a ritual and to invite them to stay or to leave as they will. The opposite of *invoke*. This term is used in Reclaiming, and it is not found in dictionaries.

DIRECTIONS East, South, West, North (also known as the quarters), and Center. Each direction has an element and particular powers and qualities associated with it. The Center is the center point of the circle. (See Elements.)

DIVINATION The practice of seeking guidance or gaining insight or foretelling the future through magical techniques, such as reading Tarot cards, scrying, or reading tea leaves.

EGREGORE "A kind of group mind which is created when people consciously come together for a common purpose . . . [It] has the characteristic of having an effectiveness greater than the mere sum of its individual members" (Gaetan Delaforgem, "The Templar Tradition: Yesterday and Today, *Gnosis*).

ELEMENTS The four substances (Air, Fire, Water, and Earth) necessary to the creation and sustenance of life. Each is associated with one of the four directions; a particular tool; certain qualities and powers that exist in the outer, physical world and within each person; certain colors, life forms, and natural phenomena that correspond to each direction.

Air: East; athame; powers of the mind, the ability to analyze and understand, to breathe, smell, and hear; the qualities of the wind—freshness, dawn light, sudden insight, rational thought, perspective; white and pale shades of yellow and pink; birds, insects.

Fire: South; wand; powers of passion and will, the ability to act effectively, to destroy, purify, and change; the qualities of the flame—heat, anger, aggression, affection, sexual desire; red, orange, gold, deep yellow; snakes, scorpions, fire ants, sparkles, the sun, the God.

Water: West; cup; powers of intuition and emotion, the ability to dream, to love, to grieve, to cleanse, to heal, to refresh; the qualities of fluid—mutability, purity, depth; blue, turquoise, purple, silver; fish, cetacea, crustacea, waterbirds, shells, seaweed, blood, tears, sweat, the moon.

Earth: North; pentacle; the powers of the body, the ability to create, nurture, nourish, sustain, to destroy, to heal; the qualities of the planet—strength, endurance, fertility, sustenance, sensuality, abundance, and diversity; mountains, rocks, trees, caves; all animals and life forms, especially bears, deer, cows; fruits and grains, birth and death, the Mother, the Goddess, and the God.

ENERGIES; ENERGY RAISING The use of various techniques, such as rhythm, movement, and voice, to increase and intensify the focused energy of a group. Such traditional techniques as chanting, drumming, and dancing are used to direct and release the energies to effect the group's intent. The most easily observable indication that energy is elevated is heat: the room becomes warm, and the people who are raising the energy sweat. Energy raising is used to magically empower a spell, healing, or other working. When energy is raised to a peak, we shape it into what we call a "cone of power" and "release" it, either by directing it towards something, or by grounding it (that is, by allowing excess energy to drain into the Earth and become absorbed).

ENTHEOGEN God within; god- or spirit-facilitating. An entheogen is a psychoactive sacramental, a plant or chemical substance taken to occasion primary religious experience—for example, peyote cactus, as used in the Native American Church.

ESBAT A monthly full-moon ritual celebrated regularly by most witchen covens.

FAMTRAD Family tradition; a Craft tradition that is kept within a family and passed down, generation after generation.

GEOMANCY Divination by means of lines and figures, or by geographic features.

GOD All that is born, grows, and dies; animal and plant life. Sometimes, the sun is considered to be the God because every year it grows bright in summer, fades, dies, and is reborn. The qualities of the God are those of plants, such as growth, vitality, reaching maturity, rising, and falling; they are also the qualities of animals, such as wildness, freedom, vulnerability, innocence, and ecstasy in Nature. (See Deity.)

GODDESS The Earth, also called "the Mother" and "the Great Goddess", because the Earth is the source of life. When we die, our bodies are returned to the Earth. Through the Earth, we are connected to the mystery and beauty of the cosmos, and Witches consider her sacred, worth dedicating their lives to protecting. Qualities of the Goddess are those associated with the Earth, such as endurance, fertility, abundance, sustenance, compassion, creativity (birth), destruction (decay), and rebirth. (See Deity.)

GROUND To consciously become connected to the energy of the Earth, usually through a meditation. This is considered essential to being able to focus and do magical work, and to prevent psychic distress.

HIGH PRIESTESS; HIGH PRIEST A trained and skilled woman who conducts rituals or who embodies Goddess, and her male working partner, who conducts rituals with her and may aspect God. These are standard roles in most older and many newer traditions. These terms are not used in the Reclaiming tradition.

INVOKE To call a spirit or deity into the circle.

MAGIC The art and practice of changing consciousness at will.

MIGHTY DEAD Those who have died and who are widely acknowledged as great priestesses, priests, and/or teachers of the Craft. The term is used in Reclaiming and Faery traditions of Craft.

OPEN To "open the circle" is to dissolve, erase, or unwrap the boundary of the circle created at the beginning of a ritual, to end the ritual, and to remove the designation of sacred space from the location.

PATHWORKING A specific guided meditation, to be done with one person or with a coven.

PENTACLE A five-pointed star figure, with one point at the top, which is enclosed in a circle. Tool of the North. The pentacle is used to achieve psychic balance and to enable people to experience various connected energies in a concentrated way; each of its points is associated with different powers and qualities. Reclaiming and Faery traditions of the Craft use two, and sometimes more, tradition-specific Pentacle schema: the Pentacle of Iron, the points of which are sex, self, passion, pride, and power; and the Pentacle of Pearl, the points of which are love, law, wisdom, knowledge, and power. In addition, each pentacle point corresponds to a "point" of the body when it assumes a pentacle position (arms straight out to the side, legs wide apart): head, hands, and feet.

POPPET A small, handcrafted doll, created to represent a particular person, used in spellcasting. A poppet may contain cloth, hair, or an object belonging to the person it represents.

PURIFY To cleanse spiritually and mentally; to get rid of any thoughts or feelings that might interfere with participation in the ritual or the ability to focus and do magical work. (See Asperge, Cense.)

QUARTERS See Elements, Directions.

REINCARNATION Most, but not all, Witches believe in some kind of reincarnation or rebirth—either in the sense that we all get recycled because everything comes from the Earth and our bodies go back into the Earth when we die, or in the sense that our individual identity, our spirit, becomes connected to a new person or life form.

RITUAL An occasion when an individual or a group uses traditional practices to focus energy for an identified purpose, such as healing, transformation, empowerment, protection, or celebration. The basic elements of a ritual in the Reclaiming tradition are grounding and purifying; casting the circle; invoking the elements; invoking deity (or deities); magical working; sharing food and drink; and opening the circle.

SABBAT One of the eight days of the solar year, which mark the turning of the Wheel. (See Wheel of the Year.)

SCRY A technique of divination. It usually means to gaze into a crystal, a bowl of water, or some other clear substance until a vision appears that can be understood directly or interpreted.

SKYCLAD Nude, clad in the sky.

SOLITARY A Witch who practices alone, not in a coven.

SPELL Focused energy, directed towards a particular result, using a carefully chosen set of objects and ingredients, words and incantations, gestures and timing (such as a particular lunar phase). The purpose of a spell is to create a change in physical or non-physical realms. In most traditions, spells are governed by ethical principles. A spell may be created in the form of a physical charm, or something may be charmed. The act of creating a spell is called "spellcraft" or "spellworking." (See Charm.)

SPIRIT The spirit is the center of the circle: it is life, which is created by the elements of Air, Fire, Water, and Earth; some Witches consider spirit itself to be an element. Witches sing "Air I am, Fire I am, Water, Earth, and Spirit I am." Many Witches believe that spirit is the external individual consciousness that exists independently of our bodies and is eternal, and most believe that all life forms (animals, plants, rocks, mountains, rivers) have a spirit. Some believe that the spirit of an individual enters into another being after death.

TAROT A set of cards with five suits and symbolic pictures, used for divination. There are many different versions, and most have a guidebook. Tarot cards are the precursors of modern playing cards, and they are known to have existed in Europe as early as the fifteenth century. The cards are believed to have been used primarily by gypsies and Witches until recent years, when their use became widespread.

TOOLS Objects, which have been sanctified or magically charged, that are used for magical purposes. There are particular tools associated with each of the five directions.

TRIPLE GODDESS The Maiden, Mother, and Crone, associated with the new, full, and waning phases of the moon, are the most familiar triad in the Reclaiming tradition. Other Triple Goddesses recognized in various cultures and historical periods are the Fates, Clothos, Lachesis, and Atropos; the Moirae or Graeae Sisters; the Norns or Wyrd Sisters; and the Morrígan. The Goddess Brigit, or Bhride, is associated with the forge, the flame, and the well.

WAND Tool of the South. A wand is usually handcrafted by its owner from wood, metal, or stone. It is a rod or stick, from a few inches long to an arm's length, which may be embellished with carving, crystals, feathers, or other objects of significance to its owner. Used to direct energy.

WHEEL OF THE YEAR Witches describe the cycles of the seasons as the Wheel of the Year. There are eight major holidays, called "sabbats," four of which are based on solar events, and all of which mark the "turning of the Wheel." Some holidays are celebrated on the "eve"—the night before. The following calendar dates reflect the perspective of the Northern Hemisphere. These are the holidays as they are observed in the Reclaiming tradition.

October 31, Samhain A Celtic word, pronounced "sow," to rhyme with "cow," and "win": sow'-win; it is also known as **Halloween**, **Hallows**, or **Hallowmas**. Occurring midway between the Fall Equinox and the Winter Solstice, Samhain is a major holiday. On it, we honor and mourn those who have died in the past year, celebrate our ancestors (see Beloved Dead and Mighty Dead; some departed souls are both), and seek to contact the spirits of the dead. Samhain is the Witches' New Year.

December 21/22, Yule A Norse word. The Winter Solstice, the shortest day and longest night of the year, and the birthday of the sun. We watch the sun set and then stay up all night, keeping the yule log burning as we midwife the rebirth of the sun. We gather together at dawn to sing the sun up. Many of us have a yule tree (with presents!) in our homes, representing the tree of life and regeneration, known among our Norse kin as Ygdrassil.

February 2, Brigid Also known as **Candlemas**; it refers to the return of the light, or **Imbolc**, or **Oimelc**, meaning "the lambing season" or "in the belly." The midpoint between Yule and Spring Equinox. This is a time when we honor Brigid, the goddess of the forge, the flame, the well, and of work, poetry, and healing. We make pledges at the holy well, in front of the sacred flame. We celebrate the gentle signs of early spring and of light returning after the darkness of winter.

March 22, Spring Equinox Also known as **Ostara**, **Oestar**, or **Easter**, and named for the Goddess of Spring. The days and nights are of equal length, and it is time to start the garden, to sow the seeds. We try to do this in our lives as well as in the Earth. We celebrate the renewal of life, the endless cycle of rebirth, symbolized by the egg.

May 1, Beltane This is also called **May Day** and, in some traditions, May Eve is called **Walpurgisnacht**. It is the midpoint between Spring Equinox and Summer Solstice. Traditionally, it is a time for lovers to celebrate. We dance around a maypole, weaving ribbons; we leap over the Beltane fire to enhance fertility and creativity of all kinds, love of all kinds, and for healing.

June 21, Summer Solstice Also called **Litha**. The longest day and shortest night of the year. After this night, the days will begin to shorten, so we call it the death of the Sun King, build a big figure out of sticks and straw, then burn it. We watch the sun set and celebrate the beauty of midsummer.

August 2, Lughnasad Pronounced "loo'-noss-sah." This sabbat, also called **Lammas** ("lom'-mus," like "Thomas," meaning "loaf mass"), celebrates the Celtic god Lugh. It is the midpoint between Summer Solstice and Fall Equinox. It is the early harvest, when we rejoice in the first fruits of the season. Also, we begin to prepare ourselves for the coming winter and think about what we will need to store up to make it through the dark, cold season.

September 22, Fall Equinox The major harvest or thanksgiving festival, also known as **Mabon** or **Harvest Home**. It is again a time when day and night are in balance—that is, they are of equal length. We have a feast and perhaps also plant a winter garden. We remember to slow down, to rest, to enjoy our blessings, especially our families and friends.

SELECTED BIBLIOGRAPHY

Abrams, David. *The Spell of the Sensuous: Perception and Language in a More-than-Human World.* New York: Pantheon, 1996.

Adler, Margot. *Drawing down the Moon: Witches, Druids, Goddess-Worshippers, and Other Pagans in America Today.* Boston: Beacon, 1979, 1986.

Arthur, Shawn. "Technophilia and Nature Religion: The Growth of Paradox," essay presented at the IAHR quinquennial world conference in Durban, South Africa, 10 Aug. 2000, and at the AAR (American Academy of Religion) annual meeting in Nashville, TN, 18 Nov. 2000.

Bunt, Gary. *Virtually Islamic: Computer-Mediated Communication and Cyber Islamic Environments.* Cardiff: U of Wales P, 2000.

Califia, Pat, and Drew Campbell, eds. *Bitch Goddess: The Spiritual Path of the Dominant Woman.* San Francisco: Greenery, 1997.

Clifton, Chas S., ed. *Witchcraft Today,* 3 vols. (*The Modern Craft Movement; Modern Rites of Passage;* and *Witchcraft and Shamanism*) St. Paul, MN: Llewellyn, 1993-94.

Devereux, Paul, John Steele, and David Kubrin. *Earthmind: A Modern Adventure in Ancient Wisdom.* New York: Harper & Row, 1989.

DiZerega, Gus. *Pagans and Christians: The Personal Spiritual Experience.* St. Paul, MN: Llewellyn, 2001.

Graham, Harvey. *Contemporary Paganism: Listening People, Speaking Earth.* New York UP, 1997.

Graham, Harvey, and Charlotte Hardman, eds. *Paganism Today: Wiccans, Druids, the Goddess and Ancient Earth Traditions for the Twenty-First Century*. San Francisco: Thorsons, 1996.

Griffin, Wendy, ed. *Daughters of the Goddess: Studies of Healing, Identity, and Empowerment*. Walnut Creek, CA: AltaMira, 2000.

Harrow, Judy. *Wicca Covens: How to Start and Organize Your Own*. Secaucus, NJ: Citadel, 1999.

Leland, Charles G. *Aradia; Or, The Gospel of the Witches*. Trans. Mario Pazzaglini and Dina Pazzaglini. Blaine, WA: Phoenix, 1998.

Lewis, James R., ed. *Magical Religion and Modern Witchcraft*. State U of New York P, 1996.

Marshall, Peter. *Nature's Web: Rethinking Our Place on Earth*. Armonk, NY; London: M. E. Sharpe, 1992, 1996.

Monaghan, Patricia. *The New Book of Goddesses and Heroines*. St. Paul, MN: Llewellyn, 1998.

Orion, Loretta. *Never Again the Burning Times: Paganism Revived*. Prospect Heights, IL: Waveland, 1995.

Pike, Sarah M. *Earthly Bodies, Magical Selves: Contemporary Pagans and the Search for Community*. Berkeley: U of California P, 2001.

Rosen, Jonathan. *The Talmud and the Internet: A Journey between Worlds*. New York: Farrar, Straus, and Giroux, 2000.

Wood, Robin. *When, Why . . . If: An Ethics Workbook*. Dearborn, MI: Livingtree, 1996.

INDEX

Note: the author names numerous friends and sources by first name only. These are listed in the index, followed by the designation "(source)".